Agents of Terror

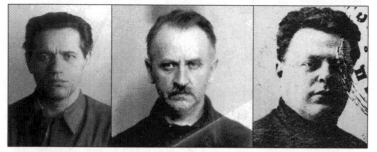

AGENTS OF TERROR

Ordinary Men and Extraordinary Violence
in Stalin's Secret Police

Alexander Vatlin

Edited, translated, and with an introduction by
Seth Bernstein

Foreword by
Oleg Khlevniuk

THE UNIVERSITY OF WISCONSIN PRESS

The University of Wisconsin Press
1930 Monroe Street, 3rd Floor
Madison, Wisconsin 53711-2059
uwpress.wisc.edu

3 Henrietta Street, Covent Garden
London WC2E 8LU, United Kingdom
eurospanbookstore.com

Library of Congress Cataloging-in-Publication Data

Names: Vatlin, A. Iu., author. | Bernstein, Seth, editor, translator. |
    Khlevniuk, O. V. (Oleg Vital'evich), writer of foreword.
Title: Agents of terror: ordinary men and extraordinary violence in Stalin's
    secret police / Alexander Vatlin; edited, translated, and with an
    introduction by Seth Bernstein; foreword by Oleg Khlevniuk.
Other titles: Terror raionnogo masshtaba. English
Description: Madison, Wisconsin: The University of Wisconsin Press,
    [2016] | "Originally published as Terror raionnogo masshtaba:
    'Massovye operatsii' NKVD v Kuntsevskom raione Moskovskoi
    oblasti v 1937–38 gg. © 2004 by Alexander Vatlin and Rosspen,
    Moscow."—Title page verso. | Includes bibliographical references
    and index.
Identifiers: LCCN 2016012947 | ISBN 9780299310806 (cloth: alk. paper)
Subjects: LCSH: Soviet Union. Narodnyi komissariat vnutrennikh del—
    History. | Political persecution—Russia (Federation)—Kuntsevskii
    raion—History.
Classification: LCC HV8225.7.N37 V3813 2016 |
    DDC 363.28/3094709041—dc23
LC record available at https://lccn.loc.gov/2016012947

ISBN 9780299310844 (pbk.: alk. paper)

Contents

List of Illustrations   vii
Foreword by Oleg Khlevniuk   ix
Preface to the English-Language Edition   xvii
Introduction to the English-Language Edition by Seth Bernstein   xix
List of Abbreviations   xxxiii

Introduction: Why Kuntsevo? Setting the Stage   3

Part I: Executors of Terror   11

Part II: Patterns of Victimization   79

Epilogue: New Kuntsevo Forgets the Past   141

Notes   145
Index   167

Illustrations

Manor at Troitse-Golenishchevo	5
NKVD officer Iakov Baglikov	13
NKVD officer Isai Berg	16
NKVD officer Aleksandr Kuznetsov	18
Petr Barulin from Mnevniki	26
Petr Shushunov from Mnevniki	26
Andrei Puzankov from Mnevniki	27
Adolf Sommerfeld's act of execution	39
Kuntsevo administrator Sergei Muralov	103
Nikolai and Ivan Presnov	110
Vasilii Presnov	110
Tat'iana and Ivan Presnov	111
Luise Hadrossek	115
Alexander Feyerherd	123
Berta Feyerherd	123
Wilhelm Feyerherd	124
Friedrich Feyerherd	124
Lidia Feyerherd	125
Bones at the Butovo firing range	142
Memorial at the Butovo firing range	143

Foreword

Oleg Khlevniuk

Over the last twenty-five years, the study of Stalin's terror has flourished in the field of Soviet history. The remarkable surge of interest in Stalinist repression was the product of several factors. Above all, after the fall of the USSR researchers were able to access formerly secret archives. These new materials shocked a public that remains fascinated with the history of the terror and the Gulag. Today, interested readers can find a mountain of published documents, monographs, popular books, and articles about Stalin's terror. They number in the thousands—perhaps even more.

What have we learned from all this new research? In an important sense, these studies have confirmed and strengthened an old conclusion: terror was the foundation of the Stalinist system. Without understanding the unfolding of mass terror, we cannot understand Stalin's government, the lives of Soviet people, and the postwar development of the Central and Eastern European states of the socialist bloc. But these new findings also revealed aspects of the terror that transformed old understandings about the design and implementation of mass repression.

More than forty years ago, Alexander Solzhenitsyn pointed out the centralized nature of Stalin's terror in his *Gulag Archipelago*. One of his assertions was that Moscow sent quotas to the provinces. Writing about 1937, he observed, "Old prisoners claim to remember that the first blow allegedly took the form of mass arrests, striking virtually throughout the whole country on one single August night."[1] Solzhenitsyn's writings on the terror were fragmentary and unsystematic, relying on memoirs rather than archival sources. However, we now know that his "old prisoners" were right. The archives revealed that Stalin's terror was far more organized and centralized than even Solzhenitsyn imagined. The imprisonment and execution of most "enemies" and "suspicious elements" occurred in large-scale campaigns initiated at the highest echelons of the country's leadership. Its orders often provided detailed instructions: how many people to execute and how many to send to labor camps in each province. The secret police who carried out these plans not only fulfilled their orders but often overfulfilled them. In cases of overfulfillment, though, the leadership—frequently Stalin himself—also approved the increased plan.

The term historian Robert Conquest gave to the repression of the late 1930s was the Great Terror.[2] This shorthand will undoubtedly endure—with good reason. The terror was truly massive. However, new information has clarified the chronology of the terror and its purpose. We now know that the core of repression was a series of so-called "mass operations" the secret police of the People's Commissariat of Internal Affairs (NKVD) conducted at Stalin's behest from August 1937 to November 1938. Smaller campaigns occurred after the murder of party leader Sergei Kirov in December 1934. These episodes helped to lay the foundation for the Great Terror. However, they were miniscule in scale when placed against the orgy of violence in 1937–38.

Studies of the terror written before 1991 focused primarily on victims from the upper ranks of Soviet society. The targets supposedly were leaders in the party-state, or cultural elites. It was difficult not to focus on these figures in the absence of archival evidence. Members of the intelligentsia were responsible for almost all of the memoirs about the terror published during Khrushchev's de-Stalinization of the 1950s and 1960s. In addition, politicians during Khrushchev's Thaw asserted that party members were the main victims of Stalinist repression and documents released at the time supported this view. Historians who used Soviet official sources like Khrushchev's "Secret Speech" at the Twentieth Party Congress could hardly avoid emphasizing these same victims. This portrayal of the Great Terror and its victims is still widespread today. But new evidence shows that privileged groups accounted for only a fraction of arrestees. Above all, they came from the ranks of ordinary Soviet citizens.

The regime did not blindly arrest members of Soviet society. Rather, Stalin's regime had specific target groups whose arrest leaders believed would achieve concrete goals. Among the targets were not only former oppositionists but also many other segments of the population. They included millions of so-called "kulaks"—supposedly rich peasants whom the regime had sent to the Far North and Siberia during collectivization in the early 1930s. By the mid-1930s, they were slowly returning from exile. They included former prerevolutionary elites and people who had served in the White armies during the civil war. They included entire nationalities—Poles, Germans, Latvians, Lithuanians, Estonians, Finns, and many others—suspected of sympathizing with foreign enemies. The list of potential "enemies" and "suspect groups" could go on longer. In addition to these "enemies" themselves, members of victims' families and their coworkers became targets. Although there were specific groups whom the regime marked for arrest, mass repression also created chance victims. During the mass operations, when the secret police had to fulfill plans for arrests and executions, people outside suspect categories became victims of arbitrary terror. For this reason, the Great Terror was both highly centralized and chaotic. Stalin did not sign arrest warrants for every villager in every provincial backwater, although he signed orders for ranking party workers and other elites. However, without Stalin's directives initiating the mass operations, these villagers and others would not have faced arrest or execution.

Why did Stalin give these orders? Historians have long debated the purpose of the terror as part of the Soviet system as a whole and as part of Stalin's ruling style in particular. One purpose of terror and state violence was to forge a new social-political system and create an industrial economy. Compulsion was a key method of stimulating labor. Political violence also allowed the regime to suppress the smallest displays of dissent, not to mention open opposition. Alongside a powerful propaganda machine, repression ensured social stability. Repression had political purposes as well. When he ordered the arrest of leading party workers, Stalin at once strengthened his personal dictatorship and made these fallen leaders into scapegoats. All the shortcomings of the system he had built and the resulting problems that plagued millions of Soviet people he readily attributed to these purged "enemies." In the broadest sense, the terror was part of the regime's experiment in twentieth-century social engineering. It built a homogenous society of "new people" that had no room for the old and unreliable.

These reasons and others are undoubtedly important for understanding the impetus toward terror under Stalinism. State repression was the backdrop of daily life and a significant method of governance in the Soviet state. But besides everyday repression, Stalin also oversaw volcanic eruptions of violence that occurred over relatively short periods of time. These campaigns deserve special attention. They were at once products of the general system of state violence and the leadership's reaction to immediate crises. At the beginning of the 1930s, Stalin's leadership group initiated a campaign of repression against "kulaks" as part of collectivization. "Dekulakization" attempted to isolate and destroy those elements of the population that could have organized resistance to collective farms, the most politically active members of the village. In contrast, the mass operations of 1937–38 were most likely an attempt to destroy a "fifth column" of supposed enemies that Stalin feared would rise as the threat of war grew.

The centralized nature of the mass operations enabled their extraordinary scale and brutality. Emanating from Moscow, a series of orders called for the arrest, execution, and exile of huge portions of the population, including entire ethnic groups. The size of the terror and the process of its implementation have become clearer with the opening of the archives. Formerly secret sources have revealed the number of people who became victims of state violence. From 1930 to 1952, the state officially executed approximately 800,000 people. However, the real number of people whom state repression effectively murdered was much larger. Secret police statistics were often incomplete or simply did not include all those executed. Another factor was that torture in the interrogation rooms of the NKVD was sometimes fatal. Moreover, after prisoners arrived in the labor camps, conditions in the Gulag were often so devastating that the camps effectively transformed into sites of mass extermination, even if these deaths were not premeditated. Approximately twenty million people from 1930 to 1952 went through labor camps, labor colonies, and prisons. No fewer than six million people, primarily from the ranks of "kulaks" and national groups among the wartime "punished peoples," faced exile in Siberia or the Far North. In total, Stalin's regime sent an average of one million people per year to prison, camps, exile, or death.

People convicted for nonpolitical crimes were among those executed or sent to labor camps, too. At the same time, it is important to recognize that the harsh laws of Stalin's state had turned an extraordinary range of activities in social, economic, and political life into crimes. Many "felons" were ordinary people who had committed minor infractions or who ran afoul of the latest political campaign. For example, it was possible to receive a term in the labor camps for being late to work. In addition to those people executed, exiled, or imprisoned, tens of millions of citizens received noncustodial corrective labor sentences for various offenses, or lost their jobs and homes because they were relatives of "enemies of the people." Put in the broadest terms, no fewer than sixty million people, a considerable proportion of the population, faced either "hard" or "soft" repression during the twenty-some years of Stalin's rule.[3]

Stalin's victims included not only those who faced state repression but also those who died from famines that occurred during his rule. These famines were at least partially the product of political decisions. Undoubtedly, hunger was a weapon that helped to suppress peasant resistance to collectivization. In the famine of 1932–33 alone, five million people died. The huge numbers of people touched by the various forms of state violence demonstrate that Stalinism made political repression a part of everyday life in the USSR. It is almost impossible to imagine that any Soviet citizen was unconscious of the threat of their arrest or, at the very least, was unaware of ongoing repression in the country. How did this situation affect everyday behavior and strategies of survival? Mass terror was an important reason, although not the only reason, that people rapidly assimilated the values of the new regime and demonstrated their loyalty to it. Terror and the pervasive ideology of "class war" encouraged intolerance, facilitated the constant search for "enemies," and spread xenophobia. In the face of terror, deeds that might today seem ordinary took enormous strength of character. Only the brave acknowledged the injustice of false accusations or helped the victims of terror and their relatives. Nonetheless, these types of courageous people existed even under Stalin's regime.

Historians will surely continue to debate the motivations and effects of the terror. One scholar looking at the experience of one social group in the terror will come to different conclusions than a second historian who studies another group. Within a single segment of the population, too, individuals' behavior was not predictable. Even the most striking examples can only represent part of the story of the terror, but not its whole.

The book that awaits the reader holds a special place in the literature on the Great Terror. Like many other products of the explosion of studies on Stalinist repression, it addresses the major issues this foreword has raised. But Alexander Vatlin's book is also one of the first, and perhaps the very first, microhistory of Stalin's terror. It tells the story of how

NKVD agents organized and carried out Moscow's orders for the mass operations in one of the thousands of districts of the USSR—Kuntsevo district of Moscow province.

Why did Vatlin write about Kuntsevo? Sources dictated the author's choice. After many years of work with previously secret documents in the former KGB archive of Moscow province, a group of files drew his attention. These were the investigation files of arrestees from Kuntsevo district in 1937–38. Although good fortune led Vatlin to the set of Kuntsevo investigation files, they demonstrate how the terror unfolded more broadly.

To appreciate Vatlin's work, it is important to understand what documents are in these investigation files and how they can inform historians. And it is only possible to understand these files by following the path of people who fell into the grinder of repression during the Great Terror. Their first step was arrest by the local NKVD. Arrest orders were issued based on evidence of a person's past and current "hostile activity." It was common for NKVD officers to fabricate these accusations. For example, they enlisted so-called "staff witnesses" who blindly signed testimony with invented accusations. In each case, these materials became part of the investigation file and allow us to analyze the process of arrest.

The next stage in a victim's journey was the investigation. The typical investigation consisted of NKVD agents forcing the arrestees to sign a fabricated interrogation protocol in which they confessed to a fictitious crime. Officers obtained confessions using various tactics, most often through torture and beatings. These tactics were the norm for Stalin's secret police before and after the Great Terror. However, during the mass operations the NKVD undertook falsification on an industrial scale. Agents had to create a huge number of documents each day as evidence against arrestees. They included the interrogation protocols— if they can be called that—in the investigation files. Today these documentary reminders of human suffering have become important sources for historians.

Hastily finishing their paperwork, secret police officers then sent cases to the leadership. Ranking leaders in turn determined who would face a term in the Gulag and who would be executed by list. Hundreds of thousands of people were murdered because of the decisions of these extra-judicial commissions that issued hundreds of verdicts in a matter of hours.

The bloody wheel of terror could not turn forever. Moscow leaders issued an order in November 1938 for the end of the mass operations. The terror concluded in the same centralized manner in which it started. A reversal of the campaign began as soon as the mass operations ended. However, this countercampaign was just as much a product of Stalinism as the terror itself. A small number of victims were freed and some NKVD officers faced prosecution for their "sabotage" of police work. This procedure was one of Stalin's typical strategies. Having done their job, the executors of Stalin's orders were themselves purged. A key result of this "purge of the purgers" was that the NKVD was put back in its place after the dramatic increase in its powers in 1937–38.

In most cases, the victims of the Great Terror did not live to see better times. Hundreds of thousands of executions preceded hundreds of thousands of deaths in the Gulag. Those who survived their term in the camps frequently faced new charges and another sentence to hard labor. Anyone who had a reason to hold a grudge was a potential enemy according to the regime.

The state's reliance on political repression changed only after Stalin's death. Under Khrushchev, victims of the terror received rehabilitation, often posthumously, but the process only began after victims petitioned or their relatives appealed on their behalf. As they considered these appeals, authorities reviewed all material concerning the victim. Among the materials were the testimonies of NKVD officers arrested in the "purge of the purgers," where they spoke openly about their falsifications. This evidence, among other sources, became the basis for rehabilitation, and investigators incorporated it into the files.

Investigation files thus became one of the most important sources for understanding the process of the terror and the subsequent rehabilitation. The documents they contain present a challenge to historians. They are a combination of facts, outrageous falsehoods, and a mixture of both, where real events bled into investigators' inventions of political crime. Nonetheless, Vatlin was up to the task of working with these sources. Carefully and impartially, he analyzed the investigation files and sorted fact from fiction. The result is a vivid picture of terror at the district level.

The main actors in this book are the terror's victims and its executors. Although we already know much about the victims, Vatlin's work helps us understand the experience of Soviet citizens who fell into the jaws of repression. How did people become targets for arrest and what was the role of chance in the terror? What makes Vatlin's work truly pioneering, though, is its treatment of the executors of terror, presenting details from the lives of district-level NKVD bosses and a handful of ordinary agents in the terror. Lower-level bosses are particularly vivid in the book because they were the officers who most often faced repression after the completion of the mass operations. Under arrest, they gave some of the most striking testimony on the terror.

In studying these agents, the author shows us that NKVD agents were the products of a system. Every one of them was part of a professional patron-client network. These networks existed throughout the Soviet Union, and each had considerable strength and durability. In many cases, the foundation of these groups was mutual protection to guard against the constant threat of arrest. Each arrest of a group member or coworker dramatically increased the danger to other members of the group. NKVD agents knew better than anyone how repression spread and fiercely guarded against arrest among their group. In undertaking Moscow's plans for repression, secret police workers scrambled to overfulfill their quotas, engaging in "contests" to increase arrest numbers. As Vatlin shows, these contests were not a product of ideological conviction or fanaticism. Secret police officers, at least many of them, acted cynically under pressure from above. Their choice was simple: either fulfill the plan and participate in the murder of innocent people, or face one's own arrest.

The circumstances made criminals out of the police. It made officers lose their sense of humanity. Some did not only murder people to fulfill orders or to advance their careers. They stole from victims, appropriating belongings or even entire apartments. Vatlin's work provides a remarkable portrayal of these officers. In cases in Kuntsevo, investigators' greed alone could become the motivation for arrest. After the terror, a few NKVD agents received sentences for their "misappropriations." However, the majority escaped without receiving even the lightest punishment.

In the Soviet Union and in post-Soviet Russia, state and society have transitioned from Stalin's system of governance slowly and inconsistently. Many of the executors of Stalin's terror continued to work in the Soviet state after the dictator's death. Their successors are now trying to rehabilitate Stalinism and Stalin himself. This book serves as a barrier to the re-Stalinization of Russia. It reminds us how easily dictatorships destroyed, and can still destroy, millions of people throughout the world.

Preface to the English-Language Edition

Alexander Vatlin's local study of Stalinist repression appeared in 2004 in Russian as *Terror raionnogo masshtaba: "Massovye operatsii" NKVD v Kuntsevskom raione Moskovskoi oblasti v 1937–38 gg.* (Terror on a Regional Scale: The NKVD's "Mass Operations" in Kuntsevo District of Moscow Province, 1937–38). It remains a path-breaking study of the terror under Stalin, refreshing in its fluid, journalistic style. The challenge of translating and editing this work was both linguistic and cultural. Although Vatlin's ideas in the work remain untouched, the author and editor have worked together to accommodate an English-language audience.

Unlike Anglo-American academic studies, Russian works typically include only a short introduction that forgoes a detailed discussion of historiography, context, and the work's place in the literature. Because the Russian original lacks a traditional Anglo-American framing, *Agents of Terror* compensates in two ways. First, the editor has provided an introduction to the Great Terror that situates the work in the broader historical and scholarly contexts of Stalinist repression. Second, the editor has expanded Vatlin's introduction by moving a section on source analysis from later in the book and incorporating his discussions with the author into the text.

The remainder of the translation itself has undergone minimal changes from the original. It includes minor stylistic reorganizations of paragraphs and sentences. The citations in the English-language edition are more robust than in the original. The editor has updated the notes with citations from the latest scholarly works on the Great Terror. The author shared his notes with the editor, who added archival citations where there had previously been none. The editor cut sentences in the few cases where the author could not provide a source for an uncited piece of evidence. This edition also includes brief contextualizing explanations of events and places familiar to a Russian audience but unfamiliar elsewhere. Finally, the Russian-language original included a list of the known victims of the Great Terror in Kuntsevo that does not appear in the current edition. The author and editor agreed that this information was superfluous for an audience outside of Russia.

The author and editor would like to write a few words of thanks to those who supported the research of the Russian original and its adaptation into English. A special thanks must go to the director of the State Archive of the Russian Federation, S. V. Mironenko, deputy director L. A. Rogovaia and department head D. Ch. Nodiia. Writing the original manuscript was made possible with the help of L. A. Golovkova, N. S. Grishchenko, W. Hedeler, M. Junge, L. K. Karlova, F. McLoughlin, A. I. Mikhailova, R. Mueller, N. S. Musienko, N. V. Petrov, A. B. Roginskii, and Iu. T. Tutochkin. M. P. Prostov donated several photographs of historic Kuntsevo.

Jadwiga Biskupska, Susan Grant, and Katherine Zubovich read parts of the translation and introduction. Their comments, and those of the anonymous peer reviewers, helped this edition stay true to the original while adding perspectives and information necessary for an Anglophone audience. Lynne Viola also deserves special thanks for her reading of the manuscript. The enthusiasm of Gwen Walker and her staff at the University of Wisconsin Press for this project made adapting it a pleasure. The translation was written at the University of Toronto and at the International Center for the History and Sociology of World War II and Its Consequences of the Higher School of Economics in Moscow.

Introduction to the English-Language Edition

Seth Bernstein

In 1937–38 an unprecedented wave of repression washed over Stalin's Soviet Union. Among former elites, a series of show trials and high-profile arrests targeted the ranks of the party and intelligentsia. Beyond these well-known proceedings, more than a million people disappeared in secret "mass operations" run by the People's Commissariat of Internal Affairs (NKVD), the ministry that oversaw the criminal and secret police. Over two years, the NKVD arrested a minimum of 1.5 million people and saw roughly 700,000 sentenced to death for crimes they did not commit or for activities that could hardly be classified as crimes at all.[1] But aggregated statistics belie the way that repression occurred on the ground, where officers conducted arrests and extracted confessions victim by victim. In each of the USSR's several thousand districts, the equivalent of a county, an NKVD office with a handful of investigators operated the machine of terror.

The years 1937–38 have been a topic of horror and fascination for nearly eight decades. Known alternately as the Great Terror, the Great Purge, and the *ezhovshchina* (the reign of Nikolai Ezhov, NKVD commissar), it was a subject where politics and lack of sources obscured what scholars could know about one of the largest incidents of state violence in history.[2] Depending on who wrote the history and when, interpretations of the Great Terror changed drastically. Once conceived on both sides of the Iron Curtain as an elite purge above all, new evidence from the partial opening of Soviet archives has transformed this understanding of repression under Stalin. Above all, scholars learned about the

mass operations, overlapping campaigns where NKVD officers conducted preemptive arrests by quota of nonelites among "anti-Soviet
elements" and "hostile nationalities." Much of the writing on Stalin-era
repression has focused on the culpability of the leading figures in the
terror, above all on Soviet dictator Iosif Stalin, and historians have continued to generate new findings about the terror as planned in Moscow.
However, as ruthless as Stalin was, he did not beat the prisoners being
interrogated himself. Even NKVD commissar Nikolai Ezhov, who did
interrogate high-ranking victims, did not take to the countryside or the
factories to find ordinary "enemies of the people."[3] Lack of evidence
about the interactions of arrestees and NKVD officers has meant that
few works have examined Stalinist repression at the local level. Although
there are a wealth of studies about the production of mass violence in
other contexts—above all by the Nazi German regime—the story of the
executors of repression has been a blank spot in the history of Stalinism.[4]

Alexander Vatlin's *Agents of Terror* fills this gap with a detailed
history of the NKVD in Kuntsevo district of Moscow province during
1937–38. Although Kuntsevo was near the capital, its story represents
how the terror unfolded among nonelites throughout the USSR. Using
the investigations of the district's victims and of its NKVD officers, Vatlin
is able to reconstruct the events of the mass operations at the local level.
The majority of arrestees were not politicians but instead were peasants,
workers, and national minorities. The executors of terror were not revolutionary ideologues but fearful and ambitious officers desperate to
fulfill the plans of their bosses in the clan-like system of the NKVD. In
exploring their world, Vatlin challenges readers to go beyond the central
figures in the terror, assessing notions of historical agency and moral
responsibility in Stalin-era crimes.

This introduction places Vatlin's work in the broader context of the mass
operations and evolving interpretations of the terror. During the partial
opening of the Soviet archives in the 1990s, the greatest secret the de-
classified documents held about the Great Terror or perhaps any other
aspect of Soviet history was the mass operations. What was shocking
about them was their scope, targets, and directed nature. Only when
the Russian press published orders from the mass operations in 1992 did
it become clear that nonelites made up the vast majority of victims of
repression in the Great Terror.[5] Historians learned that the terror was
not a singular, massive campaign but a series of operations the NKVD
undertook in 1937–38 targeting specific groups of "anti-Soviet elements."

The discovery of the mass operations in the archives has forced historians to revise the familiar story of political terror into a history of social repression and ethnic cleansing.

Cold War–era studies of Stalinist repression often drew a direct line from the murder of Leningrad party leader Sergei Kirov in 1934 to the mass terror of 1937–38. However, new research has placed the origins of the Great Terror earlier, in 1929. At the end of that year, Stalin pushed for the wholesale collectivization of agriculture as a means of extracting resources for the forced-pace industrialization of the Soviet Union. During collectivization, the United State Political Administration (OGPU), the regime's state security organization, forced families to join collective farms through coercion, above all through the threat of "dekulakization." The term kulak initially referred to wealthy peasants, supposed enemies of Soviet power, but it became a comprehensive charge leveled against all those who resisted collectivization.[6] In each province, OGPU leaders received control figures for numbers of supposed kulaks to exile to "special settlements," often in desolate landscapes far from their home villages.[7] The result of collectivization and overzealous grain requisitioning ordered by Moscow was a mass famine in 1932–33 that caused the deaths of millions.

Collectivization unleashed chaos in the USSR. Peasants flooded from the starving countryside to the cities and dekulakized peasants fled from exile. This turmoil sparked a shift in policing strategies in the OGPU. Under the influence of deputy chief Genrikh Iagoda, the OGPU began to undertake sweeps of the urban population to remove "socially harmful elements" from the cities. In 1932 the Soviet state introduced a passport system under the control of the criminal police (part of the OGPU since 1930) that became another tool in monitoring social groups in the Soviet Union. This method of policing was prophylactic. Rather than punishing citizens for the crimes they committed, Iagoda's police searched for members of groups Moscow identified as likely to be the cause of social disorder.[8]

In 1934 the OGPU reformed as the NKVD with Iagoda at its head. The OGPU-NKVD had become a massive policing organization whose subunits included the civil police, the Gulag, registrars, and firefighters. But its leading division was the Chief Administration of State Security (GUGB), which was responsible for espionage, counterintelligence, and policing of economic and political crime. This structure repeated in the non-Russian republics of the Soviet Union and in every province. At the lowest level were the NKVD's state security offices in rural and municipal districts. Even at these lower levels, the commissar in Moscow had to confirm all appointments at and above the level of district chief, ensuring central control over policing.[9]

Although Iagoda's appointment as head of the NKVD seemed to indicate that mass policing techniques had won over political accusations, the latter technique returned forcefully after the murder of Sergei Kirov. On December 1, 1934, Leonid Nikolaev, an unstable former party member, entered Kirov's office and shot him dead. Khrushchev-era denunciations of Stalin asserted that the dictator himself masterminded the assassination to eliminate a supposed rival in the party, although new evidence has shown that Stalin almost certainly did not plan the murder.[10] However, Stalin used the assassination as a pretense to intensify repression in the country, in particular against old political enemies. When news of the murder reached the Kremlin, he immediately drafted a law that allowed the state to bypass judicial procedures in punishing acts of "terrorism" like Kirov's assassination. Then, rather than assigning the murder investigation to the NKVD, he called upon Nikolai Ezhov, the head of the Party Control Commission (the party's administration charged with internal discipline), to lead the case.

As Ezhov would later recall, at a party Central Committee meeting in early 1937, Stalin told him to "look for the killer among the Zinov'evites," the followers of Grigorii Zinov'ev, the defeated opponent of Stalin's who had been Leningrad party leader before Kirov. Ezhov went on to say that NKVD officials had not wanted to follow this line of inquiry, but that Stalin himself had called Iagoda and said, "Watch it or we'll beat your face in."[11] Ezhov returned from Leningrad with accusations against Zinov'ev and his fellow former oppositionist Lev Kamenev. Stalin ordered their arrest and the two admitted under duress at a secret trial to "moral complicity" in the assassination. Although Kamenev initially received five years in prison, both were eventually sentenced to ten years of confinement.

When NKVD leaders proved unenthusiastic about continuing to press upon the supposed conspiracy of oppositionists, Stalin again enlisted Ezhov, who effectively acted against Iagoda within the NKVD. With Ezhov handling the case, Stalin's regime brought new charges against Zinov'ev and Kamenev, and from August 19 to 24, 1936, the two headlined a show trial of sixteen former party leaders. The group, now framed as the "Trotskyist-Zinov'evite Center," confessed that they had conspired to assassinate Stalin and other figures. Successfully demanding their execution, Prosecutor General Andrei Vyshinsky shouted at the trial's closing, "Rabid dogs must be shot!" The front page of *Pravda* printed these words in bold on August 23, alongside articles calling for "death to murderers of Kirov"—other former oppositionists named during the trial whom Stalin would send to two subsequent show trials.[12]

Soon after the first show trial, Ezhov presented Stalin with accusations that the leadership of the NKVD had failed to uncover other conspiracies within the party. Stalin, who seems to have desired this kind of material, replaced Iagoda with Ezhov.[13] Iagoda himself would be sentenced to execution at the third Moscow show trial in 1938. Ezhov lost no time replacing Iagoda's subordinates with his own loyalists.[14] With the demise of Iagoda, it seemed that mass policing was also on the decline. Ezhov's specialization was intraparty policing, and he did not believe in using the political police for controlling social order like Iagoda.[15] In late 1936 at the higher reaches of the party, Ezhov arrested provincial party leaders and in the spring of 1937 undertook the arrests of military leaders like Mikhail Tukhachevskii. The fall of these leaders usually preceded the arrest of their subordinates.[16] At the February–March 1937 Central Committee plenary meeting, Stalin announced that large numbers of Trotskyists and other enemies had penetrated the party and called for members to unmask them.[17] Local party meetings became trials where members attempted to discover enemies hidden within their midst or face accusations that they themselves lacked vigilance.[18] Arrest followed expulsion from the party in a matter of days or even minutes. NKVD officers, who often provided the incriminating information against party members, were sometimes on hand at meetings to detain the expellees.

In the midst of the hunt for enemies within the party, the mass operations began. On July 2, 1937, the Politburo issued a secret message to provincial party leaders announcing that large numbers of kulaks and criminals roamed the country and were responsible for "anti-Soviet crime." It called for the preemptive mass arrest and execution of "the most dangerous" of them. The directive seems to have appeared without any significant provocation. It asked provincial party chiefs to return control figures for the number of hostile elements in their territories. At the end of the month, Ezhov signed NKVD Order 00447, often called the "kulak operation" because it targeted dekulakized peasants alongside recidivist criminals and other "anti-Soviet elements." The operation established quotas (*limity*—limits) for arrests for provincial NKVD administrations to fulfill in category one (execution) and category two (forced labor). In each province, an extrajudicial "troika" (committee of three), usually made up of the province's head of the NKVD, head of the party, and state prosecutor, reviewed cases and passed sentences. Subsequent orders in the mass operations targeted national minority groups who had a homeland outside the USSR: Germans, Poles, and Finns among others.

The campaign used a radicalized version of earlier mass policing, in which authorities had acted preemptively against various "socially harmful elements." In 1937–38, however, the punishment for arrestees was not exile but death or a term in forced labor camps. Accusations against the victims took on a political character, as indictments for terrorism and espionage became common. The quotas drove the campaign. Although the term used was "limits," the orders made it possible for provincial leaders to ask for increased "limits." Unceasing pressure from Moscow and provincial centers made these supposed maximums into control figures to fulfill. NKVD operatives at the local level produced more than a million arrests in the mass operations from August 1937 through March 1938.[19]

In 1938 new arrests largely stopped, although the operations formally continued to be in effect. Meanwhile, Stalin had become convinced that the search for enemies was undermining the party's ability to govern the country and perhaps the NKVD.[20] The January 1938 Central Committee plenum acknowledged that "mistakes" had been made in the search for enemies within the party.[21] In August Stalin took the first steps toward replacing Ezhov when Lavrentii Beria became the commissar's first deputy. On November 15, the Politburo disbanded the troikas. By that time, several ranking NKVD officials had gone into hiding or fled the country. Apparently they sensed a pattern between Beria's rise and Ezhov's ouster of Iagoda. Ezhov took responsibility for allowing these enemies to penetrate the NKVD and resigned on November 23.[22] Beria replaced him almost immediately.

Beria's first steps as commissar were predictable. As Ezhov himself had done, the new police head replaced his predecessor's lieutenants with his own loyalists, arresting the former commissar and his underlings in a "purge of the purgers." The campaign against Ezhov's personnel was in some aspects a reversal of the mass operations. A key charge in many of the investigations was that NKVD officials had falsified cases and the NKVD undertook a limited review of cases based on petitions. Although many of the NKVD personnel involved in the mass operations would face punishment, few of their victims were ultimately released before their terms ended.

Before the partial opening of the Soviet archives, writers understood the apex of Stalinist repression through contemporary newspaper sources, memoirs, and limited official documents. The main questions they asked about the terror concerned the magnitude of repression, the extent of Stalin's personal role, and the purpose of the elite purge. The traditional perspective, exemplified by Robert Conquest's *The Great Terror* (which coined the term), asserted that victims numbered in the millions, and that Stalin's role was large and motivated by his mad desire for control.[23] In contrast, revisionist works, exemplified by J. Arch Getty's *The Origins of the Great Purges*, argued that the number of victims may have been smaller and that while Stalin presided over the terror, other dynamics within the party and society played a role in repression.[24] Few scholars doubted that urban elites were the main targets of a politically motivated purge and that it stemmed to some degree from Stalin's desire for power and centralization of authority.

With the release of previously classified data in the 1990s, researchers quickly gained answers to these contested questions. They learned from internal reports of the Khrushchev period that police counted approximately 1.5 million arrests, including 681,692 people executed for the years 1937–38. These figures continue to be a point of dispute for several reasons. They do not include the execution lists that Stalin signed personally, accounting for roughly forty thousand additional people.[25] Others argue for counting mortality in the Gulag alongside executions.[26] Still others contest the validity of the data from Soviet police sources altogether.[27] Documents show that more than presiding over the terror, Stalin was its architect. His role is particularly visible in his initiation of Order 00447 in July 1937.

The mass operations made it impossible to envision the Great Terror as strictly or even primarily a campaign against Stalin's perceived political foes. Instead historians like David Shearer and Paul Hagenloh have convincingly shown that Stalin directed the terror as a deadly prophylactic campaign against elements of society he believed were dangers to the Soviet state.[28] Although historians have learned a great deal about the planning and operation of the Great Terror in the last twenty-five years, their findings have raised new questions. We have operational documents from the mass operations—orders providing limits by

province, and procedural instructions. However, materials on the motivations of the terror are scarcer. The campaign against Stalin's political
enemies began immediately after the murder of Kirov. In contrast, no
particular event seems to have sparked the mass operations.

In interpreting the motivations behind the terror, Oleg Khlevniuk
has offered the most convincing view, that Stalin believed the campaigns
were necessary to eliminate a potential "fifth column" in the event of a
seemingly inevitable foreign invasion.[29] When interviewed in the 1980s,
Stalin's chief associate Viacheslav Molotov claimed that this threat had
motivated repression in 1937.[30] In May 1937, during the Spanish Civil
War, when the Soviet-backed coalition of Republican forces faced off
against the German and Italian-supported Fascist and conservative
forces, members of the leftist coalition rebelled.[31] Khlevniuk argues that
a similar fear of wartime internal discord among disaffected Soviets
drove the terror. In June 1937, days before Stalin initiated the mass
operations, Western Siberian party secretary Robert Eikhe sent the
Politburo an alarming report about "anti-Soviet elements" who were
prepared to rebel in the event of a Japanese invasion.[32] Although neither
Stalin's orders nor Order 00447 presented themselves as preparation
for war, the timing of the Eikhe report and Molotov's remembrances
provide the best explanation for the campaigns.

An alternate interpretation of the impetus behind the mass operations comes from Rolf Binner and Marc Junge. In their view, Order
00447 was in part an attempt to create a utopian society. In 1934, Stalin
declared that the Soviet Union had become a socialist country, having
defeated class enemies within its borders. Yet the continued presence
of various "anti-Soviet elements" was a black mark on socialism that
Stalin could eliminate finally in a massive wave of repression.[33] However, this view provides a weak explanation for the timing of Order
00447 in the summer of 1937. It also has trouble accounting for the
national operations. The mass arrests of Germans, Poles, and other
"hostile nationalities" seem more plausible as a measure to eliminate
potential spies and wartime collaborators than as a means of perfecting
a socialist society.

The first two interpretations of the mass operations assume that
central leaders, above all Stalin, were the primary drivers of the terror.
In contrast, J. Arch Getty suggests that regional chiefs played a crucial
role in pushing for the mass operations. Getty asserts that party leaders
intended to allow free elections to the Supreme Soviet promised by the
1936 Soviet ("Stalin") constitution. However, regional party leaders

feared that disaffected citizens in their provinces would vote for non-party candidates from the clergy or elsewhere. In Getty's interpretation, these regional leaders demanded repression to solve the problem of disaffected people. The center's limits were not quotas but instead served as "maximums more than minimums" that Stalin used to ensure party leaders in the regions did not use repression excessively against their own enemies. However, Getty's evidence linking the mass operations to the elections comes exclusively from prisoners themselves, who could hardly have known the inner workings of the Politburo.[34] And while *limity* might literally translate to "limits," it is clear from Kuntsevo and elsewhere that NKVD officers, based on verbal orders from above, understood the numbers as quotas to be fulfilled.[35] It seems more likely that provincial officials fulfilled and increased their plans for arrest because they believed it was what Stalin desired. In this sense, they would have exhibited what Ian Kershaw described in the Nazi German context as "working toward the Fuhrer," where the murder of the Jews developed from ranking Nazis' competition to meet Hitler's wishes in the absence of direct orders.[36]

These debates about the origins of the mass operations analyze the motives of political elites for instigating repression. Yet the terror was not just a set of quotas imposed from above; it was also the arrest, interrogation, and sentencing of more than a million individual people. How much influence could Stalin have exerted on each of these investigations and how much did local pressures and circumstances shape their outcomes? Were victims truly members of the campaigns' target groups or did victims produced by societal input (e.g., denunciations) and expediency fill the quotas?

A number of studies of Stalinist society have argued that while Moscow retained and frequently used a monopoly on violence, local conflicts could shape who exactly became the victims of repression. A classic treatment of this issue is in Jan Gross's study of the Sovietization of Eastern Poland from 1939 to 1941. When the Red Army crossed into what became Western Ukraine and Western Belorussia, it counted on locals who could identify opponents of the new regime. This reliance allowed locals to use the repressive power of the state to achieve their own goals. Gross argues, "The real power of a totalitarian state results from its being at the disposal of every inhabitant, available for hire at a moment's notice."[37] Similarly, local show trials during the terror channeled popular dissatisfaction toward representatives of Soviet power. Although central authorities initiated the trials and determined their "master plot," peasants took part in the proceedings and relished the downfall of their immediate oppressors.[38] In Kuntsevo, too, denunciations to the police—and actions by NKVD officers themselves—were instrumental in gaining apartments, removing unwanted coworkers, or even getting rid of in-laws.[39]

In the Great Terror itself, perhaps the most important factor that contributed to the expansion of repression from below was fear. Wendy Goldman's studies of Moscow factory party organizations during the 1930s reveal a dynamic of panic that drove the terror at the local level. A common accusation in party meetings was that a member had failed to unmask a colleague or mentor whom the party later expelled or the NKVD arrested. The shocking arrests of seemingly loyal local leaders suggested that anyone could potentially be an "enemy of the people." Repression was planned in the Kremlin but among rank-and-file party members it seemed random. This atmosphere of fear and mutual suspicion encouraged party members to denounce preemptively or face charges that they had protected a masked Trotskyist.[40] Gabor Rittersporn proposes an alternate interpretation: that many citizens' belief in the reality of spies, wreckers, and saboteurs motivated their denunciations.[41]

Those that denounced others were sometimes days or weeks from their own arrest, and the malleability of roles in the terror makes assigning agency and blame complicated. The best-studied case of mass murder is Nazi Germany and any instance of large-scale repression inevitably draws this comparison. In the German case, the line between victims and perpetrators was clearer than under Stalinism. Of course, some Jews became participants in genocide as Kapos in concentration camps or officials in ghettos. However, they could not become members of the Einsatzgruppen—the mobile killing detachments that operated in Eastern Europe.[42] Likewise, the Einsatzgruppen did not face genocidal murder at the hands of their former unit. In contrast, Soviet party members whose accusations had sent friends and colleagues to the Gulag one day could find themselves in an NKVD interrogation the next.[43] Moreover, many of the NKVD officers who had conducted those interrogations found themselves under arrest after Beria replaced Ezhov as commissar. It is clear that outside of the Kremlin itself, Stalin's Soviet Union was filled with "gray areas," as Lynne Viola asserts, where victims and perpetrators switched places continuously.[44]

Alexander Vatlin's case study of the Great Terror in Kuntsevo cannot address all the questions that have come out of new research on

Stalinist repression. Its main actors, the NKVD officers of Kuntsevo, were not concerned with the far-reaching policy of Moscow leaders. They worked in a semirural district on the edges of the capital where they oversaw a population of peasant farmers and factory workers. Although *Agents of Terror* presents a view of Stalinist repression at the local level, any case study has particularities that cannot be generalized. Kuntsevo's population was not full of Muscovites but the concerns of the victims and perpetrators in the district reflected the influence of the city. Victims included peasants who came into contact with vacationing German embassy officials. The ambitious officers of Kuntsevo's NKVD commuted from Moscow and tried to fulfill and overfulfill their quotas for arrests as a Stakhanovite might overachieve on the plan for iron.

Nonetheless, *Agents of Terror* presents one of the most complete pictures of the terror on the ground since historians discovered the mass operations. Vatlin searched through hundreds of the investigation files of Kuntsevo's victims to create a sprawling treatment of the terror. He guides readers into the political theater of the district, the show trials in miniature, before taking them into the interrogation cell to learn how the NKVD produced confessions. He examines popular opinion as registered in the case files of the mass operations and then explores the history of the group of German communists in the district. Indeed, his writing is so wide-ranging that it can be difficult to identify the book's main claim. At the core of the book, though, is the assertion that planning and pressure from above created a system of arbitrary policing on the ground. Although the mass operations targeted specific groups, the investigators implementing the plan for arrests often chose their victims through expediency or even for personal gain. They used violence, deception, and widespread falsification to enact Stalin's terror.

Vatlin is skeptical about NKVD officers' belief in a pervasive anti-Soviet conspiracy but treats their personal convictions as a secondary issue. Whatever they believed, investigators had their *limity* to fulfill and the hierarchical structure of the NKVD allowed superiors to compel underlings to complete their quotas for arrest. Many NKVD workers were well aware that their bosses had incriminating information about them, as was the case for virtually every ranking officer in Kuntsevo. In turn, bosses in provincial NKVD administrations faced similar pressure from Ezhov, who was himself surely aware that hesitation to fulfill Stalin's orders would mean his demise, as it had for his predecessor Iagoda. This top-down compulsion, as well as a camaraderie between police, created a clan-like system of mutual protection in the NKVD.

Throughout the Soviet Union, bureaucratic "families" within the Soviet party-state contained patrons and clients who helped one another survive the dangers of Stalinist politics.[45] In the state security organs, these groups ensured that officers were willing to undertake any task, no matter how unjust. Refusal to fulfill orders or betrayal of the clan meant the destruction of the officer. Particularly in March 1938, as orders came to finish arrests in the campaigns, the rush to fulfill quotas with arrestees mattered more than if the accused fit the specific campaign—if an arrestee in the Polish operation was truly a Pole, for example.

With so many falsified cases and confessions signed under coercion, is it possible to believe any of the materials that the NKVD produced in this period? This question is especially pertinent for *Agents of Terror*, whose main sources are police investigation files, including those of Kuntsevo NKVD agents themselves. Vatlin's source methodology will strike some as inconsistent. He dismisses the interrogations of victims in the mass operations as falsified. However, he largely accepts the interrogations of arrested NKVD officers as genuine, although Vatlin acknowledges that they, too, were extracted under coercion. In 1939 Kuntsevo officers who were not arrested had to compile reports about their activities in the mass operations and used the opportunity to denounce their arrested colleagues as the main villains of the terror. Vatlin treats these accounts as the mostly truthful explanations of fearful men trying to escape punishment. Yet read differently, these reports might be the best proof that investigators were utterly cynical and willing to follow whatever policy the leadership handed them, perhaps even providing false accusations against their former bosses.

Nonetheless, Vatlin's treatment of sources has sound logic. Investigators' interpretations were false in virtually all cases, as were their most outlandish accusations, but many interrogations contained detailed evidence about events or conversations that would have been difficult to fabricate entirely. The investigations of NKVD personnel provide meticulous retellings of the mass falsification of cases and corruption that occurred in Kuntsevo. These crimes surely happened even if they were not the work of a counterrevolutionary Trotskyist cabal, as investigators asserted.[46] Vatlin is careful to use these materials, as well as investigators' reports from 1939, in conjunction with corroborating evidence from victims' appeals and testimony from rehabilitation proceedings in the Khrushchev period. Other interpretations would have been possible, particularly about the investigators' motivations. However, Vatlin provides a convincing account of the methods and impulses that drove the terror from below.

Agents of Terror recognizes that secret police workers faced repression and coercion but never absolves them of their roles as perpetrators. Kuntsevo's NKVD did not enjoy a great deal of agency in undertaking repression. Pressure from the center meant that its officers could hardly have gone against their superiors without losing their freedom or even their lives. However, Vatlin does assign officers responsibility for performing "the leading roles in a play written in the Kremlin and at Lubianka."[47] The example of Kuntsevo suggests a stark moral dichotomy between NKVD investigators and the accused whom they routinely forced to sign false confessions under torture.

Vatlin's engagement with the issue of responsibility in the terror is not only a matter of academic inquiry but an attempt to achieve a measure of justice in a country that has often ignored Stalin-era crimes. During Khrushchev's Thaw, particularly after the "Secret Speech" in 1956, the party rehabilitated limited numbers of purged and executed party members but not the huge numbers of victims in the mass operations. After the failed communist coup of 1991, Russian president Boris Yeltsin introduced legislation to rehabilitate victims of Stalinist repression. Archives allowed victims and researchers inside the repressive machinery of Stalin's regime.

Despite these efforts, the USSR and post-Soviet Russia never grappled with the Stalinist past as Germany has dealt with its history of Nazism, or as some former socialist republics have engaged their pasts through lustration. A year after Yeltsin banned the Communist Party in 1991, it returned as a powerful force that opposed any attempt at a reckoning with the past. Moreover, the issue of de-Stalinization was remote from the problems facing Russians in the turbulent 1990s. Since the rise of Vladimir Putin, the country has experienced a partial rehabilitation of the historical image of Stalin.[48] In the minds of some Russians, the dictator was the hero of World War II and not the chief cause of millions of deaths. The main push to commemorate the victims of Stalinism has come from human rights organizations. Attempting to fulfill poet Anna Akhmatova's call to "name them all by name" in her "Requiem," these organizations have been especially active in publishing martyrologies—books containing the names and sentences of victims of political repression.

Vatlin is a Moscow State University professor who works primarily on the history of the Communist International (Comintern, the Moscow-led organization of the world's communist parties) and German-Soviet relations. Yet in the 1990s he became involved in a project to commemorate the thousands who died at the Butovo execution site in Moscow.

Although the Russian version of *Agents of Terror* transcends the martyr-ology genre, it also contains a list of the known victims from Kuntsevo and to some degree is a tribute to them. In other ways, too, this work is a clear product of the research environment of the first years after the fall of the USSR. From 1992 until 2006, the archival files of victims were available for researchers like Vatlin. Today, a study like *Agents of Terror* would be impossible because only victims themselves or their family members can access this information. Because of political changes in Russia, the window for any formal judgment of actors in Soviet repres-sion, let alone the long-dead people who took part in Stalin's terror, has likely closed. However, Vatlin insists that a moral reckoning is still possible by understanding how mass repression worked outside the walls of the Kremlin and by remembering whom it victimized.

Abbreviations

d.	delo (file)
f.	fond (collection)
op.	opis (subcollection)
FSB	Federal'naia sluzhba bezopasnosti (Federal Security Bureau)
GARF	Gosudarstvennyi arkhiv Rossiiskoi Federatsii (State Archive of the Russian Federation)
GUGB	Glavnoe upravlenie gosudarstvennoi bezopasnosti (Chief Administration of State Security)
KIM	Kommunisticheskii internatsional molodezhi (Communist Youth International)
KPD	Kommunistische Partei Deutschlands (Communist Party of Germany)
MVD	Ministerstvo vnutrennikh del (Ministry of Internal Affairs)
NKVD	Narodnyi komissariat vnutrennikh del (People's Commissariat of Internal Affairs)
OGPU	Ob"edinennoe gosudarstvennoe politicheskoe upravlenie (United State Political Administration)
OKhDOPIM	Otdel khraneniia dokumentov obshchestvenno-politicheskoi istorii Moskvy (Department for the Preservation of Documentation of the Social-Political History of Moscow)

RGASPI   Rossiiskii gosudarstvennyi arkhiv sotsial'no-
                politicheskoi istorii (Russian State Archive of Social-
                Political History)

Agents of Terror

Introduction: Why Kuntsevo? Setting the Stage

The residents of today's Kuntsevo, a prestigious municipal district in Moscow, cannot imagine that fifty years ago their neighborhood was a quiet provincial town. With its small train station and pine trees scattered about the abandoned estates of the prewar era, it hardly differed from thousands of other small towns in Russia. In 1937 *The Great Soviet Encyclopedia* listed Kuntsevo's population as 40,637 and noted that it had received the official designation of town only in 1925.

Located on the right bank of the Moscow River southwest of the capital, Kuntsevo's history was linked to many of the great figures of Russia's past. The boyar family Miloslavskii first owned the estate that gave the town its name before it passed to the illustrious Naryshkin family. Visitors to the town included Catherine the Great and King Frederick Wilhelm III of Prussia. Both stayed at the palace in Kuntsevo that stands to this day, albeit in heavily reconstructed form. In the nineteenth century, the picturesque slopes near creeks and gulches became the site of dachas and the backdrop of classic Russian literature. Turgenev's gentlemen and their breathless beauties gave way to successful businessmen and bankers at the turn of the century. With them came Kuntsevo's first automobiles, tennis courts, and charity balls. The Naryshkin estate soon became the property of the cinema tycoon Soldatenkov.

In 1871 the Western train line connecting Moscow with Minsk and Warsaw was built through Kuntsevo. Train traffic fostered new light industry like textile factories, and tradespeople as well as dacha-goers populated the roads beside the railroad tracks. Kuntsevo was still just a village with seventy-four estates and 496 residents. Gradually, however, the face of the ancient Russian village in the land of the Naryshkins changed. Ambitious peasants, positioning themselves to address the demands of Muscovites, began to deliver dairy products to the capital and learned to produce vegetables in hot houses.

The revolution of 1917 brought devastation to the area around Moscow. The gentlemen disappeared and ordinary people had bigger concerns than vacation homes. The regime nationalized many of the luxurious dachas and divided them into communal apartments. These houses often became the last haven for their former owners—those who had been unable or unwilling to flee the country. Workers settled nearby, attracted by the opportunity to make money in the capital or evicted from their homes in the course of collectivization and the removal of the so-called kulaks (rich peasants) in the early 1930s.[1] The slope near the ravine at the Mozhaisk Highway grew into a shanty-town, called "Shanghai" in the surrounding villages.

The state highway that spans the district from east to west then, as now, carried Russia's grandees in their limousines. Stalin's own dacha was located in the valley near the river Setun'. To this day, the older generation of Muscovites swear that a secret subway line links it to the capital. Ordinary dacha-goers tried to avoid the grounds around the heavily guarded, green batten fence. Average people had their own concerns, much smaller than those decided in that dacha. In the town itself, there was an inconspicuous two-story wooden building at 5 Zagorskii Street, painted in a standard lettuce-green hue. It was the Kuntsevo district office of the People's Commissariat of Internal Affairs (NKVD), the main setting of this book. The office was just one cog among thousands in a machine of state terror set in motion in 1937–38.[2]

Any reference to these years conjures visions of the notorious show trials at the House of the Soviets and the "execution lists" of the party's old guard signed by Stalin. The Great Terror evokes the shadowy outline of the NKVD headquarters at Lubianka prison and its chief the "iron commissar" Nikolai Ezhov. These images all represent the standard interpretation of the terror as seen through the prism of the capital— history from above. This vantage point has prevented historians from understanding the institutional dynamics of state terror in Stalin's regime.[3] The terror emanated from the Kremlin to the outermost corners of the state. The history of the Great Terror told from Lubianka alone cannot explain the scale of repression in 1937–38. Even recent studies of

A ruined manor house of "former people" from Troitse-Golenishchevo, just outside the Moscow city limits. (from the author's collection)

republic and provincial police administrations largely ignore the NKVD unit closest to the ground—the district office.[4]

Understanding the workings of the NKVD at the lowest level is essential for comprehending how the center's quotas for mass repression were interpreted in their implementation.[5] NKVD chiefs in the districts lacked necessary equipment, cadres, and facilities. They had to produce regular reports on informants, create lists of potential "enemies of the people," and carry out arrests. Yet their bosses in the provincial and central NKVD administrations cared little about the limitations district offices faced or the content of their investigations. These leaders wanted one thing: to fulfill the quota for arrests. In exchange, high-ranking NKVD bosses promised impunity and promotion when district leaders accomplished their plan for arrests and confessions.

In the Great Terror, the absurdity of Stalinist repression reached its apex. It was an era where identities written in boiler-plate phrases on bureaucratic forms and arbitrary chance decided life and death. And it was at the district level that the majority of Soviet citizens experienced the oppressive power of Stalin's totalitarian regime. Nonetheless, Khrushchev hardly mentioned repression at the local level in his famous "Secret Speech" at the Twentieth Party Congress in 1956. Nor does repression at the local level appear in the memoirs of those who returned from the Gulag. However, ordinary people remembered the arbitrary crimes of the state. Those it murdered were not only distant "enemies of the people" among Moscow elites but relatives, friends, and loved ones.

In September 1937, Moscow province had fifty-two administrative districts. The capital itself included twenty municipal districts. The population of Moscow province was 3.8 million before the war, not including the city itself. A crude calculation of population over districts shows that for every NKVD district office, there were some seventy thousand Soviet citizens. The tight coverage of the population by Chekists—the term for Soviet secret police derived from its revolutionary incarnation, the Cheka—was the main factor that contributed to the speed and magnitude of repression.

Agents of Terror is a book about state terror at the district level. The project grew out of my work with an organization called the Group for the Commemoration of the Memory of Victims of Political Repression. Our mission was to catalog those buried at Butovo, a village in Moscow province. The settlement was the site of an NKVD firing range that turned into the execution ground for over twenty thousand victims from August 1937 to October 1938.[6] NKVD investigators from municipal and district offices charged most of those executed with crimes against the state. However, in the majority of cases the investigators knowingly fabricated these crimes. Moscow province was not exceptional in this regard but utterly typical. Post-Soviet martyrologies—enormous lists of victims from nearly every province—confirm the ubiquity and scale of the terror.[7]

Evidence about the district-level NKVD is often scarce. Most archival documentation from the period before World War II was lost. Internal documents (e.g., office correspondence) were supposed to be destroyed after twenty years. Moreover, many NKVD offices destroyed files during the evacuation of Moscow in the fall of 1941. The main resource left for reconstructing the history of the terror at the local level is individual investigation files. Regulations required that the police retain these files permanently. When the process of political rehabilitation for victims began under Khrushchev's Thaw in the 1950s, new evidence was added to the investigation files—the testimony of local NKVD operatives who worked during the Great Terror. The NKVD had gathered the material immediately after the mass operations. Investigators answered questions about the atmosphere within the commissariat in 1937-38, the pressure applied by their leaders, and the methods they used to fulfill the center's quotas for arrests. The purpose of the NKVD's internal investigation was supposedly to catalog the criminal excesses of the terror. In fact, the information primarily served as a weapon in the NKVD's internal clan struggle as Lavrentii Beria attacked Ezhov's appointees after replacing him as commissar in late 1938.

The materials from the NKVD's internal investigation are invaluable. In contrast to the leaders of the NKVD, the biographies of its sergeants and lieutenants are largely unknown. Only those officers who survived and then climbed to higher posts became the objects of interest for memoirists.[8] How did they live during the terror? What did they feel as they filled and overfilled the orders of the mass operations?[9] The materials from Kuntsevo district cannot represent every case. However, they paint a vivid picture of the officers and the atmosphere in state security at the lower levels.

Researchers must read these sources with care. Investigators wrenched the testimony from former NKVD workers in interrogation rooms. The interrogators used methods that were hardly different from those they employed against the victims of the mass terror. Officers wrote self-serving reports in a desperate struggle to save their jobs or even their lives. How are we to know that NKVD officers under investigation gave statements that reflected reality? Could it be that their testimony was falsified, like the accusations they made against their victims? Where do the hints of truth end and where do outright "lies, slander and torture" begin?[10]

It is true that these files and the investigation files of victims are filled with falsifications and that they "exclude testimony that might contradict the accusations of the investigator."[11] However, there is another side to these files. Despite all the phantasmagoric self-denunciations, above all about supposed espionage and terrorism, investigation materials include evidence reflecting the realities of those years. There were arrestees who were truly responsible for explosions and accidents in factories, although these incidents were not the consequence of conscious sabotage. The NKVD frequently created groups of supposed conspirators from the real bureaucratic families in the party, economy, and the police when the bosses of these groups lost out in factional struggles. It is important to throw out the investigators' conclusions in the cases— that these groups were consciously undermining the regime as spies and Trotskyists.[12] However, the evidence in the interrogations is often too specific to be falsified. Interrogators were able to force arrestees to

make political self-denunciations, to call themselves counterrevolutionaries or saboteurs under torture. But it would have been difficult for
investigators to invent all the mundane details that appear in case files.
To cite a prominent example, arrested Kuntsevo NKVD investigator
Viktor Karetnikov admitted that he obtained an apartment using coercion from people he arrested. Multiple victims and colleagues confirmed
that Karetnikov had committed these abuses of his office. Other NKVD
investigators faced similar charges. It is easy to believe that Karetnikov
stole the apartment from his victims, even though it is impossible to
accept the core allegation that he participated in a counterrevolutionary
conspiracy. When read carefully, the details of NKVD investigation
files can allow a reconstruction of events on the ground.

Specific conditions in Moscow province and Kuntsevo made it a
logical choice for this study. In contrast to the other provinces and republics of the USSR, Moscow province's NKVD did not have an operations
sector that coordinated the mass operations. Each district reported to
the provincial administration directly. Of all the districts in Moscow
province, the author chose Kuntsevo district as the setting of this study
because materials on its NKVD were more numerous than other districts.
In Kuntsevo the criminality of local security officials reached unusual
heights, even under the conditions of the Great Terror. The corruption
in Kuntsevo's NKVD was sufficient to draw the attention of superiors
who made its officers the subject of a special investigation. Among the
materials the investigation collected were reports and testimony of operative workers in the district. Kuntsevo investigation materials also include the interrogation protocols of district bosses, Aleksandr Kuznetsov and Viktor Karetnikov. The NKVD arrested both in the summer of
1938, and their confessions became the center of an enormous, fabricated
Trotskyist conspiracy in the Moscow NKVD. Although their case files
remain classified in the Moscow archive of the Russian Federal Security
Bureau (FSB), sections of the materials from NKVD investigations into
their activities appear in the case files of their victims. The documents of
this investigation, which ended with the Kuntsevo officers' death sentences, are extremely informative. They allow an account of the terror
from below, demonstrating its dependence on signals from above, the
role of informal connections in the internal politics of the NKVD, and to
what degree individual officers enjoyed autonomy in the implementation of repression.

Despite the particularities of Kuntsevo district as a case study of the
NKVD, in other ways it was an average district. It had a population of

nearly 200,000, including one town and thirty-eight villages. Statistically, it was a typical region in central Russia in the interwar period. This ordinariness suggests that what happened in Kuntsevo represented broader aspects of the terror, although the comparison to a study of repression in a rural region farther from Moscow would be illustrative.

A final reason that Kuntsevo was a likely choice for this study was the large number of available case files from the district in 1937–38. An online database cataloging executions among victims of political repression in Moscow province gives three hundred names of Kuntsevo inhabitants.[13] This database aided the search for the remaining victims of Kuntsevo's NKVD, listed in archival files by their name alone. Many cases in the district were grouped together into falsified conspiracies where the mythical organization's leader received a death sentence and was thus included in the list of executions. The file of the leader included the names of lesser "coconspirators" whose archival files I could then find.

In the mid-1990s, archival records of political crimes were moved from the archive of the FSB to the State Archive of the Russian Federation (GARF).[14] The study of these documents has become a veritable discipline of archival research in Russia. Each file includes a standard indictment signed by the victim and executioners, and an unassuming notice of execution. The rest of the file is made up of dozens of documents concerning the victim's rehabilitation. Without these sources it would be difficult to comprehend the spirit of the era, as terrible as it was, or even to start a study of the Great Terror, if only in one district. When I conducted research for the book, most of the archival files I read had no page numbers. A new Russian law on privacy of information in 2006 closed the files to all researchers except family members, making it impossible to order them. For this reason, I have cited most of the investigations by the archival file number alone.

Based on the available archival records, it is possible to count 560 people from Kuntsevo district who were arrested from the summer of 1937 to the following spring. However, this number does not include even the complete figure of those executed, not to mention those sent to the Gulag. Identifying victims who passed through the Kuntsevo NKVD is problematic for several reasons. The interrogation records of employees in defense industry factories listed only their identification number but not their place of residence. Additionally, some workers, mostly the managers and engineers, commuted to Kuntsevo from the capital and thus were Moscow residents in the case files. In other cases, the district NKVD even arrested people who had no real connection to the district—unlucky wanderers or passengers at the train station—although these were isolated instances and do not change the general profile of victims in Kuntsevo.

The available data allows several conclusions about the composition of victims. Most important, it shows that the peak of arrests occurred in March 1938, with that month accounting for a third of all those repressed in the district. The arrests then stopped suddenly at the beginning of April. The list of victims contains forty families—not only husbands and wives but brothers, nephews, parents, and children. In most cases, the NKVD arrested them as a group in a single spy or counterrevolutionary conspiracy, although sometimes the charges fell under different categories. And in Kuntsevo, the proportion of women arrested, 8 percent, was greater than in the rest of Moscow province, just 3.6 percent.[15]

The search for people sent to the Gulag or freed after the end of the mass operations is even more difficult than the search for those executed. Documentation linking a specific case to the corresponding NKVD office was not saved. Finding all the victims of a single district would require access to catalogs and materials in today's FSB and Ministry of Internal Affairs (MVD) archives, now classified in government storage. The best figure available comes from the chief of the district NKVD Kuznetsov. He testified that the department arrested around one thousand people. This number does not seem inflated. During the mass operations, approximately one-third of all arrests ended in execution per central NKVD quotas. Extrapolating from available figures, the number of repressed persons in the district was probably not more than a thousand, even if Kuntsevo's "shock workers" labored with more enthusiasm than investigators in other district offices. Nonetheless, researchers still have a considerable job ahead of them if they want to fulfill the poet Anna Akhmatova's wish to "name them all by name." Only when that happens will the picture of repression in 1937–38 in Kuntsevo be complete—a picture that includes its motivations and methods of implementation on the ground.

Part I: Executors of Terror

The School of Chekist Cadres

Kuntsevo district was located on the outskirts of Moscow. It was the site of Stalin's dacha and those of lesser party officials, an element that led to heightened security in the district. The presence of these grandees placed the district under the careful watch of the NKVD and gave it an air of being under total surveillance. Still another factor made Kuntsevo's NKVD a school for Chekists: Leaders from the Moscow provincial administration frequently visited Kuntsevo to unwind. Their gracious host in the district, its NKVD chief, had to be a person capable of keeping secrets. The holders of these secrets, officers working in the district, considered the post a launching pad for their careers, and so worth the daily commute from their Moscow apartments to the modest building on Kuntsevo's Zagorskii Street.

Before and during the Great Terror, Kuntsevo had validated its reputation as a fast track to success. Until May 1936, Iakov Baglikov was head of the district office. From Kuntsevo he eventually became the acting head of the Moscow province NKVD's second department, the "operations" division, whose main function was watching over suspects and conducting arrests, among other tasks. Baglikov's replacement Ivan Sorokin worked in Kuntsevo just a half year before he, too, moved up to a post at Lubianka. Another former Kuntsevo worker, Isai Berg, took up the highly desirable position of chief of the administrative-economic department in Moscow's NKVD in the summer of 1937.

Besides sharing a connection to Kuntsevo, these men all had pasts filled with serious mistakes at previous positions. Baglikov left Kuntsevo under a cloud after he tried to interfere with the district procurator's investigation of his friend, a Kuntsevo notary. An investigatory commission in the provincial NKVD did not find that Baglikov's actions had been illegal but nonetheless considered it best to transfer him to a post in distant Egor'evsk district, in the southeast of the province.[1] In all likelihood, a more important factor in his removal was that operations work in the district was in shambles. Baglikov had formally assigned his deputy to monitor operations but informally charged his follower Berg with managing it as well.

After Baglikov, Sorokin moved to Kuntsevo following a fire at his office in the Dzerzhinsky district (Moscow province) NKVD. Sorokin immediately dismissed Berg, declaring to the Kuntsevo office that with his departure "the air would become fresher." However, Berg, like the other Kuntsevo Chekists, proved resilient and he landed on his feet as the chief of the NKVD office in Vereia district in the province. His rise through Moscow's NKVD came even as rumors spread that he used forbidden, coercive methods of conducting investigations—methods the NKVD preferred to keep quiet.[2]

The entrenchment of ranking cadres in bureaucracies throughout the Soviet Union in the first half of the 1930s was a key cause of the terror.[3] Workers in state security were no less inclined than bureaucrats in any other administration to embed themselves in their organizations. NKVD leaders were reluctant to sacrifice workers, even those whom they had penalized, because they were nonetheless "our people." Leaders' unwillingness to bring their subordinates to responsibility cultivated a sense of personal loyalty to superiors among district chiefs. Moreover, this lack of culpability gave rise to district heads' condescension toward their own underlings and a feeling of invulnerability about their actions within their jurisdiction. The dynamics that existed between workers and superiors in state security are crucial to understanding why NKVD officers repressed their fellow citizens in the Great Terror.

In addition to their frequent job changes and the presence of embarrassing information in their personnel files—most were not from favored proletarian backgrounds, for instance—Kuntsevo NKVD workers shared another important connection. They were all members of the professional clique of Aleksandr Radzivilovskii, deputy head of Moscow's NKVD from March 1935 to July 1937. From NKVD personnel files, one gathers that police bosses like Radzivilovskii especially valued

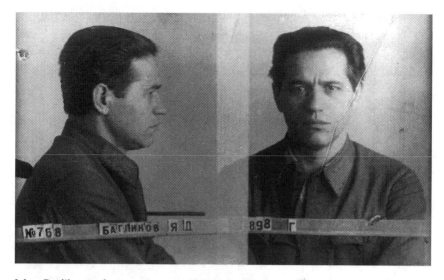

Iakov Baglikov under arrest in 1939. (GARF, f. 10035, op. 1, d. p-7698)

employees who had erred in the past, since these workers were prepared to fulfill any order given by those who knew about their troubled
history. Ivan Favorov, former head of the Moscow NKVD's cadres department, was arrested in 1938 and declared in his interrogation, "Radzivilovskii asked me to give him a detailed list of personnel files for officers
in the Moscow NKVD where there was incriminating material.... After
ten to fifteen days, I made a list of about 150–180 persons (I don't remember exactly) and I gave it to Radzivilovskii in January 1937. Then and
there, Radzivilovskii gave me an order to have the cadres department
cultivate operatives with serious compromising material in their files."[4]

It is possible that Favorov's interrogator altered parts of the testimony
for the sake of the investigation. But even if this was the case, the basic
premise of the episode shows that the leadership of the Moscow NKVD
used methods for recruiting similar to those that espionage organizations used to enlist secret agents. Information about the stains in the
biographies of underlings guaranteed their absolute loyalty. It even
allowed leaders to give them assignments that fell outside the bounds
of their official duties. These kinds of relationships served as fertile
ground for growing informal groups that would work toward mutual
protection and collective survival.

Professional clans like those in the NKVD were common in various
areas of Soviet officialdom in the 1930s. The high stakes of life and work

under Stalin turned career advancement into a game of "Soviet roulette": one false step could undo all previous good work. Party and government officials lived in a world of constant, often unofficial inspections, any of which could uncover something incriminating or even illegal in their work. Under these circumstances, the selection of "our people" and the use of collective protection served as a defensive reaction to the political environment.

Despite party purges and repression, bureaucratic cliques full of "our people" constantly expanded to guard against external foes. In each clique, members knew enough about one another to cultivate an atmosphere of mutual respect and fear. Moreover, clan activities did not stop at the office but extended into members' free time, too. Often their ideas of leisure did not follow official representations of Bolshevik morality. Carousing and drinking sprees not only demonstrated the coarse behavior of cadres, but these binges also relieved the psychological stress that was a product of the unending assault of urgent new assignments at every turn of the party line.

Radzivilovskii's right-hand man was Grigorii Iakubovich. Under his patron's protection, he achieved a dizzying rise through the NKVD apparatus. Beginning as assistant to the head of a department, he became deputy head of the Moscow province NKVD. Iakubovich actively exploited his informal connections in Kuntsevo's NKVD office for his own purposes. His sister-in-law moved into the building designated as the living quarters for Kuntsevo's officers. Baglikov then moved into a room in the apartment. Similar incidents raised muted protests among rank-and-file operatives and this episode figured into a number of complaint letters sent to the province's NKVD administration. One worker wrote, "Baglikov gave a whole apartment to Iakubovich's sister while we workers in the Kuntsevo NKVD slept on the couches in our offices for seven months."[5] An investigation based on the letter ended with its author's termination from the NKVD in 1936.

When influential guests from Moscow made their getaways to Kuntsevo, district Chekists accommodated them, their wives, and acquaintances in local resort houses. Radzivilovskii himself had a dacha in the district near the village of Odintsovo, and Berg was responsible for "Chekist amenities." "Cliquishness, immorality, and degeneracy" were transgressions that Berg and other NKVD officers later acknowledged under interrogation. However, these offenses did not occur in just one district or even in the NKVD alone.[6] Rather, these practices reflected a system that new elite groups throughout the Soviet Union had developed to shield themselves from the control of higher authorities. At the February–March 1937 plenum of the Central Committee of the Communist Party, Stalin made the notorious assertion that various hostile elements had infiltrated the party. The resolutions of the plenum also included the following lines about enemies in the NKVD: "Many people have received promotions not as a sign of their loyalty to the party, ability or knowledge, but as a sign of servility and toadying. As a result, various sections of [the organs of] state security have been penetrated by alien and criminal elements."[7] However, attempts to combat the clan system in the NKVD both before and after the plenum went no further than shuffling cadres, as the example of Kuntsevo shows.

Another factor that enabled these professional and personal clans to flourish in Soviet officialdom was leading administrators' unprecedented professional mobility. The Soviet bureaucracy was constantly in need of new workers who could meet the demands of the never-ending flood of new and always urgent campaigns. A cursory examination of any NKVD leader's résumé reveals that he never held one position for long.[8] To deal with new assignments from the party and state, each high-ranking boss moved trustworthy people with him from project to project and department to department, knowing he could rely upon them. These groups assured that normalcy would return to the new post as quickly as possible and provided a defense against hostile outsiders.[9]

After Radzivilovskii was transferred to Ivanovo province in the summer of 1937, he tried to take along trusted subordinates from Moscow province. Berg later described Radzivilovskii's attempt as follows: "Radzivilovskii knew me well as 'his' man. When he had already become head of the NKVD in Ivanovo province, he took a business trip to Moscow where he met with Redens [the new head of the Moscow NKVD] at Dinamo Stadium. In my presence, he asked [Redens's] permission to let me work in Ivanovo. Then, after Redens refused this, Radzivilovskii recommended me for the position of head of the administrative-economic department of the Moscow NKVD."[10] Berg, who had a long history of official reprimands, went instantly from being a minor figure—the assistant secretary to the head of the province's NKVD— to a person with considerable authority. Later, it would fall to him to prepare the Butovo firing range for the mass execution of people from greater Moscow and to ensure that these executions occurred without interruption.

Clans in the upper echelons of the NKVD thrived despite the official slogan that Bolsheviks "can keep no secrets from the party." This

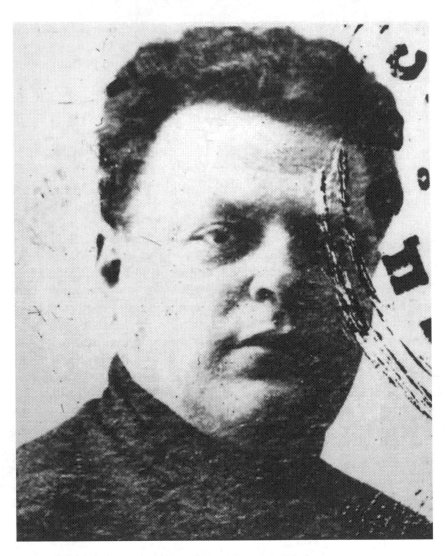

Isai Berg's official party photo. (RGASPI, f. 17, op. 99, d. 68623)

mantra was undoubtedly connected to Stalin's own pathological hatred
of "the champions of special interest"—bureaucrats who carried out
their own affairs behind the backs of the party and its leader. However,
to repurpose another of Stalin's phrases, it seems that "cadres decide[d]
everything."[11] Stalin believed that the basis for clan-like behavior lay
in intraparty ideological splits like "Menshevik wavering" and other
factions from the Bolsheviks' past. This notion formed the basis for the

first phase of repression (1936–37), directed above all against supposed enemies in the party-state apparatus.

In this first campaign of repression, bureaucratic clans in industry and government transformed into counterrevolutionary groups and spy rings. The real connections between clan members facilitated the work of NKVD operatives at all levels. When Beria replaced Ezhov and repressed the former commissar's appointees, secret police clans also transformed into supposed anti-state conspiracies. Radzivilovskii's Moscow NKVD clique met the same fate as the rest of Ezhov's police groups. Most of the clan's members had met in the early 1930s in the province's secret-political department of the United State Political Administration (OGPU), the predecessor of the NKVD. Some had been associates even earlier. Sorokin began to work with Radzivilovskii in 1925 in Crimea.[12] The former's brief tenure as chief of the Kuntsevo NKVD laid the foundations for a Radzivilovskii-Iakubovich clan just outside the capital. An NKVD investigation in 1938–39 made the group into a "counterrevolutionary Trotskyist conspiracy." The documents of this investigation provide a window into the brief existence of the clique.

The personnel worker Favorov described the development of the clan in his interrogation: "In March 1937 the cadres department found incriminating material about Kuznetsov. He was the son of a kulak and had participated in a revolt. I called him in. He was very nervous and said, 'All that's left for me is to shoot myself.' Fifteen minutes after he left, Radzivilovskii called and asked [me] to bring in Kuznetsov's file. After looking at it, he said: 'There's nothing unusual here. Kuznetsov is one of ours, we need to move him to a more important district.'"[13] Kuznetsov was soon after transferred from Ramenskoe district to Kuntsevo, opening his career to brilliant prospects. Radzivilovskii gave a warning to Kuntsevo's new head that if outgoing chief Sorokin should leave him cases missing documentation, Kuznetsov should not ask questions.

Aleksandr Kuznetsov came from a well-off peasant family. They were so prosperous that in 1918 he had gone with neighbors from his village to threaten the local executive committee about the tax in kind that the Bolshevik government had imposed. This kind of act would later be classified as banditry. Nevertheless, in the following year he joined the party as a soldier in the civil war–era Red Army. He never returned to his village after he went to work for the OGPU. However, the black spot on his biography followed him. In 1931 he found himself

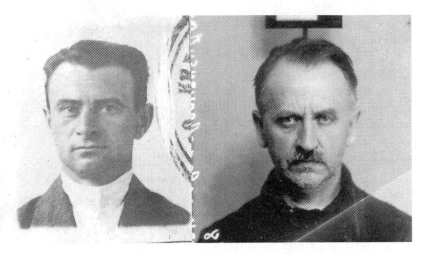

Kuntsevo NKVD chief Aleksandr Kuznetsov, from his party file and under arrest. (RGASPI, f. 17, op. 99, d. 78310)

under investigation for "participation in an anti-Soviet uprising." His new appointment to the Kuntsevo NKVD office seemed to indicate that his act of protest during the civil war was a problem of the past. However, Kuznetsov's record meant that the newest member of Radzi-vilovskii's informal collective would need to prove himself to his bosses at the Moscow NKVD.

The Ultimate Insider

When Sorokin left to work at Lubianka, he recommended that Kuzne-tsov take NKVD sergeant Viktor Karetnikov as his right-hand man. Sorokin had known Karetnikov for several years. His career deserves special attention as an example of the shocking violations of law and order that occurred in the Stalinist system. Karetnikov was the very opposite of the professed ideal Chekist—someone with "a cool head, a warm heart and clean hands." Petit-bourgeois origins minimized Karetnikov's chances to rise through the ranks of the secret police. Nonetheless, he went to work in the security organs. An energetic young man, he started to work on special assignments in the secret-political department of the Moscow OGPU. Soon he made himself irreplaceable and accumulated important connections. His colleagues called him "the ultimate insider" (*blatmeister*). Karetnikov later said during an in-terrogation, "My work exclusively involved taking care of the personal and family affairs of Radzivilovskii, Iakubovich, and [G. A.] Solomatin [the secretary of the secret-political department]. My relationship with Radzivilovskii, Iakubovich, and Solomatin was so close that I was considered an intimate friend in their homes and my mother mended underclothes for all the families."[14]

The career of this irreplaceable agent faltered in March 1933. He was fired from his position after he was arrested for "debauchery with gunfire in a drunken state." In other words, Karetnikov had discharged a firearm while drunk in downtown Moscow. Although Karetnikov beat up the police officer who attempted to pacify him, the affair did not go to trial. The imposing reputation of the OGPU and the personal intervention of Radzivilovskii saved him. Removed from his position in the provincial administration, Karetnikov then worked for the state security office in Dzerzhinsky district, where Sorokin was chief. When Sorokin transferred to Kuntsevo, he not only took Karetnikov with him but also made him into an operative. All the while, Karetnikov had maintained his informal contacts with former patrons. He continued to pay them friendly visits and provide them with various services.

Upon his arrival in Kuntsevo, Kuznetsov understood at once that Karetnikov was a person whose status in the informal hierarchy was higher than his own. He made peace with Karetnikov's place as a grey cardinal of sorts in the department. The other employees of the district office also recognized this state of affairs. Kuntsevo operative worker A. A. Tsyganov said, "Karetnikov had Kuznetsov on a string and wherever he wanted Kuznetsov to go, he pulled him there."[15] The new sergeant, assured of his Moscow patrons' protection, had bigger goals. On one occasion when Berg ran into Karetnikov at Lubianka, he asked why the latter had not become the head of the Kuntsevo NKVD after Sorokin left. "Karetnikov answered: In order to become chief of a district office you need to be a full member of the party, but I am still a candidate member. Soon Iakubovich will help me join the party and in the summer name me head of the Kuntsevo district office."[16] It is worth noting a final detail about the "ultimate insider": At the beginning of the mass repressions, where his criminal talent would bloom, Karetnikov was just twenty-five years old.

The District NKVD and the First Stages of the Mass Operations

From the beginning of the 1930s, the OGPU's permanent representative (*postpredstvo*) in Kuntsevo bore responsibility for state security operations in the district. His office conducted operations in two main directions. The first was to suppress the "incursions" of former kulaks in the countryside. The second was to provide security for the district's armament factories. When the newly formed NKVD inherited and expanded the functions of the OGPU in 1934, district offices became the core of the apparatus of security and control over the population in the Soviet Union. In addition to secret police work, they controlled the ordinary police and its subdivisions, the fire department and registration services.[17]

As part of these reforms, the policing functions of the OGPU became the responsibility of the NKVD's Chief Administration of State Security (GUGB), with subdivisions in all republics, territories, and provinces. The district office of the NKVD had operative workers who studied the mood of the population, conducted work with informants, and undertook investigations into political cases.[18] Soon the work of these operatives overwhelmed all other functions of the NKVD. Bureaucratic correspondence during the period of mass repression sometimes referred to the district office as the "district department of the administration of state security," reflecting the dominance of the secret police within Kuntsevo's NKVD.

Until the summer of 1937—the start of the mass operations—political cases generally prevailed over mass-social categorization as state security agents searched for "anti-Soviet elements." Agents investigated individual members of former oppositions within the Bolshevik party, prerevolutionary political figures, and members of non-Bolshevik parties who were too active in public affairs or had retained old connections. Still another category of victims in the first stages of repression was *nomenklatura* workers—ranking members of Soviet officialdom. These administrators, above all those who worked in the economic sphere, frequently faced accusations of being hidden saboteurs when their enterprises failed to fulfill the state's plans. If the charges "stuck" (the term of NKVD workers), agents observed procedural and judicial norms. For example, they acquainted suspects with the charges before sending them to trial or to extrajudicial proceedings.

But shifting winds from Moscow blew through the provinces too. In the infamous Moscow show trials of August 1936 and January 1937, Soviet prosecutors accused "unmasked" politicians of masterminding conspiracies against the state and individual leaders. At the district level, operatives replicated these accusations among local state workers. On February 21, 1937, Karetnikov initiated the arrest of the members of "a counterrevolutionary-terrorist group in the system of the Kuntsevo town council." This group included five men—stablemen, wagon

drivers, and their immediate superiors from the town's communal facilities. The investigation uncovered no wrongdoing besides generic anti-
Soviet statements. However, Karetnikov had calculated correctly. The
stablemen's kulak pasts and their boss's five prior convictions convinced
the special collegium of the Moscow provincial court to convict the
men.[19] The victims were fortunate that Karetnikov got to them before
the mass operations. Had the arrests occurred under Order 00447, they
would have received a harsher sentence.

Begun under Sorokin, the case of the stablemen gave the district's operatives a taste of the "class approach" to selecting victims. This method
was rare before the summer of 1937. Karetnikov's zeal was not always
supported among higher-ups in the Moscow NKVD. A case against
wreckers at the Moscow province cropping station ended with the indictment of the station's leadership. However, other potential arrestees
among its research staff remained free. Similarly, provincial NKVD
leaders did not sign arrest orders for Zabel'skii, the director of a textile
factory, or for construction engineers at Kuntsevo arms Factory 46,
where a roof collapsed in a building they had assembled. Later, when
Karetnikov and Kuznetsov themselves were under investigation, they
would offer these uninvestigated cases as evidence of a conspiratorial
organization within the Moscow province NKVD that had protected
counterrevolutionaries.

Arrest criteria changed radically following NKVD Order 00447.
NKVD commissar Nikolai Ezhov signed the order on July 30, 1937,
beginning the period of the mass operations. Demanding "the removal
of anti-Soviet elements" from the entire country, the directive gave para-
mount importance to fulfilling quotas (*limity*) for arrests, broken into
two categories: prison sentences and executions. Order 00447 listed
figures for each category down to the republic and provincial levels of
the NKVD. At an extraordinary meeting of NKVD republic and provincial chiefs in Moscow, Ezhov guaranteed complete immunity in the
execution of the order.[20] Undoubtedly, quotas for repression filtered
down to the lower echelons of the commissariat just as plans for economic development had in other state agencies. The order to begin the
mass operations was disseminated at provincial meetings of district
NKVD chiefs who in turn acquainted their underlings with its contents.

How did local operatives receive the order? It is easy to imagine
that many investigators welcomed its simplified judicial procedures,
which allowed them to finish investigations where the evidence was
weak. Many previously tenuous investigations suddenly became work-
able. In 1957 the secretary of the Luga district (Leningrad province)

NKVD V. P. Grinko testified, "The main materials that we used at the start of the campaign of mass and illegal repression were from archives [of investigations] that had been abandoned by the OGPU and NKVD. These materials included official and unofficial documents, cases that had been sent to the archive unfinished because they were unsubstantiated or were trivial. These cases included correspondence with relatives from abroad, belonging to a socially alien group or to another [supposedly hostile] group, having national loyalties, and other accusations of anti-Soviet activity that were not proven."[21]

In effect, operatives had a free hand in choosing their victims. Indeed, they had to think broadly about whom to arrest to meet their quotas. Order 00447 contained no provision for arresting citizens who had contacts abroad. Nonetheless, Kuntsevo residents whom police had arrested for "suspicious contacts with foreigners" before the summer of 1937 became its victims during the mass operations.[22] In rural districts, the anti-kulak aspect of the operation played an important role. When formerly exiled peasants came back to their home villages, villagers who had remained understood return as rehabilitation. These homecomings led to new social tensions in the countryside between those whom the regime had exiled and those whom it had not. Order 00447 called for "a final and decisive battle" with the kulaks. When they received the order, lower-level operatives realized that they would bear the primary responsibility for filling the arrest quotas in the city and the countryside.

Immediately after the issue of Order 00447, work in the district office on Zagorskii Street heated to a boil. The staff urgently refitted offices for investigative work. They set up additional cells in the basement for prisoners. Several Kuntsevo victims whom the secret police arrested remarked that they had been kept in the holding cells of the district criminal police.[23] Nonpolice personnel like firefighters and passport registry workers had to move into cramped quarters to make room for new operatives. The influx of investigators fulfilled the demands of the party Central Committee's February–March 1937 plenum for the expansion of the NKVD with new cadres from the party. The party mobilized recent graduates and students who had some kind of legal education. After two or three months of training in the NKVD, they began operative work—recruiting informants, conducting arrests, and leading interrogations. Tsyganov was mobilized to the NKVD from the Moscow Institute of Government and Law. He began working in Kuntsevo in December 1937 and by February was already leading investigations independently.[24] Assistant operative sergeant A. V. Solov'ev, who joined the

Kuntsevo NKVD in July 1937, later described in a report how he learned to conduct investigations:

> Two days after I began working, I came to see former chief Kuznetsov to show him the results of my work. Karetnikov was in Kuznetsov's office. After reading my interrogation protocol aloud, Kuznetsov dressed me down, "Is this really a protocol? Here, look here at the kind of testimony you need to get from the suspect." At his command, Karetnikov gave me an interrogation record with the suspect's signature. I read the protocol with great interest and, I must say, I was horrified that I was still such a bad investigator. Then I decided to see how Karetnikov conducted investigations but when I entered his office, I saw the following picture: The accused sat and read the interrogation protocol. Having read the protocol, the suspect categorically refused to sign it, saying that nothing in it was true. Then Karetnikov yelled at the suspect and finished by using physical measures, that is, he beat the accused so that he would sign the protocol. I didn't have to stay in Karetnikov's office any longer because it all became clear to me, that is, I had learned how to conduct investigations. Without delay I approached Kuznetsov and said I could not work like that. Kuznetsov insisted, "In the fight against enemies all methods are valuable and it is necessary to purge the Soviet Union of foreign agents."[25]

These lessons from senior comrades were effective. Out of the approximately ten investigators on staff between July 1937 and March 1938, there was not a single man who refused to use torture and humiliation against detainees according to the petitions of the survivors among their victims.

The indisputable leader of the anti-kulak operation in the Kuntsevo NKVD was veteran operative S. I. Rukodanov. A career worker in the state security apparatus, Rukodanov received his first reprimand in April 1937 for falsification of materials in an investigation. His experience in fabrication would be needed later that year. However, it would be too simple to say that Rukodanov and his helpers invented accusations completely. They could draw upon the entire district NKVD archive, full of testimonies detailing unrest in the countryside. The most common records were complaints about misappropriations by local authorities in village councils. The second most common records were denunciations from peasants who claimed to be harassed by kulaks

who had returned from exile. While city-dwellers usually wrote to
newspapers and party organs—letters then forwarded to the NKVD—
the noticeable majority of peasant complaints were meant as signals
to authorities of wrongdoing, many of whose authors remained
anonymous.

These files do not reveal how the district NKVD systematized materials. The district chief examined those accusations that seemed
authentic—as well as those forwarded from other institutions—and
assigned them for further investigation to one of the operatives. He sent
illegible letters from semiliterate authors to the archive immediately.
Accusations in denunciations were general and often involved several
persons. For this reason, the office probably sorted the letters not by
the individual accused but by "place of illegal activity": an enterprise,
collective farm, or even an entire village. The investigations of counterrevolutionary agitation from the summer and fall of 1937 came from a
standardized set of files labeled "registered materials." Only a few of
the files from "registered materials" contained evidence from an informant. Informant reports were formulaic, containing the date of the investigator's meeting with the informant, the informant's code name, and
the incriminating material received. The advent of Order 00447 had a
paradoxical effect on informant work. It allowed investigators to act
upon all existing leads from informants. However, the office had too
few operatives to cultivate new leads through the lengthy process of
recruiting and meeting informants.

Even before the "kulak order," operatives had conducted cases as
part of the virtual civil war the state waged against the supposed exploit-
ing classes in the countryside. However, their accusations were not outright falsifications. The Kuntsevo NKVD carried out an operation called
"Creepers" from 1933 onward. In the "Creepers" investigation, operatives monitored collective farm chairs who had been dekulakized. After
being exiled from their villages in collectivization and branded enemies
of the Soviet state, some dekulakized peasants managed nonetheless to
"creep" into positions of authority on collective farms. Although these
farms were among the most productive in the district, the high yields
did not guarantee the chairs' immunity from repression. As Order 00447
arrived in the summer of 1937, a directive from Moscow demanded that
Kuntsevo finish the "Creepers" operation. The operation had already
produced a few indictments, but Order 00447 allowed officers to put all
the gathered information into action. Iakubovich even suggested that
K. M. Kulmanov, a "Creepers" arrestee already sentenced to seven

years in a labor camp, be brought in to give testimony that would lead
to even more arrests. The reopened investigation, conducted jointly by
Karetnikov and Rukodanov, ended with eleven death sentences.[26]

The investigation of the "Creepers" and their henchmen had begun
a considerable time before Order 00447, making it an exception in the
"kulak operation." Operatives in the provinces, especially those in rural
areas, had mostly depleted their reserves of archived investigation materials during the repression of *nomenklatura* workers from 1936 to the
first half of 1937. Once investigators had exhausted these materials, they
did not play a large role in the terror. In the early stages of Order 00447,
evidence was limited to witness testimony. Occasionally arrest files contained a reference to an arrestee's previous convictions, including those
connected to dekulakization during collectivization. Sometimes they
contained negative character references from a village council or workplace. In most cases, though, it seems operatives compiled these documents after detaining their victims and forged the dates on them so that
they preceded the arrest.

In Kuntsevo Order 00447 primarily affected the rural population.
NKVD operatives recognized it as a continuation of the familiar battle
with supposed "kulak incursions." During the "kulak operation," the
number of arrestees rose sharply compared to previous campaigns
and each case, which could contain a number of individual arrestees,
included more victims. From August 1937 onward, these investigations
no longer went to trial before the Special Counsel of the NKVD. Instead,
they went to an extrajudicial organ, the provincial troika (committee
of three). Moscow's troika included the province's head of the NKVD,
its procurator, and the secretary of the Moscow party committee. Each
provincial troika had the right to sentence as many people as Order
00447's quota provided for that province. While provincial NKVD investigators also sent cases to the troika, the committee received the majority
of its investigations from district NKVD offices.

As they rounded up victims in the countryside, Kuntsevo agents conducted group arrests in villages to save labor. From June 15 to 19, 1937,
agents arrested six inhabitants of the village of Matveeskoe. On August
19, they arrested ten peasants from the village of Mnevniki. On September 5, they arrested nine people from Nemchinovka and surrounding
villages. On September 24, they arrested seven people from the village
of Orlovo.[27] On the night of October 6–7, agents carried out arrests in
the town of Bakovka and the nearby villages of Vyrubovo and Izmai-
lovo.[28] In January 1938, the district NKVD organized group arrests in

Petr Barulin from Mnevniki, sentenced to death for "C[ounter]-R[evolutionary] activity" on October 25, 1937. (GARF, f. 10035, op. 1, d. p-47579)

Petr Shushunov (age 56) from Mnevniki, sentenced to death for "C[ounter]-R[evolutionary] activity and a[nti]-S[oviet] agitation" on October 25, 1937. (GARF, f. 10035, op. 1, d. p-47579)

other villages, Teplyi Stan and Troparevo.[29] Agents combined arrestees from each village into a single "terrorist-subversive group."

The scale of repression in Kuntsevo district's villages contradicts historian Sheila Fitzpatrick's assertion that "the Great Purges in the countryside in 1937–38 were a lesser event than the Great Purges in the towns."[30] This only seemed to be the case because rumors about arrests circulated differently in villages and in cities. Word spread more easily in urban spaces than in the countryside, where information traveled only through relatives and neighbors. Conducting arrests from an entire

ВЫПИСКА ИЗ ПРОТОКОЛА

заседания тройки при Управлении НКВД СССР по МО от „25 " X   1937 г.

Ф. 896

СЛУШАЛИ:	ПОСТАНОВИЛИ:
63. дело № 9443 по обв. ПУЗАНКОВА Андрея Ивановича, 1909 г. р. ур. МО, Кунцевск. р-на, дер. Мневники, из семьи крупного кулака. За к... деят. высл. ОГПУ на 3... отбыл. Обвиняется в к... тельности.	ПУЗАНКОВА Андрея Ива- новича, - РАССТРЕЛЯТЬ.

Секретарь тройки

Andrei Puzankov (age 28) from Mnevniki, sentenced to death for "C[ounter]-R[evolutionary] activity" on October 25, 1937. (GARF, f. 10035, op. 1, d. p-47579)

village at once, operatives extinguished any advanced warning peasants may have had. From Kuntsevo it is clear that the early victims of Order 00447 were ordinary peasants rather than local bosses, whose turn would come in March 1938.

In addition to revived investigations from the archive, local authorities in the villages largely determined whom officers would arrest as part of the "kulak underground." The mass operations provided rural leaders with an opportunity to have their denunciations acted upon, and they used the chance to get even with personal enemies. Although the NKVD could settle their scores for them, local leaders faced new problems. It was impossible to conceal anything in the countryside, and local bosses soon faced the resentment of fellow villagers. The chair of Bakovka village council Oganes Uzunov asked Kuznetsov to protect him from the furious wives of arrestees in the village. At the same time, he requested that Kuznetsov "give agents an order not to use my name." Investigators had told others about his willingness to "help the investigation." Rumors led the heads of neighboring village councils to visit Uzunov and ask for a model they could use when writing their own denunciations.[31] Of course, village council heads did not just participate in the mass operations to settle scores. They found themselves in a difficult situation in the period of mass repression, incriminating themselves if they refused to cooperate with the NKVD. In a number of villages, investigators accused the council chairs of being the leaders of counterrevolutionary conspiracies.

In late October this accusation was the basis for the operation against "anti-Soviet elements" in Nemchinovka. Near the village was Deputy Defense Commissar Semen Budennyi's dacha, whose presence changed the gravity both of the accusations against the villagers— terrorism rather than counterrevolutionary agitation—and of their sentences. Ten people from Nemchinovka received death sentences.[32] The summer homes of other grandees had a similar effect. Eight peasants from the village of Matveevskoe, near head of state Mikhail Kalinin's dacha, received death sentences. Arrestees from Barvikha, according to relatives, were repressed because they lived near the country home of Commissar of Agriculture Mikhail Chernov.[33]

Despite including some social input, the operations from the summer and fall of 1937 were generally not initiatives from below. Instead, these arrests reflected the attempts of rank-and-file operatives to meet the overwhelming demands of the provincial leadership. Provincial authorities determined the minimum number of investigations to be undertaken. It is unclear what exact directives the heads of district offices in Moscow province received about the evidence required for cases. In neighboring Iaroslavl' province the requests were the following, according to historian Sergei Kudriavtsev: "It was enough to provide the 'social profile' of the arrestee and two testimonials 'exposing' him. At the same time, they [the provincial leadership] provided another directive: give the troika only group cases. As a result, district administrations began to combine the cases they had prepared."[34] Operatives in Leningrad province received the same instructions.[35]

Few documents reveal the influence district-level investigators had over sentencing in the cases they sent to the troika. The troika made the final decision but its conclusion was based on investigators' evaluations and summary letters. Undoubtedly, district NKVD workers were able to influence the severity of punishment. It is possible that operatives indicated arrestees who they believed deserved the death sentence. Nikita Petrov and Arsenii Roginskii note that it was common for operatives to recommend a sentence in the later "national operations": "In the localities, after an operative made a report [for the extrajudicial organ] he and his boss from the office or department also suggested a sentence."[36] These recommendations probably occurred in the "kulak operation" as well.

At weekly meetings of NKVD personnel, the provincial administration singled out Kuntsevo for special praise. Leaders noted the district office's success in unmasking "enemies of the people" without regard for their rank or status. Sorokin himself visited his former post to urge the fulfillment and overfulfillment of their Chekist plans. In turn, the district leadership inculcated the ideology of state terror into each investigator. Conditions in other districts in the province varied little from those in Kuntsevo. An operative from the town of Mytishchi explained the instructions he received in 1937 from Kharlakevich, the head of that district's office: "We received a 'limit' for arrests and every one of us had to complete no fewer than one case per day. Whoever didn't want to work cases like that—let him write a report about it. He [Kharlakevich] would send it to the Moscow administration. After that, Kharlakevich added that the head of the Pushkin district office had refused to carry out the mass arrests and was now arrested himself."[37]

Kuznetsov provided general oversight for the mass operations in Kuntsevo, signing arrest warrants and demanding his underlings collectively provide six to seven confessions per night.[38] Investigative work was entirely under Karetnikov's command and he became de facto deputy head of the district office, with his authority resting upon rumors that he was the "son-in-law or brother-in-law of Iakubovich."[39] He quickly mastered the art of falsification and managed to overtake Rukodanov in arrest totals after the focus of the repression turned from the countryside to the city. The Kuntsevo NKVD mobilized all available resources to fulfill the plan for repression in the district. Dispatchers and fire department instructors joined regular secret police staff to conduct arrests. In order to cut down on wasted time and energy, the criminal police called victims to its office, located in the same building as the secret police. There an investigator was waiting to make the arrest.

There were places in the town of Kuntsevo where terror struck as cruelly as it did at Moscow's House on the Embankment, the elite Moscow residence where hundreds of officials were arrested in the terror. In Kuntsevo agents combed over private housing uniformly. The number of arrests in each residence depended largely on the diligence of the individual operative. Densely populated factory settlements became the main targets for district investigators during the mass operations. Fifteen workers from the barracks of the Communist Youth International (KIM) factory and fourteen from the settlement near Factory 95 went to the Butovo firing range.

The residence where the fewest people faced repression was building 8, a modest wooden structure where factory managers lived. On October 31, 1937, agents arrested Factory 46's head mechanic M. M. Avdeenko, a Ukrainian from apartment 9 of that building. On November 23, they arrested Factory 95 engineer I. A. Deich, a Latvian from apartment 11. On December 23, they arrested the factory's office of technical supervision head P. I. Verakso, a Latvian from apartment 3. On January 18, they arrested workshop mechanic R. S. Kliat, a Pole from apartment 5. Finally, on February 2 they arrested the factory's chief metal worker V. I. Dvoretskii, a Pole from apartment 12. All were executed.[40]

Until the first interrogation, the Kuntsevo NKVD held arrestees in the holding cell of the local criminal police, where conditions were insufferable. During the fall of 1937, the district NKVD only sent arrestees to Moscow on the eve of the troika's meeting. After the troika made its decision, they went to the Gulag or to the execution pit at Butovo. In cases where the investigation took longer than expected, arrestees went to one of three Moscow prisons: Butyrka, Taganka, or Novinskaia. Operatives were unable to go to Moscow regularly and check on developments in the cases because of their heavy workloads. According to the dates on some of the case files, an entire half-year elapsed between the first and second interrogations. No documents about prolonging cases were produced. In all likelihood, "forgotten" arrestees' experience of an extended prison stay contributed to their willingness to sign false confessions.

Investigatory Techniques in the Period of Mass Repression

NKVD operatives on Zagorskii Street found their rhythm quickly during the mass operations. Their main form of evidence in the terror was the arrestee's confession to a crime. In the absence of genuine confessions, the officers' work consisted primarily of fabricating this testimony. Investigator Solov'ev later wrote, "During the day we usually made up fabricated interrogations for the accused and at night we made them sign under compulsion."[41]

Investigators created interrogation protocols most often from denunciations and informants' reports. Less frequently officers used notes from informal interrogations—preliminary questioning sessions with detainees that were unrecorded. The most experienced agents conducted interrogations. V. F. Petushkov, the party instructor at the registration bureau, said, "Karetnikov dictated interrogation records and afterward he ordered workers at the registration bureau to rewrite the text of the interrogation onto a piece of stationary."[42] Workers familiarized themselves with the arrestee's place of work before writing the protocol in order to make the accusation seem more plausible. Then the investigators and their helpers forced innocent people to sign the protocols using methods that hardly fit into the framework of "revolutionary legality."[43]

Investigators' main technique was threats accompanied by endless nighttime interrogations. "I signed out of fear of being hurt—a revolver and blackjack were on top of the investigator's desk," said Etgard Shidlovskii, an Estonian who could not read Russian.[44] The investigators often worked in teams. One victim wrote, "Four or five people interrogated me at the same time and made me sign their fabricated confession."[45] When threats were insufficient, beatings followed. Not a single agent shrank from violence. "When I refused to sign the confession," wrote A. A. Gailesh, "investigator Solov'ev hit me and then called the policeman to take me to the cell, saying he would give me a couple hours to think things over and then he would talk with me less nicely."[46]

Another form of pressure was to appeal to the accused's Bolshevik conscience while simultaneously promising a deal. Gailesh also encountered this form of coercion: "The investigator said that he knew that the entire interrogation record was utterly fabricated, but that I should recognize that the international situation was very tense and that for the benefit of the motherland I should admit to all the accusations and sign the confession."[47] How the accusations might benefit the motherland varied from case to case. Sometimes it meant cleansing the capital's outskirts of unwanted foreigners. Other times it meant collecting evidence to close a consulate. Unable to make sense of these fantasies, arrestees offered to leave their homes voluntarily. Investigators replied that cooperation with the investigation would give them an advantage and that their exile would only last three to five years.

Terror victims noted that investigators used a good cop-bad cop approach. A year after her interrogation, ethnic Greek Nadezhda Sidiropulo described the following scene: Petushkov was interrogating her, urging her to sign the investigation protocol. "The party demands it," he insisted. Sidiropulo later wrote, "He knew that I was not guilty but [he said] I had to sign the confession like a conscientious Soviet young woman. When I refused, Karetnikov began to shout threats from a neighboring room. Then he entered the room and beat my head until I lost consciousness. Then he gave me a pen. It was in that condition that I signed the interrogation protocol."[48]

Judging by the petitions of victims, none of the interrogators pretended to believe the fabrications they made the accused sign. For example, E. V. Breivinskaia described her only meeting with investigator Solov'ev on March 16, 1938: "The investigator gave me a prewritten confession that stated that I had given information about the workshops and all sorts of other things [to foreign intelligence agencies] while working at Factory 46 in 1935. He didn't give me a chance to read the whole confession. Instead he asked why I wanted to read it. You will be even more scared when you finish [he said]. When I said it was all lies, the investigator answered: In the NKVD we know that and have nothing against you but it is necessary. Because I was a Pole I was arrested and had to sign the protocol."[49] Members of the first generation of Soviet people had experienced radical shifts of the party line, each twist and turn creating a sense of emergency and unveiling new adversaries of Soviet power. When party leaders introduced a new campaign against the next enemy, many people may have accepted it as normal.

Evgeniia Babushkina was only twenty-eight years old at the time of her arrest. After graduating from a mining institute, she worked at the aviation instrument factory in Kuntsevo. Later she became a researcher at the Institute of General and Inorganic Chemistry at the Academy of Sciences. Her life would have been perfect if not for one detail in her biography: until she enrolled at the institute, she had lived at the residency of the Polish Consulate in Moscow, where her mother had worked as a maid. This detail transformed Evgeniia into the ideal candidate to play a resident spy in a fictitious conspiracy. Sixteen years after her conviction, she wrote to the procurator general of the USSR about the methods Kuntsevo's NKVD had used in her investigation:

> The investigators' explained that Soviet power needed my confession in order to shut down the network of foreign consulates

and for this reason I had to "suffer" but that I would receive a short term and so on.

I resisted these "arguments," the swearing, investigators' threats to shoot me, and similar techniques. This team worked me over one at a time at first but then one night they appeared with Efremov leading the way and beat me, demanding that I sign the protocol they had written—my "confession" of counter-revolutionary activity.

I was a young woman who was brought up by Soviet power. First I had been a member of the Pioneers and then the Komso-mol [Young Communist League]. I had absolute trust in Soviet legality and respect for human rights. I was shocked by every-thing I saw, heard, and lived through in the month after I was arrested. It had driven me into a state of insanity. The beating drove me even further. They had to call an ambulance to the holding cell to revive me. But only a few hours later, before I fully came to my senses, investigator Dikii called for me again and told me to sign the fabricated protocol. My confession contained everything those people were able to imagine—leadership of some kind of counterrevolutionary organization where there were people whom I not only did not know but whom I had never seen, espionage, sabotage, an attempt on the life of Stalin, subversion. And all that in the Polish Consulate. I don't re-member everything because I was in such a state that I could barely hold the pen in my hand. Nonetheless, I refused to sign the "confession" once again so Dikii threatened to call Efremov back to "work me over." To be fair, when Efremov began to beat me, Dikii left and did not participate. Then, pitying me, he [Dikii] explained person-to-person that they had to make me sign a protocol one way or another because I was the best candidate for this confession. I had a connection to the Polish Consulate.

In short, I had no more strength to resist. By that time it was all the same to me, shoot me or convict me. I signed everything that they asked. That night they took me from the district to Moscow and then to the camp.[50]

Babushkina was arrested on January 17, 1938, and her confession was dated February 14. She resisted her interrogators and the inhuman conditions of jail for nearly a month.

Other accounts also confirm that S. K. Efremov, party secretary of the Kuntsevo NKVD, acted as the office's designated tormenter. In 1956 the former head of the Soviet Sulfite Trust, Zhan Miklau, a Latvian, petitioned Khrushchev for political rehabilitation, writing of his case:

> The day after my arrest, they told me to sign the protocol confessing to my alleged counterrevolutionary activities. After I firmly refused to sign the fabricated interrogation protocol, that very night they sent me to Butyrka prison where I received hideous beatings—beatings I have been unable to describe in any of my recollections. Over the course of a month, interrogators regularly beat me to the point that I could no longer stand on my own legs. Under constant physical coercion they made me sign the protocol. After that no one touched me or interrogated me.[51]

Miklau's case file contains a short confession dated February 2, 1938. On the next day, he signed another, longer document with the names of his coconspirators—a document that had clearly been written long before Miklau agreed to sign. Underneath both of the records is the signature of the interrogating officer at the Kuntsevo NKVD, Efremov.

Investigators did not use sophisticated methods of torture. Their technique was limited to "manhandling," as it was called in official discourse. However, beating out the needed evidence proved effective enough. What broke people was not so much the physical pain as it was the humiliation and stress. I. Ia. Konon-Kononov wrote in his petition from 1956, "The investigator punched me in the cheek and said that he would kill me and write on the death certificate that I had died of a heart attack if I did not sign what he wanted. The monitor in the cell, the chief engineer of one of Kuntsevo's factories, confirmed that it could really happen. A prisoner in our cell had almost gone deaf and was coughing up blood after multiple beatings in Rukodanov's office. Another prisoner returned from the same office to the cell with a swollen neck and face. They had beaten him with a rubber boot."[52]

In addition to violence, the terrible conditions in the jail cells were their own kind of torture that encouraged arrestees to confess to fabricated crimes. People slept in turns in the overpopulated cells of the local police station. Investigators refused them the right to take walks. Prisoners shared a single dish for food. The officers then enlisted those who had already signed confessions to convince those who had not yet broken down. G. G. Ferapontova, a German language teacher at

Kuntsevo's School no. 3, wrote in protest from a prison camp: "After long protesting I signed the false confession. You should be honored, the investigator then told me, that we are now giving you the task of convincing others in your cell that they should sign their protocols or else it will be even worse for them."[53]

Evgeniia Ligeropulo, a Greek, signed the interrogation protocol on the advice of her cell mates who told her life would be easier once she went to the prison camp. Her jail mate, Liubov' Papakhristodulo, came to prison without her glasses. Karetnikov read her an edited version of her interrogation protocol.[54] Bookbinder A. P. Demidov, a former member of the Socialist Revolutionaries (SR), waited nearly ten days after arrest for his first interrogation with Rukodanov, who asked him, "Did you see the people who didn't want to sign, what they are like? If you sign I'll make a call and they'll bring you your package [a parcel Demidov received from outside]."[55] Other petitions by Kuntsevo's inhabitants reveal similar incidents. Gailesh wrote that after signing the protocol, "I was allowed to fill out a document for my back wages and government bonds, and I was allowed to meet with my family."[56] In some cases Kuntsevo's agents hoped the arrestees themselves would make true the scenarios they had written for them and held groups of alleged spies or saboteurs in the same cell. A. R. P. Vizula wrote in his rehabilitation petition, "They tried to indict me for being in Kuntsevo to organize a group of Latvians [as spies]. For that reason they put me in a cell with arrested Latvians whom I had never met."[57]

For some arrestees, belief in the reality of anti-Soviet conspiracies drove them to sign confessions. Against the backdrop of press accounts about spies and terrorists, the confessions investigators put in front of arrestees did not seem like absolute lies. A. A. Popov, arrested in the case of a counterrevolutionary conspiracy at the provincial cropping station, wrote in one of his petitions, "Karetnikov played on my patriotic feelings toward the motherland and took advantage of my desire to be of maximum help to the police in their struggles against enemies of the people. He was only able to make me sign the protocol because newspaper articles from the Moscow papers about the show trials and the situation at the cropping station, which everyone was aware of, made [Karetnikov's scenario] seem likely."[58] Investigators had called Popov to the district office as a witness but after he signed the protocol, they arrested Popov himself.

Witnesses like Popov, most often the neighbors and coworkers of victims, faced the same coercion as arrestees. Family members only became involved as witnesses when their denunciation caused the arrest. In most cases, the witness protocols contained evidence that belied the hand of the investigator. When the NKVD reviewed these investigations at the end of the 1930s, the majority of witnesses renounced their testimony. Several of these witnesses said that the investigator forced them to sign a blank piece of paper, promising to copy their words onto it later.[59] In an atmosphere of spy-mania, witnesses who had any reservations about their testimony stifled their hesitation when they learned about allegations of the accused's loyalty to a "hostile nationality." Police simultaneously exploited witnesses' fear of the NKVD and their unfamiliarity with the law. Authorities regularly produced secret laws (classified as "not for publication") and secret orders for state security administrations. In the words of historian Galina Ivanova, "Soviet society developed a peculiar understanding of the word 'rights.' In the collective consciousness, it was not identified with the constitution or laws, and even less so with the natural rights of man, but with the real actions of law enforcement agencies."[60] This understanding of rights explains what would otherwise seem to be a paradox: In their petitions, a significant number of the victims wrote that they signed false confessions not because investigators used torture but because they had used persuasion. Younger arrestees and those with less education proved especially susceptible to the coaxing of the investigator.

In Kuntsevo and in other districts, authorities employed so-called staff witnesses to simplify evidence gathering.[61] Former police officers, the chairs of village soviets, and their acquaintances often filled this role. In many villages, the same witnesses appeared repeatedly to denounce various inhabitants. One of the staff witnesses in Kuntsevo was M. T. Shchadenko, the head of the Kuntsevo NKVD garage. In 1939 he described at length how investigators recruited him: "One time a trainee named [Aleksandr] Nikitin stopped by my apartment and asked who do you know from Bakovka, reading me a list of people. I answered that I knew them all and listed a few of them. He then asked me to sign a couple interrogation protocols. I refused. Nikitin suggested that I go see Rukodanov." Try as he might, Rukodanov was also unable to persuade his colleague from the garage. Karetnikov then took charge. Shchadenko reported his discussion with Karetnikov, "He asked me, 'Do you know Pavlenkovich?' I said that I knew him because we lived near each other. Karetnikov then asked me, 'Have you gone hunting with him?' Yes, I had been hunting with him, I answered. 'You know — he was arrested as an enemy of the people, so while it's not too late, go to Rukodanov and sign the [witness] questioning protocol.'"[62] Under the coercion of investigators G. I. Smirnitskii and Rukodanov, M. M. Kolesnikov, a former member of a cavalry platoon in Kuntsevo's police department, made false accusations against B. P. Brevdo (a Latvian). He even repeated these accusations during his official confrontation with Brevdo—a common investigatory practice where officers arranged and recorded the meeting of accuser and accused.[63]

Shchadenko's confession to false testimony appeared in the case file of A. I. Zaitsev, an investigation that Rukodanov handled with lightning speed. The arrest and first interrogation occurred on November 19, 1937. The investigator wrote the indictment the following day. On November 23, the troika heard the case.[64] Another Zaitsev, named Stepan Mikhailovich, had the opposite experience. He became the record holder among Kuntsevo's prisoners for days spent in preliminary detention. Arrested on January 18, 1938, he appealed to Beria in November 1939 to accelerate the investigation. He had spent twenty-two months in Butyrka prison. While he was in prison, the investigators had sent his case to the troika multiple times, but it always returned from the procurator with a request for further investigation. When the case finally went under review, it became clear that one of the witnesses, a supposed Kozhevnikov, was entirely invented. Exactly two years after his arrest, Stepan Zaitsev was free again.[65] The name Zaitsev proved fateful for Rukodanov. In the case of the first Zaitsev, he wrote the testimony for Shchadenko. In the second case, he created an imaginary witness named Kozhevnikov. During a review of the cases, his explanations for both errors were deemed insufficient. For the newly promoted lieutenant Rukodanov, they became a stain on his record.[66] But Rukodanov was not the only investigator to invent a witness.[67]

The conveyor of repression accelerated at an incredible rate from August 1937 onward. Nonetheless, district investigators managed to produce reams of documentation for review at the provincial NKVD. Investigators confiscated all typewriters they encountered on searches and appropriated them as NKVD property. The office mobilized typists from the district's largest enterprises, even those without clearance for classified work, to complete documentation for investigations. Office stationary was always lacking and the typists had to create it on typewriters. The staff typed so many copies of interrogation records on imported carbon paper that the text became illegible.

Kuznetsov signed most of the orders opening cases in the district. An exception was when cases fell into the hands of the local police, in which case its head Chugunov signed the documents. Depending on the nature of the accusation, Sorokin or Mikhail Persits (both department chiefs in the Moscow province NKVD) also signed the orders. However, at the peak of the mass operations, these higher-ups could not manage to sign even the indictments. The assistant head of the provincial NKVD should have confirmed the order to open cases but only a few investigations contained Iakubovich's signature on this document after the beginning of 1938, as district offices became busier due to involvement in the "national operations." At that same time, but perhaps for unrelated reasons, Kuznetsov began to write out arrest orders, indicating the agent who would conduct the arrest. Occasionally Karetnikov would sign orders as the self-appointed assistant head of the district NKVD. The opposite side of the paper usually contained the signature of the arrestee and sometimes the date and even the time of arrest. Because arrests occurred at night, the date on the back of the order was frequently a day later than on the front.

Investigations ended when the district office issued an indictment, indicating the nature of the crime and that the arrestee had confessed. Then the case went to Moscow where the corresponding department in the provincial administration examined it. Typically each district office had its own "curator" at the province. Sometimes the curator himself questioned the arrestee, although the questioning was usually a formality. For example, during an examination with Petukhov from the fourth (secret-political) department, the Moscow NKVD officer asked a single question about a Kuntsevo arrestee's prerevolutionary social status.[68] Following the inspection, the reviewer wrote a decision in the case file with the first bullet point, "The indictment corresponds to the material in the file and the guilt of the accused is demonstrated in full." After the review, the investigation went before the troika or the dvoika—the committee of two made up of the province's NKVD leader and procurator—who pronounced the verdict having never seen the accused.

It is likely that the province's NKVD returned some cases for further investigation because of fabrication that was too obvious. Even during the peak of repression, the provincial administration monitored and corrected cases—red pencil marks on the page margins of investigation files are evidence of readings. In one case, the reviewer underlined "vile" in the phrase "I undertook vile wrecking work" as awkward.[69] Nonetheless, obvious errors made it past the supervision of the provincial administration. One indictment charged the arrestee Anton Shteklian with recruiting himself in a spy conspiracy.[70] In another case, investigators asserted that Eduard Sommerfeld, a German, had attended a Polish club in Moscow where he met with German spies.[71] It was the job of reviewers

Act of August 28, 1938, for the execution of Adolf Sommerfeld. (GARF, f. 10035, op. 1, d. p-49580)

at Lubianka to catch these mistakes and ensure that paperwork was complete. They returned the case of V. V. Shematovich to the Kuntsevo NKVD after Shematovich had already been executed; district officers had failed to produce a receipt for the typewriter and camera they confiscated.[72] Despite their diligence, central administrators surely were aware that they, too, were participants in falsification on a national scale. Like their colleagues in the district offices, though, Moscow NKVD officials felt the sword of Damocles over their heads in the form of clan-based collective responsibility.

It is unclear how many cases officers at the district level sent to the provincial NKVD. Although Kuntsevo's operatives, especially Ruko-danov, often complained that workers in the central administration poached the juiciest cases, these incidents were few. They occurred during the initial period of repression, particularly in cases of spying which were then under the auspices of the provincial administration. For example, after Karetnikov first interrogated Ernst Meier, a German, the third department (counterespionage) of the provincial NKVD soon took over the case.[73]

The March Peak

Directives from the center determined the narratives that district NKVD offices used in investigation reports. Until the end of 1937, central authorities placed an emphasis on counterrevolutionary propaganda and wrecking. These orders and the provisions of Order 00447 allowed district investigators to use evidence their offices had already accumulated. Investigators at higher levels, in the third department of provincial administrations, conducted investigations involving "spy networks." For example, the Kuntsevo NKVD began an investigation into the Monich family, migrants from Belorussia to Kuntsevo. However, investigators from Lubianka took over the case, transforming the family into a spy ring in the pay of the Polish General Staff from the early 1920s. The NKVD arrested eighteen people from Kuntsevo alone in the investigation and six members of the Monich family were executed.[74]

From the beginning of 1938, district offices in the NKVD became directly involved in the Chekists' most important fight—the battle against foreign spies. Counterrevolutionary agitation in the indictments of the district NKVD gave way to spying, terrorist plots, and diversion. Above all, this shifting emphasis affected members of "hostile nationalities" such as Latvians, Poles, Germans, and Finns—"nationals," in the language of the NKVD. Repression found its second wind. The massive scale of the terror and its direction from above remained constant features in the new operations. However, investigations now focused on the discovery of large counterrevolutionary organizations with connections abroad—either spies from Western governments or Trotskyists.[75] In a political system based on collectivism, no other outcome was possible.

Propaganda about conspiracies and spy rings provided Soviet leaders a scapegoat for the problems the country met on the path to the radiant future. These accusations formed the basis for the show trials of former Bolshevik leaders, one-time comrades of Stalin who had turned into his political enemies. In district NKVD offices, investigators carefully read accounts of these trials in the national press and applied the logic of Stalinist justice to their jurisdiction. Karetnikov, in an aside about the trial of Nikolai Bukharin, Genrikh Iagoda, and others accused in the "Right-Trotskyist center" at the third Moscow show trial, said, "I bet they also coerced those confessions."[76]

The "spy turn," to use the agents' own jargon, did not emerge from below. Ezhov's orders outlined the target groups, punishment, and scale of "national operations." According to Petrov and Roginskii, "[The orders] created entirely new procedures for trials by the OGPU-NKVD. After an investigation ended, a summary report was created 'with a short review of investigation and informant evidence that characterize the level of the arrestee's guilt.' Individual summaries of the files were then gathered into a list every ten days for review by the committee of two [dvoika]."[77]

Available summary reports in investigation files suggest that district offices prepared them or at least signed off on them. Each page, set in a standard, horizontal orientation, included the information gathered about the accused on the left half of the page. At the bottom of the page was the case number and a mark indicating that the case came from the Kuntsevo district office. The right half of the page included information about the crime taken from the indictment. In contrast to the indictment, the case summary included the verdict. In the case of A. A. Sim, a Latvian worker at the Moscow province cropping station, the right side of the summary concludes with the words "TERRORIST (SABATEUR)."[78] NKVD chiefs reviewed and signed the collected summary reports, sentencing hundreds to death in a few hours.[79]

Over the course of the "national operations," the procedures also changed for documenting investigations. In spy conspiracies, each arrestee's investigation file contained copies of the interrogation records from all of the spy group's members. Duplication of the materials allowed the pretense of a thorough investigation and gave agents a means of standardizing their work. At the peak of repression in March 1938, the Kuntsevo police had no time to produce evidence through investigation methods such as an official confrontation where coparticipants in a supposed crime could identify one another.

As was the case with Order 00447, the deadline for completing the "national operations" was extended several times. Only after district-level operatives became involved in these operations was the NKVD apparatus able to fulfill and overfulfill its quotas for repression.[80] The shift in emphasis to spy groups at the beginning of 1938 has another, more practical explanation. By that time, district NKVD offices had exhausted their reserves of archived evidence against anti-Soviet elements, kulaks, and "former people" (prerevolutionary elites whom the new regime had stripped of rights). Gathering new evidence demanded the kind of work with informants that district offices did not have the labor or resources to conduct. Moreover, indictment on charges of counter-revolutionary agitation required confirmation by witnesses. In contrast, investigations of espionage were extremely simple because they required neither witnesses nor character evidence. District officers understood this change. An officer working under Mytishchi district (Moscow province) NKVD head P. A. Solov'ev reported that his boss once announced, "Subversion cases require serious investigation, cases with documentation, and at that moment there was no time to undertake this work. He demanded that we only get [confessions] from arrestees about espionage because in spy cases it was easier to complete the investigation and to indict the arrestee."[81]

Workers at the district level faced the constant threat of their own arrest if they did not fulfill orders from above.[82] NKVD chiefs admonished their subordinates, confronting them with incriminating evidence. Fear for their own safety motivated officers to conduct mass arrests more than did appeals to Bolshevik vigilance against enemies. Kuznetsov went to see Sorokin in February 1938 to receive instructions about the "national operations." As soon as Kuznetsov entered his boss's office, Sorokin mentioned that he had compromising information on the Kuntsevo NKVD head. Under interrogation later, Kuznetsov claimed that he had then asked Sorokin to destroy the material and recruited him into the conspiracy. However, it is more likely that Sorokin demanded Kuznetsov fulfill the plan for arrests at any cost and sent him to his assistant, Petrov, for further instruction. According to Kuznetsov, the conversation with Petrov was as follows:

> Petrov asked me what materials I had on the nationals. I answered that the district office had no such materials. After this Petrov directed me to gather the names of nationals from industrial enterprises, from the address bureau, and from other places. Based on these lists I should compile summary reports to conduct arrests, charging the arrestee with espionage in each report. Then he gave me a quota for how many I should arrest for the first round. When I noted that we would not be able to get confessions to spy activity during the investigations, Petrov said: You should do it like this. You yourself write the protocol. You indicate how the charges relate to the arrestee's work, what kinds of information he could have given as a spy, or attribute acts of sabotage to him. Just do this. Don't worry, we won't be sticklers. If the accused won't sign the protocols you write, beat them until they sign. That was the end of our conversation.[83]

Returning to Kuntsevo, Kuznetsov gathered the district office's workers and repeated the instructions he had received from the NKVD chief, promising full immunity for falsifying protocols. Undoubtedly, other district chiefs received similar orders, although implementation was different from district to district. Some district heads undertook only

the minimum number of cases and received reprimands for their lax-
ness. Others attempted to overfulfill their quotas. However, the furious
pace of work at the lower levels of the NKVD did not mean that provincial administrators gave up control. Instead, the peak of repression
created a flood of bureaucratic correspondence for the provincial
NKVD to monitor.

In May 1938, Il'ia Il'in, the head of the eleventh department (policing
of transport and communications) in the Moscow provincial NKVD,
wrote to the new head of the provincial administration Vasilii Karutskii
on the situation in the administration under former provincial chiefs
Leonid Zakovskii and Iakubovich. "The system worked out by the provincial administration for daily reporting on operative work created
destructive methods where offices competed for larger numbers of
arrests and confessions. They [the provincial leadership] viewed some
operative departments (XI, VI departments) as lagging behind in this
competition because they did not produce large numbers of confessions.
Investigators [in these departments] tried to question arrestees conscien-
tiously, more or less. The goal of the leadership was to catch up with
Leningrad, that is, to gather no fewer than 200 confessions per day in
the Moscow administration."[84]

The spirit of competition was in full swing in the districts as well. At
several meetings, Zakovskii singled out the Kuntsevo office as a model
for lagging districts to emulate.[85] A Kuntsevo operative later recalled,
"In the March operation, Kuznetsov was competing with Kolomna
[district]. At one of our meetings, Kuznetsov demanded that operatives
produce even more arrest reports so that Kolomna would not overtake
our office. I said 'soon this competition will hang us' pointing to the
hook in the ceiling of his office. Kuznetsov called me an alarmist who
did not want to fulfill the decisions of the party and the government."[86]
When the new operative asked for normative instructions about the
spy operation, Kuznetsov answered, "You're just a young operative
and don't understand what's going on here. After all, we are carrying
out an operation to remove Germans, Poles, and other alien nationalities
by order of the Politburo of the Central Committee of the Communist
Party."[87] The mention of this authoritative body was enough to remove
doubt from the operatives' minds about the legitimacy of their actions.

During the March operation, Karetnikov made specific demands.
"No fewer than five [interrogation] protocols per day from every operative because according to him the directive of the provincial NKVD was
no fewer than fifty cases [from the entire district office] per work

week."[88] Investigative work during the peak of repression in March consisted of one interrogation (or more accurately, the extraction of a signature on a prewritten report) and an indictment no more than two pages long. Operatives added copies of the testimony from all members of the same "spy group," even if those testimonies made no mention of the person in the current case. The addition of the copied testimony prevented the cases from looking suspiciously thin. These methods allowed the district office to arrest almost two hundred people in March. In all likelihood, the district office finished and sent approximately this many cases to the troika and dvoika that month.

It is clear from the reports of Kuntsevo's NKVD operatives that the Politburo's quotas for arrest translated into a personal assignment for each operative. Approximately ten operatives in the district had the right to conduct investigations (including criminal police). This number fits the count of agents who signed investigation documents—although a much larger circle of people (e.g., typists) became involved in the mass operations.[89] Simple arithmetic—"no fewer than fifty cases per week"— suggests that each of the workers had to contribute roughly five cases per week.

The state of affairs in Kuntsevo was similar to district offices of the NKVD throughout the country. According to the testimony of head of the Mtsenskii district (Orel province) NKVD M. F. Pikalov, "[The provincial NKVD administration] sanctioned arrests by list. Moreover, it demanded that we create a list to arrest a large number of kulaks and gave us two days to compile it. The investigations of fifty arrestees were to take no more than five days."[90]

Despite appeals to Bolshevik resolve, the nerves of Kuntsevo's operatives could not withstand the physical and psychological strain. On February 26, investigator B. D. Smirnov shot himself in his own office. On March 7, operative Solov'ev's assistant began to have nervous fits and took a leave of absence. As those who remained continued to work on cases, Kuznetsov dressed the March peak in familiar slogans: they were taking part in socialist competitions, fulfilling and overfulfilling the plan, overtaking the neighboring region. It was as if Kuznetsov was talking about norms for grain requisitions or steel, not the arrest of hundreds of people.

During the peak of repression in March, district criminal police became involved in investigations of those accused under the infamous article 58, against "counterrevolutionary activity." Kuznetsov took criminal police chief Chugunov to meetings of the provincial NKVD.

Criminal police cases that resulted in an indictment under article 58 looked more reputable and occurred only after they received approval from M. I. Semenov, the head of province's police. However, when criminal police wrote indictments or beat arrestees, they did so under the guidance of secret police operatives. S. G. Zudin, arrested during March 1938 in a case against prerevolutionary entrepreneurs, wrote that Novikov from the criminal police led his investigation but did so with the help of Dikii. "He [Novikov] and investigator Dikii told me to sign the prewritten protocol and beat [me] until I lost consciousness. Then both investigators beat me at once, one from behind the other from the front. They beat my face, chest, stomach, saying that if I didn't sign I would be beaten even worse."[91]

One of the last victims of the mass terror in Kuntsevo was B. B. Cherskii, the son of a tsarist officer and himself a cadet before the revolution. It seems that after investigators exhausted the ranks of counterrevolutionary "fathers," they went after the "children." Another NKVD employee named Smirnov, a worker in the anticorruption department, conducted the investigation with the speed of a shock worker. Cherskii was arrested on April 4 and no less than five days later his case went forward to the troika.[92]

The speed of these cases would have been impossible without the extreme simplification of investigatory practices. Using these methods, Kuznetsov scrupulously turned Lubianka's directives into reality:

> During the operations against the kulaks and national counter-revolutionaries, Kuntsevo district finished investigations concerning almost a thousand people. These cases included a considerable number of people . . . arrested and tried using testimony obtained through physical coercion. I arrested foreign nationals who lived in Kuntsevo district using a list gathered from the enterprises and institutions in the district.
>
> I grouped together arrestees working at an enterprise or institution and charged them as members of a counterrevolutionary group. The crime depended on the character of the enterprise or institution where the members of the group had worked. If the group of arrestees worked at a military enterprise, then that group was charged with spying and diversion.[93]

At the end of March, the Kuntsevo NKVD "cleansed" each arms factory in the district two or three times. When police exhausted their lists of

people with appropriate backgrounds for arrests, this method of selecting victims was no longer viable. Without the lists of "nationals," investigators' fantasies lost their last anchor to reality and gave rise to ever
more outlandish stories. Operatives Dikii and Solov'ev constructed one
of the final falsifications—the case of the Norwegian spies. The spy group
included three men arrested back in August–September 1937 whom
investigators had clearly forgotten in the fever of the repression that
unfolded. One of them, a Czech named L. P. Blakh, allegedly "was
found in communication with an agent of Norwegian counterintelligence" and was supposed to have led the spy ring.[94]

Rank-and-file members of the Norwegian group were arrested on
March 28–29 for no other reason than the foreignness of their names—
and sometimes just their patronymic.[95] They included an elementary
school teacher, an accountant at a framing shop, a stoker at a print shop,
and a digger at a brick factory. The object of their alleged machinations
was the airplane factory at Fili (constantly "saved" by the efforts of
Kuntsevo's investigators) and, inexplicably, a worsted-textile factory.
Over the same days, investigator G. I. Smirnitskii arrested spies at the
neighboring Nogin leather and oilskin factory. One of these spies allegedly gave foreign agents information about the resin and dyes used for
the production of kitchen oilcloth.[96]

Final Accord

February and March 1938 also marked the peak of arrests along the
"secret-political" line that Rukodanov directed. At the start of the mass
operations, Kuntsevo's NKVD had exhausted its leads from informants
and from its list of dekulakized peasants and other counterrevolutionary
elements. The stream of denunciations had run dry after the January–
February 1938 Communist Party Central Committee resolution had
condemned "excesses" in the purge of the party. Although materials
for arrests had dissipated, the provincial NKVD administration made
even more intense calls for "shock work" among the Chekists. In the
"secret-political" line, the last reserve of victims in the district were
former members of the Socialist Revolutionary (SR) and Menshevik
parties—one-time allies of the Bolsheviks against the tsar.

After these parties lost the political and military fight against the
Bolsheviks, former SRs and Mensheviks preferred to forget about the
past. The majority of these people were approaching retirement age
and had long ago disappeared from public life. Nonetheless, their turn

had come in the terror. On March 19, the passport department of the district NKVD received the documents of twenty-three arrestees. As it turned out, these people had been prerevolutionary SR or Menshevik "sympathizers"—not full members.[97] In constructing this "SR-Menshevik conspiracy," Rukodanov employed a significant new technique. Alongside the central conspiracy, supposedly named "Our Cause" and directed by A. I. Kudriavtsev, Rukodanov asserted that the group had affiliates at the village level. In effect, the construction of this conspiracy repeated the Kuntsevo NKVD's "autumn levy," when it arrested former kulaks in the countryside. It allowed Rukodanov's assistants to prepare interrogation protocols without leaving the district seat, inventing evidence to match any village.

In the "SR conspiracy among pedagogues," the NKVD arrested seven schoolteachers from the villages Nikulino, Mnevniki, Amin'evo, Ochakovo, and Odintsovo. The investigation connected each individual with A. G. Zverev, a teacher in the village of Rumiantsevo who took on the role of the conspiracy's leader. Each teacher was supposedly the head of a military unit in their village that would be at the forefront of a peasant uprising. Perhaps when Rukodanov created the conspiracy he had in mind the fact that SRs in the village had once been influential among teachers.[98] However, ordinary members of these groups had no idea who Zverev was—or for that matter who the SRs were.[99]

For unknown reasons, the case of the SR conspiracy did not result in the arrest of all the teachers. It seems that the case failed because its accusations against the teachers were too apolitical—hitting students on the back of the head, holding back students, a damaged portrait of Stalin in a classroom, and so on. Under the guidance of the investigator, witnesses had to construct political crimes from the everyday life of a school: "At a teachers' conference, Zverev did not act like a Soviet person. He said that students who spent two to three years in the same grade were themselves responsible for their low level of achievement in their studies. From his statement, it would appear that Soviet children are idiots incapable of learning."[100]

Approximately half of those teachers mentioned in the interrogation records as members of rural counterrevolutionary cells ultimately were not arrested. Rukodanov had already shifted his focus to falsifying a promising "rightist conspiracy" and it is clear that the district NKVD did not have the manpower to unmask two major conspiracies simultaneously. In the end, most of the SR investigations turned into cases of "counterrevolutionary agitation" and the Special Counsel of the NKVD gave them a "lenient" five-year sentence. However, Rukodanov's technique of uncovering local affiliates, developed during the case of the teachers, would prove its usefulness later.

The terror of 1937–38 in Kuntsevo ended with two of the largest of the operations, led by Karetnikov and Rukodanov. Karetnikov's operation represented the district's efforts in counterespionage (the NKVD's third department). Rukodanov's operation represented its efforts on behalf of the secret-political (fourth) department. These two departments were perhaps the most important in the NKVD's hierarchy. The cases in the two operations bore the mark of their respective leader down to the scenarios invented for the investigations. Karetnikov was a master of extracting confessions from the accused themselves whereas Rukodanov focused on compiling witness testimony.

It seems that in the rush to meet the plan and stay in the good graces of the leadership, both men began to see their victims as statistics. The thrill of the hunt for numbers overtook whatever decency they had. The struggle between the veteran officer's experience and the young man's energy ended with a draw. Karetnikov purged Factory 46 for a third time, taking around fifty arrestees. Rukodanov responded by expanding the case of the "counterrevolutionary organization of rightists" in Kuntsevo to no fewer than forty arrestees, copying the scenario of the third Moscow show trial of Bukharin and other former Bolshevik leaders.

Karetnikov's technique was to increase the number of members of a given spy conspiracy crudely, occasionally confusing who recruited whom. In contrast, Rukodanov refused to place arrestees together without a conspiratorial logic to their grouping. He learned from the case of the schoolteachers how to construct a conspiracy with village affiliates. Using the confession of Sergei Muralov, the former chair of the Kuntsevo district executive committee, he built an organizational chart of sorts for counterrevolutionary groups in the district. Effectively, Rukodanov's conspiracy mirrored the party-state apparatus of the USSR in the 1930s. Later the investigator asserted that he received instructions to organize the conspiracy this way from the provincial administration. Of course, it is possible that his modesty belied a desire to deflect responsibility for the falsifications of March 1938.[101]

As conceived by Rukodanov and his curators in Moscow, the Muralov-controlled Kuntsevo conspiracy originated with the "rightists" in the provincial center. The leadership of this conspiratorial organization was the chair of the Moscow provincial executive committee N. A.

Filatov. In turn, the NKVD implicated Filatov in the case of former commissar of agriculture Mikhail Chernov, who was executed after conviction in the third Moscow show trial. Head of the Moscow executive committee's personnel department I. A. Sviridov was supposed to have disseminated counterrevolutionary instructions to the chairs of district executive committees. As the conspiracy moved to the lower levels, the chairs of collective farms or village committees became the leaders of local terrorist undergrounds under the command of Muralov. Individual doctors, veterinarians, surveyors, and agronomists formed subunits reporting to the district executive committee. This scheme made the "rightist conspiracy" in Kuntsevo truly boundless, allowing Rukodanov to include even the most unlikely candidates in its ranks.[102]

At the beginning of April 1938, the mass arrests in Kuntsevo stopped as suddenly as they had started nine months earlier. It is apparent that local NKVD units received an order that set an end date for the activity of extrajudicial repressive organs. Rukodanov wrote in a later report that he received an order to end his current investigation and send all cases to the troika by April 5, 1938.[103] However, this deadline proved unrealistic and the Kuntsevo NKVD continued to file paperwork at the same tempo until the middle of the summer.

Although the mass arrests stopped in April, several hundred arrestees from Kuntsevo remained in the cells of the district police and in Moscow prisons. The time difference between the interrogation record containing the confession and the indictment was usually weeks and sometimes months. Not one of the arrestees was acquitted and freed. One rule held firm: Chekists do not err. After a lull in April, Butovo saw the murder of more than a thousand people in May and June. Even in August, fifty of Kuntsevo's residents who passed through the modest building on Zagorskii Street were sent to their deaths.[104]

The Bolshevik Party during Mass Repression

The role of the party during the Great Terror is a point of dispute among historians. The traditional perspective is that communists accepted Stalin's proclamations that enemies had infiltrated the party's ranks and unquestioningly sought these enemies.[105] An updated version of this argument is that genuine belief and self-conscious attempts to make oneself into an ideal party member created intense vigilance from below.[106] Other historians argue that the terror allowed party members to achieve personal goals—to settle scores with bosses or show their loyalty through denunciations. Similarly, party members' fear of being "unmasked" for their lack of vigilance led them to denounce their peers preemptively.[107] The case of Kuntsevo's party shows aspects of all these motivations, and the story of Kuntsevo's NKVD in 1937–38 can only be fully understood in the context of the district party organization.

The close connection between the district's NKVD and its party organization is indisputable. The head of the district NKVD ex officio was also a member of the bureau of the district party and executive committees.[108] Denunciations that party organizations forwarded to the NKVD became evidence during investigations.[109] Correspondence in the other direction was also frequent. On April 5, 1937, just two weeks after taking his post in Kuntsevo, Kuznetsov delivered a report to the district party committee on wastefulness at the chamomile-growing collective farm, Path of October. At first, the district party committee limited punishment to a strong reprimand for the farm's chair V. S. Chernov for "opening a workshop with hired labor at the collective farm" without the party's sanction.[110] In the case of M. K. Volkov, chair of the collective farm Red Izvarinets, the district NKVD's denunciation to the party committee was more extensive. It accused Volkov of drunkenness, taking bribes, and "policies that corrupted the collective farm and undermined Soviet power."[111] In this case and eventually in the case of Chernov, the party expelled the rural boss from its ranks and then he was arrested.

In her study of the terror in Smolensk, historian Roberta Manning had access to party documents from the Smolensk archive but did not have access to NKVD documents.[112] In this study of Kuntsevo, the opposite is the case. Files for 1937 in the party archive for Kuntsevo district are limited. They only include the records of the district party's bureau meetings. Among these records, documents dealing with the misconduct of individual communists remain classified. Materials from 1938 are not in the archive.[113] Because of these limitations, this section can only present a fragmentary account of the interaction between the district's party organization and its NKVD.

Throughout the USSR in 1936–37, party organizations carried out a "verification" of membership documents. Ostensibly, this membership operation was meant to ensure that all communists had their party card and that no nonmembers had received party documents. However, this verification was far from a formality. It was effectively a purge of the membership where party members' faults could lead to expulsion. Even at the district NKVD, two of twelve workers who went through the verification were expelled from the party.[114] The verification began in local party organizations and disputed cases made their way to the bureau of the district party committee. In cases where the party committee questioned the authenticity of members' documents or their biographies, the district NKVD became involved in the verification. The NKVD received a great deal of compromising materials on party members by these means. Many of those who faced party discipline during the verification appeared on the lists of victims in the mass operations a year later.[115]

Stalinists understood the verification as the apex of intraparty democracy, a chance for party organizations to discuss the merits of all its members great and small. Yet it was also the first phase of repression. Lasting from the fall of 1936 to the summer of 1937, its victims were party *nomenklatura*. These party members often had extensive records of service. Far from an advantage, the length of their service suggested that they might have made various deviations from the party line over their long careers. Moreover, work in leadership positions inevitably invited conflict with the party's directives and the state's laws. As early as the purge of 1933–35, central leaders had put pressure on local party committees. Occasionally the campaign against them subsided but soon after rekindled with new strength. Local bosses could only save themselves in these campaigns by gaining support from above and finding a group of loyal associates, the most important of whom was the secretary of the party organization.

Gorbatov, the director of the Moscow provincial cropping station, had gathered just this sort of group, achieving safety until 1935. In that year, the director's supposed Trotskyist past was uncovered, and he was expelled from his post and later arrested. The station was located at Nemchinovka, not far from Kuntsevo, and the district party committee closely monitored the clan struggle that followed. Local communists voiced their opposition to the "Ukrainians" that Gorbatov had brought with him and placed in key posts. New director N. P. Nikolaev, whom the Moscow land committee appointed, attempted to stay above the struggle. However, he became embroiled in the fight when he left the matter in the hands of deputy I. M. Osaulenko, a member of the "Ukrainian" faction.

Over the course of 1936, the two sides gathered compromising information on each other, flooding higher authorities with complaints and petitions. Every incident with the workers at the station took on a political meaning and became fuel in the clan struggle. In February the station's party secretary received an official reprimand for displaying lack of revolutionary vigilance and allowing the supposed anti-Soviet jest, "The worker Churkina, based on the suggestion of citizen Lobinin and several housewives, undressed and ran naked through the street, for which she received 100 grams of pork fat."[116]

The district party committee, an unwilling participant in these squabbles, resolved to bring order to the station once and for all. On September 1, 1936, the district newspaper *Bolshevik* published an article with a typical title: "The Children of Trotskyism at Selection Stations." The article assigned Osaulenko the role of the devious saboteur who "struggles against Professor Lysenko's well-known vernalization methods." The director was a hideous liberal who "is not familiar with the Stakhanovites [members of a movement of exemplary workers], the best people at the station." The article concluded that "Gorbatov's nest of Trotskyists still exists." The piece could only have appeared with the approval of the Kuntsevo district committee. Capitalizing on their good fortune, the party organization of the station took on the role of an investigatory agency. In December 1936, its representative made a special fact-finding trip to Ukraine to learn about Osaulenko's harmful activities over the last ten years.

For a time, higher authorities restrained the activity of Nemchinovka's communists, who wrote to them about rotting potatoes and unharvested rye. During Moscow party secretary Nikita Khrushchev's visit to the station, the future Soviet leader tried to laugh off the struggle, "If we have so many subversives [at the station], then just transform them [into nonsaboteurs]." The district party committee made a similar statement, "There is no Trotskyism at the station but there is inefficiency."

The situation shifted in favor of the local communists after a meeting of the station's workers in February 1937. At the meeting, Nikolaev pointedly announced that the danger of foreign intervention meant that the survival of Soviet socialism was still at risk. The argument had moved from the realm of agriculture to the theoretical plane. It ended with the station director's recanting at the district party conference in May. His admission of fault did not stop waves of criticism from above and below. When the leadership of the land administration of Moscow province was arrested, Nikolaev, too, became an enemy of the people. On June 9, 1937, an article in Kuntsevo's *Bolshevik* carried the commanding headline, "Unmask the Trotskyist Followers."

Afraid to appear as though they were behind the events, the bureau of the Kuntsevo district party committee expelled Nikolaev from the party. At the same time, it also accused the station's party organization of complacency about its own faults. Nonetheless, the vigilant communists, whom the station leadership had stripped of their bonuses but could not remove from their jobs, claimed victory. Two weeks after his exclusion from the party, Nikolaev was arrested. His investigation file, involving five other people from the administration of the station, contains all the documents of the party's examination of the case.[117] Undoubtedly, these documents aided NKVD investigators in Kuntsevo as they began the mass operations.

Because the district bordered Moscow city, it was a convenient location to hold various types of inspections and commissions. In October 1937, a commission of the Moscow provincial agricultural committee came to investigate the district. After the commission accused district party leaders of "political indifference," Kuntsevo's party committee began to take preemptive measures. Party leaders requested compromising materials from the neighboring district about N. I. Zalivalov, senior agronomist of the Kuntsevo executive committee's land department. As it turned out, in the course of the party purge of 1933 he had been charged with "rightist-opportunist negligence in the planning of crop rotation." On November 3, 1937, he was expelled from the party, and the district committee decided "to commission the district NKVD (Comrade Kuznetsov) to carry out an investigation about the activities of Zalivalov in the district land department."[118]

A week later, the NKVD returned a decision that replicated the accusation of the party committee: "For criminal planning of sowing plots in the collective farms, . . . for massive violations of agricultural laws, for lack of leadership over district agronomists, for disengagement from the supervision of hot houses . . . senior agronomist Zalivalov is dismissed from work and his case is to be sent to investigatory organs." In the Zalivalov case, the Kuntsevo NKVD kept a logbook containing regular entries from a secret agent code-named "Radish." On November 27, the agronomist was arrested, but repression among the district's agricultural managers did not stop there. In contrast to arrests in the village, the district party committee was both aware of the unfolding events and was the primary agent choosing victims from the ranks of Kuntsevo's communists.[119]

Before the arrival of the provincial agricultural commission, District Party Secretary Rostislavov and Executive Committee Chair Muralov conducted a comprehensive verification of cadres from Kuntsevo's land department and its machine-tractor station (MTS). The results of the verification went to the district NKVD. Based on blemishes in their party files, on January 27, 1938, the NKVD arrested four workers at the land department. After only a month, they were executed—unusually quickly for this period in the terror. It is unclear whether Kuntsevo's party committee had a hand in the speed of the investigation. In any case, the investigators then used these four victims as "absentee denouncers," calling on evidence they had given in order to fabricate a large-scale conspiracy among Kuntsevo's agricultural workers. The district NKVD later revealed the leader of the conspiracy as Muralov himself.[120]

Arrests of district *nomenklatura* functioned as a significant motivation to work harder out of fear—an impetus that the entire Stalinist system depended upon. On March 20, 1938, the district party committee called several of these workers to a meeting where it gave them formal reprimands. Kuznetsov delivered a speech full of political platitudes. G. M. Lopatin, the district's representative for the Commissariat of Requisitions, "was absolutely incapable of understanding how to fulfill the plan like a Bolshevik. He carries out his job like a soulless bureaucrat. . . . He did not implement the law on meat deliveries as he should have and brought major harm to the interests of the state."[121]

Another *nomenklatura* worker who received the party's castigation was I. P. Badaev, the director of Kuntsevo's MTS, who also served as Muralov's deputy in the executive committee from October 1937. The reprimand charged him with all his underlings' mistakes, even "driving a tractor into a creek." Alongside Badaev, the district committee condemned V. T. Kokhov, deputy director for political affairs of the MTS. When questioned about this affair in 1940, Kuntsevo's district party secretary, A. G. Belov, asserted that the party committee had made these denunciations under pressure from Kuznetsov. Undoubtedly he knew what had become of the NKVD chief and found in him a convenient scapegoat.[122]

After just a short period of deliberation, the party committee expelled Badaev, Lopatin, and Kokhov from the party. An NKVD operative arrested them on the spot.[123] Rukodanov was in the building for this very purpose, which was standard practice by March 1938. In another case, in September 1937, Kuznetsov delivered a report at the bureau of the district party committee about the shortcomings of party members K. V. Skoruk and I. N. Ershkov. Immediately after this denunciation, they became the suspects of an investigation.[124]

The cooperation between party organizations in factories and the district NKVD during the operations against "alien nationalities" was unusual. Most of those arrested were not party members. However, whenever a factory party committee had compromising evidence on one of the accused, it became the property of the investigation without fail. The head of the department of cadre training at Factory 46, T. S. Kokhanskaia (a Ukrainian, although listed on the investigation form as a Pole), spoke out against the mass arrest of foreigners in March 1938.[125] The party committee of the factory took up her case and expelled her from the party. After a few days, the NKVD arrested her. The investigation file contains the stenographic record and protocol of the party meeting with her case. The factory committee sent "Materials on hostile anti-Soviet elements in the factory," the record of the Kokhanskaia case, directly to the district NKVD, as well as to the party committee of the Kuntsevo textile finishing plant.[126]

It is unclear whether the secretaries of local party organizations received confidential information from their contacts in the NKVD. This information would allow them to expel party members before arrest, a sign of their vigilance. In contrast, arrests of communists who had not been expelled became a black spot for all those surrounding them.

At the same time, however, it is worth acknowledging those communists who dared to defy the local agents of state security. Karetnikov's application for full party membership is a prime example. In 1932 Karetnikov had already composed a biographical sketch in which he described himself as a "member of the party" instead of merely a candidate member. In order to move from candidate to full member in the summer of 1937, Karetnikov had to use all his cunning. At first, the local party organization in the district NKVD refused to give him a recommendation, rightfully considering several parts of his biography too murky. Only when a delegation from Lubianka—with Iakubovich himself at its head—appeared at a party meeting did his membership application move forward.

Karetnikov's application then went to the district party committee for approval. Under inspection, it turned out that Karetnikov had falsely listed himself as having proletarian roots—which would have placed him in the favored group of the Bolshevik party. The district party secretary, not wanting to upset his relationship with the NKVD, kept the documents stored away but also did not allow the application to proceed. Only after Kuznetsov, as a member of the party committee's bureau, began to investigate the documents' disappearance did the application move forward. On September 21, 1937, the bureau confirmed Karetnikov as a full member of the party. Of course, even his confirmation did not

occur without Karetnikov's usual tricks. The party admitted him under
the first category of the party's regulations, as a worker coming from
the factory bench.[127]

By the end of 1937, the scale of repression was impossible to hide
from the district's inhabitants. In the town of Kuntsevo, rumors about
nighttime arrests and people disappearing without a trace had fright-
ened its residents. They found excuses to avoid the NKVD building.
The local government, on the contrary, tried to identify itself ever more
closely with the "glorious Chekists." On December 20 in Kuntsevo, the
district's party committee, executive committee, Komsomol, and trade
unions held a ceremonial meeting dedicated to the twentieth anniver-
sary of the Cheka-GPU-NKVD. Members of the district NKVD received
gifts. While giving thanks, Kuznetsov promised to triple his administration's efforts to eradicate counterrevolutionary forces. During the cere-
mony, its participants composed a symbolic address to Ezhov: "You
are the loyal son of our party, faithful to the end to the work of Lenin
and Stalin, selflessly loving of your people and motherland. You have
developed in yourself the same outstanding qualities as the organizer
of the Cheka, Feliks Dzerzhinsky. You, having become head of the
NKVD and with the help of your nation of millions of workers, in just a
short time have unmasked and liquidated the hornet's nest of Fascist
hired lackeys, terrorists, saboteurs, wreckers, and spies. For this, all the
Soviet people send you their heartfelt thanks."[128]

Behind this endless flow of adulation, paraphrased from the front
pages of *Pravda*, hid district leaders' fear that they, too, would soon
be counted among the "hired lackeys." They were at the mercy of the
workers of the district NKVD, who had the opportunity to pursue the
arrest of nearly any party worker. After his arrest, Karetnikov declared,
"Muralov gave testimony about the counterrevolutionary activities of
Morozov—the former secretary of the Kuntsevo district party committee
who was later removed by the Moscow party committee for his Right-
Trotskyist work, [about the activities of] Krylov—the second secretary
of the district party committee, and about other members of the district
party committee. . . . When Muralov began to give testimony about
these participants in the counterrevolutionary organization, I persuaded
investigator Rukodanov that Muralov was slandering honest workers
and forbade him to record testimony in the interrogation protocol. This
is how we protected that illegal organization."[129]

The Moscow provincial party committee had released a special
resolution on November 26, 1937, blaming the bad harvest in Kuntsevo

on the poor work of the district party committee. At a plenary meeting of the district party two days later, Morozov and his deputy Rostislavov were removed from their posts.[130] Why Kuntsevo's NKVD did not use this chance to unmask a conspiracy in the top ranks of the district's party hierarchy is a mystery. It is likely that in November all its operatives were occupied with fulfilling Order 00447. When the focus of repression turned to wreckers in March 1938, mass arrests among the *nomenklatura* only occurred in Muralov's executive committee. Of the dismissed party workers from Kuntsevo, only those who had already lost their party posts were arrested—Kokhov, the political instructor of the MTS, and Petr Mishin, the secretary of the party committee of Factory 46.

Almost as surprising and inexplicable as these oversights was the reprieve given the director of the Odintsovo lumber mill, M. I. Ob"edkov. His arrested colleagues painted a picture of an enterprise in ruins. According to their testimony, Ob"edkov was at the center of a system of corruption. Despite this evidence, Karetnikov's only action against Ob"edkov was to send the collected materials to the Kuntsevo party committee "for consideration."[131]

Local agents of state security had varying relationships with their counterparts in the party. In some cases, district party secretaries in Moscow province tried to control the local NKVD, warning superiors about the lawlessness of state security agents. V. M. Sukurov, head of the NKVD in Voskresensk district (Moscow province), demanded that his underlings reveal nothing if summoned to the district party committee, citing the secret nature of their investigations. The conflict between the district party committee and the NKVD ended in favor of the latter. In September 1937, immediately after the start of mass repression in the district, the NKVD arrested Solomon Gorbul'skii, the first secretary of the party committee. Although Sukurov doubtless took part in the case, agents arrived from the provincial NKVD, including Mikhail Kaverznev, the head of the eighth office of the counterintelligence department, to arrest Gorbul'skii and search his apartment.[132]

It is difficult to generalize about the relationship between state security and party organizations at the district level. The repression of high-ranking members of the party on Moscow's outskirts was common. In Serpukhov district, the NKVD arrested Party Secretary M. N. Nikiforov and forced him to sign a falsified interrogation protocol. Moreover, one of the investigators "attempted to slander the first secretary of the Serpukhov town party committee, writing a denunciation against him to the presidium of the district party conference based on falsified incriminating evidence."[133] In contrast to this case, the communists from Bel'sk district of Smolensk province managed to expel head of the district NKVD Vinogradov from the party in September 1937.[134] The outcome of these rivalries was not predetermined and depended on the degree of personal animosity between the police and party members toward one another. Despite conflicts between the NKVD and the party, their cooperation in selecting the victims was a constant.

Spoils of Terror

By the beginning of the 1930s, state distribution of goods had displaced the market economy in the USSR. The state-dominated economy gave the government the potential to exercise unlimited control over the population of an enormous country. Ostap Bender, the hero of Ilya Il'f and Evgeny Petrov's *The Golden Calf*, obtained the million rubles he had sought for so long but could not buy a train ticket or get a hotel room in the Soviet economy. Possession of Soviet currency was far less important than access to material goods. The first way to obtain goods was to buy them. Elites had access to hard-to-find products at fixed prices in exclusive stores. Ordinary citizens paid far greater prices for the same goods on the commercial market.[135]

Buying goods was legal, although carefully concealed from the public. The second way of finding products was illegal and tightly monitored. This way was workplace appropriation—a person's illegal use of an official post to improve his or her living standard. From ordinary buffet workers to the directors of large enterprises, nearly every person conducted a covert, albeit purely materialistic, struggle against a system that demanded total control over the country's possessions. A hierarchy of jobs with "informal influence" developed. The representatives of these in-demand professions, where the goods available were exceptionally valuable or easily taken, carried the practice of workplace appropriation to wider and wider circles. This mutual aid system became part of the informal clan relationships found in the NKVD. The NKVD provided considerable salaries and the commissariat had its own system for providing for employees. However, it would be naïve to think that workplace appropriation was absent from the lives of state security workers.

Power is a substitute for money. This old Soviet aphorism was doubly true during the height of Stalinism. In the USSR of the 1930s, party-state elites created their own scale of material success. At its pinnacle was a prestigious apartment and access to an automobile, although usually state-owned.[136] Agents of state security had these luxuries and others. Mass repression opened a world of possibilities for enrichment. Arrest and search protocols recorded the square footage and number of inhabitants of arrestees' housing. If the arrestee had lived alone in an apartment or room, the real estate was transferred to the account of the administrative-economic department of the provincial NKVD. The department then assigned the housing to NKVD workers. Otherwise, if an arrestee's family members lived in the apartment, they usually continued to inhabit it. However, for every rule there is an exception and in this case it was so-called "elite housing."

The investigation files of 1937–38 provide a lens into the NKVD's appropriation of apartments. When Karetnikov searched Muralov's apartment—located in central Moscow on Petrovskii Lane—he sealed two of three rooms and warned the family that they should anticipate "consolidation." However, during their feverish work the Chekists forgot about this tempting prize. In the summer of 1939, after Muralov had already been convicted, his wife tried to recover the rooms. Her request was in vain. Two weeks later the NKVD settled one of its workers in the apartment.[137]

After his transfer to Kuntsevo, Kuznetsov received a three-room apartment in the center of Moscow on Gogol Boulevard—a dream location for an operative of his rank. In the list of repressed people from Kuntsevo, one had an address the author had seen before. As it turned out, Kuznetsov had received the apartment of San-Tagi Kim, a Korean who had worked for the Moscow city administration. Later he left for his homeland on business for the Communist International (Comintern, the Moscow-led organization of the world's communist parties). On the eve of his arrest, he was the assistant head of the workshop of the Odintsovo brick factory in Kuntsevo district. It is unclear whether the exceptional apartment itself was the motivation behind Kim's arrest or if Kuznetsov only learned about it later.[138]

In either event, the head of Kuntsevo's NKVD did not miss his chance. After Kim's arrest, his wife and two children continued to live in the apartment. However, it seems that Kuznetsov found a solution to evict them as well, although it is unclear what criminal statute or internal NKVD instructions he used. When Kim left the labor camps after ten years and went into administrative exile, he could not find his family.[139] Instead, Kuznetsov found himself in a comfortable apartment. It was far from Kuntsevo, of course, but close to the Kremlin. Undoubtedly, the same technique allowed another former Kuntsevo chief, Baglikov, to find an apartment near the prestigious Arbat Street on Sivtsev Vrazhek.

Karetnikov himself appropriated a three-room apartment near the leadership on one of Arbat's famous alleyways. It is possible to reconstruct how Karetnikov obtained this valuable property to the smallest detail. In taking it, he engaged in actions that were openly criminal. These offenses would start the process that would bring down Karetnikov and Kuznetsov—the topic of the next section. For now, it is enough to say that workplace appropriation was a common practice among the NKVD officers in Kuntsevo. With a telephone call, district NKVD officers could produce fruit from local state farms.[140] They received furniture and arranged repairs courtesy of local factories.[141] One investigator named Iosifov shared his impressions of these perks: "The couple times I was at Karetnikov's apartment I saw that he was very well set up—a radio, mirrors, and so on. All the while, Karetnikov bragged that he received it all for free thanks to his connections at the facilities he monitored."[142] To commute to Kuntsevo from his new apartment in Moscow, Karetnikov used a GAZ-A brand car. The district NKVD had requisitioned the car after the arrest of its former owner, the director of the KIM factory N. I. Lazarev. Another worker at the NKVD received the furniture from Lazarev's apartment "for safekeeping."[143]

At times, NKVD workers simply stole the belongings of arrestees. In the petitions of arrestees from Kuntsevo, several noted that officers flaunted new watches, jackets, and other objects in front of their former owners. When the chief mechanic of Factory 46, M. M. Avdeenko, was arrested, his motorcycle and sidecar were taken and subsequently disappeared without a trace.[144]

The height of the arrests drained the energies of many lower-ranking operatives. Nonetheless, Kuznetsov and Karetnikov had time for personal enrichment, professional promotion, and even for rest and relaxation. The district NKVD leaders threw boisterous parties in the courtyard of the little house where workers from the office and Iakubovich's sister-in-law had lived. Among frequent guests were Karetnikov's former bosses. Karetnikov himself ended several nights being chauffeured back to Moscow dead drunk. These drinking bouts with high-ranking guests from Moscow set Kuntsevo apart from other district NKVD offices. However, local workers in the NKVD throughout the country used the terror to enhance their material situations.

Roberta Manning asserts that Vinogradov, the head of the Bel'sk district NKVD in Smolensk province, was "the most corrupt of the Bel'sk communists." He did not shy away from requisitioning even a good pair of shoes from arrestees.[145] Baglikov took the leather furniture of an arrested colleague whom he himself had interrogated.[146] The party organization of the Ulianovsk city NKVD discovered that operatives were reselling cloth and bicycles they had taken from the factory by coercion. Later it emerged that the leaders of that city's NKVD had bought valuables confiscated from victims for almost nothing. Agents who worked during executions went even further. They took money and valuables from their victims and exchanged them for alcohol to relieve pent-up emotional stress.[147]

An anonymous letter saved in the investigation file of a worker at the Serpukhov district NKVD, V. I. Khvatov, presents a similar case. The letter claimed that Khvatov bought a motorcycle from a photographer but instead of paying, he arrested the man and saw his case through to conviction. The letter's author asked in conclusion, "How many people were arrested because of greed? The first refused to give up milk or butter, another textiles, the third a car and so on."[148] In a small town, everything was out in the open. Theft by officials—whether police officers or NKVD agents—was impossible to hide.

When discussing the ordinary men involved in Stalin's terror, it is necessary to remember that they were not standard cogs in a machine of repression. They were living people who had to answer to their own consciences. It is important to exercise care in generalizing about them. The majority of NKVD workers accepted directives from above as the latest development in the war against the counterrevolution. Others thought their orders were the expression of the great leader's genius, incomprehensible to mere mortals. However, the history of the Kuntsevo NKVD in 1937–38 shows that some workers also reveled in their power over helpless people and manipulated tragedy for their own benefit. There is still another side to this story. The leadership at all levels had an interest in cultivating these types of people. Kuntsevo's workers could not guarantee the favor of their Moscow bosses with gifts and parties alone. "Shock workers" at the lower levels received incentives because they fulfilled the endless quotas that Lubianka itself received from above. In turn, NKVD leaders in the province could boast of their own successes. Without thousands of Karetnikovs and hundreds of Kuznetsovs, fulfilling the absurd plans for the complete destruction of "anti-Soviet elements" would have been impossible.

The End of the Duumvirate

Leaders in the party and the NKVD constantly received information about Kuntsevo NKVD agents' abuses of power. These signals came not only from those under investigation but also from operatives within the Kuntsevo office. Yet as long as Radzivilovskii's group—"our people"—sat behind the desks of the province's NKVD, all those letters, anonymous and signed, were locked away. The situation changed when Radzivilovskii's group began to disintegrate. Radzivilovskii himself went to work in Ivanovo province on the eve of mass repression but Iakubovich and Sorokin remained at key positions in the Moscow NKVD.

In July 1938, those two men set off to work in the Far East, the location given on documents recommending their arrest. Members of Radzivilovskii's group who remained in Moscow fell from grace. Karetnikov approached his former colleague and Iakubovich's secretary S. I. Ermakov about what was happening in the clan. Ermakov replied, "Vitia [the familiar form of Viktor], you shouldn't worry. When Sorokin handed over cases to the new boss of the third department [counterespionage] . . . he told the new boss that he shouldn't mess around in his business or else they would both go to prison. Everything in the third department will be fine."[149] Despite these assurances, the plot continued to thicken around the associates of Sorokin and Iakubovich.

On July 12, 1938, NKVD commissar Ezhov received a message from the new head of the Moscow NKVD, V. E. Tsesarskii. The letter detailed what must have been a common occurrence in the NKVD: Karetnikov's use of his position to procure an apartment. The story of the apartment affair is worth exploring in full. At the end of March 1938, Karetnikov was conducting a major investigation of workers at Kuntsevo's Factory 46. During the arrest of the former head of the factory's department of provisioning, V. P. Kuborskii, Karetnikov took notice of the arrestee's luxurious three-bedroom apartment in the center of Moscow, on Bolshoi Vlasevskii Lane, where the factory manager and his wife occupied two rooms. Karetnikov himself had just received a room in Moscow in January 1938 but clearly did not intend to stop there. He soon learned that Kuborskii's apartment still had an inhabitant. The activity the NKVD sergeant undertook to obtain the apartment would be at home in any crime movie. Karetnikov's arrest report contains the following information:

Karetnikov used physical coercion to obtain testimony from Kuborskii that Iakob Grigor'evich Litvak, who also lived in Kuborskii's apartment, was a member of a counterrevolutionary spy-sabotage organization. Although he was an investigator without the right to order an arrest, on March 22, 1938, Karetnikov signed an order for the arrest of Ia. G. Litvak. Having arrested Mr. Litvak, a Jew by nationality [Jews were an ethnic category in the USSR], Karetnikov gave instructions to [V. F.] Petushkov, a worker at the district NKVD, to list Litvak's nationality as Polish in the investigation file. Petushkov carried out Karetnikov's orders, illegally falsifying the documents. He changed "Jew" to "Pole" in the form and left a blank space in the interrogation protocol, filling in "Pole" after Mr. Litvak signed.

After the arrest of Kuborskii and Litvak, Kuborskii's wife Mariia Alekseevna Kuborskaia still lived at the apartment. With this in mind, Karetnikov entered into a deal with the accused Kuborskii, asking to exchange his room for Kuborskii's wife's. After he received Kuborskii's approval to exchange his apartment for the apartment of the Kuborskiis, Karetnikov allowed an illegal meeting between M. A. Kuborskaia and her husband the accused Kuborskii. After this meeting, Karetnikov decided not to exchange his room for the apartment of the Kuborskiis. Through Petushkov, Karetnikov received testimony from Litvak and other accused persons that Maria Kuborskaia was also a spy and on March 29, 1938, arrested her. Wishing to hide the traces of his crime and to show Kuborskaia in the worst possible light, head of the investigation Petushkov, at Karetnikov's orders, falsified a document. He wrote on the form after her signature that her "father was a significant landowner," while Kuborskaia herself testified that her father was petty bourgeois. After Kuborskaia's arrest, Karetnikov received a note from Iakubovich, the former assistant head of the Moscow provincial NKVD, giving him official authorization [to move]. He settled into the Kuborskiis' apartment, exchanged his former room with Mr. Zaitsev who lived across the hall from the Kuborskiis, and then occupied an entire apartment with three rooms and nearly fifty square meters. Using the influence of his office, Karetnikov refurnished his entire apartment at the expense of Factory 95.

Karetnikov's intrigue was largely representative of the possibilities agents throughout the USSR enjoyed during the terror. Of course, there was a distinction in Karetnikov's case. Powers from above sanctioned mass arrests. However, Karetnikov's solution to his apartment problem had been a demonstration of personal initiative—and that was punishable. The leadership of the NKVD that had put tens of thousands of innocent people to death each month also meticulously attended to the purity of its own ranks. Karetnikov's colleagues in Kuntsevo and in the provincial NKVD who had refused to use the terror for personal enrichment saw his machinations as a chance to settle scores.

Baglikov later took credit for Karetnikov's unmasking while under questioning: "From an operational document that fell into my hands, I learned that Karetnikov, an investigator of the Kuntsevo district office and a close relative of Iakubovich, had committed an illegal act in the case of the arrestee Kuborskii. With the approval of Iakubovich, he illegally occupied Kuborskii's four-bedroom [sic] apartment and handed over property that should have been confiscated to his relatives. When Tsesarskii was assigned to [head] the Moscow provincial NKVD, I told Tsesarskii about him [Karetnikov] in a written report without the knowledge of Iakubovich." It should be noted that Baglikov's main motivation for attacking Karetnikov was probably as vengeance against Iakubovich, whom he blamed for seven years of stints in district offices on the outskirts of Moscow.[150]

Although Baglikov may have informed Tsesarskii, Karetnikov's downfall began with another source. On June 6, Litvak addressed a petition on a scrap of paper to the procurator of the Soviet Union Andrei Vyshinsky from Butyrka prison. The petition never left the hands of the NKVD but it launched an internal inspection. This petition was the final straw for superiors in the NKVD. It caused them to run out of patience and turned the scales against their professional solidarity. It is important to recognize the bravery of a man who only became embroiled in the case because he had lived in the wrong apartment. Litvak was not afraid to criticize the Chekist and he laid out in detail the circumstances of his arrest:

> I was the victim of a serious crime against the state committed
> for personal gain by Karetnikov, an investigator of the Kuntsevo
> district office of the NKVD. On March 18, Karetnikov arrested
> my neighbor from my apartment, Kuborskii. During the search
> at Kuborskii's, Karetnikov entered my room and during our

conversation he abruptly announced, "I recommend that you vacate your room." To my bewildered response, "Why?" Karetnikov answered, "Otherwise it will be worse for you."[151]

Evidently this episode looked even more unseemly to the provincial NKVD leadership because Litvak contended he had no connection to Factory 46. Tsesarskii sent a commission supervised by Nikitin, the head of the secretariat of the provincial NKVD, who questioned both Litvak and Kuborskii on July 8. The commission confirmed all Litvak's assertions and more. "Pole" was written on the arrest forms instead of "Jew." Karetnikov had beaten Kuborskii with the telephone book *All Moscow* to extract both his confession to espionage and permission to switch apartments. After Kuborskii accepted the switch, he immediately called Kuborskii's wife but Litvak answered the telephone. Karetnikov became furious and sent a subordinate to arrest Litvak. Then he set up the meeting between Kuborskii and his wife, and even promised to help her move to the new accommodations. At a later questioning, on December 2, 1938, Kuborskii added more details:

> Karetnikov arrested me and led me to his office. There he beat me severely until I lost consciousness. On March 22, Karetnikov came into the cell and asked if I could walk and I answered I could. Karetnikov then asked me if I understood everything that was happening and if he could compose my testimony. I answered that I understood. . . . When I signed the protocol, Karetnikov said to me, "Give me your apartment." I answered that another person lives there. Karetnikov said that the tenant was a bastard and he sent for him to be arrested. Later, when I was back in the cell, they brought in my tenant Litvak [it is unclear from testimony whether Litvak owned or rented the room], who had been arrested by Karetnikov.[152]

In July Karetnikov evidently sensed that the apartment affair could end badly and decided to protect himself. He hastily got married. Then he registered his new wife, her child, and her father in the apartment. Beyond these measures, Karetnikov sought the help of his old patron Radzivilovskii, who had moved to the central NKVD administration in April 1938. The latter recommended requesting reassignment to a different location and lying low.[153] But it was already too late. Five days after his wedding, on July 13, 1938, Karetnikov was arrested. At the end of the investigation, his new family was moved from the exceptional apartment—which nonetheless remained in the hands of the NKVD—to a wooden shack.

In comparison to the thousands of innocent people sent to execution at Butovo or to the Gulag, Karetnikov's apartment debacle was relatively harmless. Besides the affair with the apartment, only Karetnikov's supposed negligence incriminated him. Investigators accused him of failing to uncover and arrest "109 kulaks, sons of kulaks, and various anti-Soviet elements" at an armament factory in his jurisdiction. His arrest report is notable for another reason. Unlike so many arrestees, he was not "unmasked by the testimony of arrestees." Karetnikov was the first of his group of arrestees—and in the supposed conspiracy he himself was only a "pawn," as one of his interrogators called him. But he was a pawn on whom patrons had staked a great deal and who himself had believed in his own invulnerability.

The apartment affair determined not only Karetnikov's fate but that of several of his victims as well. When Tsesarskii released Litvak on July 22, his order contained the directive, "With regard to other people connected to investigation 9160 [the large case Karetnikov conducted at Factory 46 in March 1938], conduct addition inquiries."[154] Besides Litvak, though, none of the dozens of workers arrested in the Factory 46 case were freed in 1938. The investigation was put away unresolved and the arrestees had to wait for it to be reopened.

Now on the other side of prison bars, Karetnikov was not yet ready to surrender. Even after he lost hope in the help of high-placed patrons, he was confident of his own value. He tailored his testimony to the politics of repression current in the highest echelons of the NKVD. At his questioning on August 29, 1938, he admitted that Sorokin had recruited him for an underground organization in 1936. Sorokin, after a two-week tenure as the head of the NKVD of Ussuriisk in the Far East, was arrested on September 16. Iakubovich arrived from the Far East three days later. The arrest notice in Iakubovich's file declared that his detainment was based on Karetnikov's testimony. Besides Iakubovich, Karetnikov's evidence also instigated the arrests of Berg, Kuznetsov, Sorokin, Radzivilovskii, and his secretary G. A. Solomatin.

Later, when Karetnikov sensed a change in the mood of his interrogators, he refused to acknowledge his participation in the work of the counterrevolutionary organization. The interrogations in September produced evidence similar to previous questionings and were not saved in his investigation file. Only references to these interrogations in later protocols with Karetnikov allow the reconstruction of the content of the September sessions. In later interrogations, his questioners soothed him by saying that throughout the Soviet Union there were "nests of enemies" being unmasked. In all these counterrevolutionary organizations there were pawns like Karetnikov, they said, and for many punishment would stop with reassignment to work in the Gulag.[155] Berg was arrested on August 3, 1938, in connection with Karetnikov and his questioning unfolded in a similar manner. Interrogators persuaded Berg to admit to depravity and corruption, promising a light sentence of three years.[156] Insofar as the interrogator and the prisoner both knew the NKVD's methods of fabricating charges, their conversation turned away from what had actually happened to what kind of crimes would fit the investigation.

The situation changed radically after Beria replaced Ezhov as head of the NKVD in November 1938. The new NKVD head needed to find scapegoats who could bear the blame for the abuses of the mass operations and the Kuntsevo affair received renewed interest. Even earlier, after he became deputy head of the NKVD, Beria backed Kuznetsov's arrest on September 21, 1938. The order was clearly written in haste: Among other accusations against Kuznetsov, he was charged for his connection to Lazarev, the director of the KIM factory who had been arrested in June 1937. A clear oversight was that the arrest order failed to reference the Kuntsevo chief's brother Dmitrii, who held a high post in the Commissariat of Transport until his arrest. A denunciation about the brothers that had triggered an internal investigation even escaped notice. A neighbor of Dmitrii Kuznetsov wrote to the NKVD that on the night of August 18, Aleksandr Kuznetsov appeared at his brother's wearing his uniform. Along with Dmitrii's wife, they moved the family's belongings from the apartment in advance of possible confiscation.[157] Kuznetsov's natural urge to help relatives and the thrift learned in his upbringing in the village helped bring his promising career to ruin.

Aleksandr Kuznetsov was arrested on September 26 at a sanatorium in the Crimean resort town of Alushta. At interrogations he expressed his willingness to confess to any charge, no matter how absurd. "I stood against Soviet power from the first days of its existence," he claimed. However, as in the case of Karetnikov, the investigators waited for the leadership to determine the direction the investigation should take. At the beginning of 1939, haste replaced the lull of the fall. In both investigation files, a resolution dated January 17 extended the investigation and marked the beginning of a new series of interrogations. On February 10,

Kuznetsov and Karetnikov had their only face-to-face confrontation and that very day the accused learned that their cases had moved to the courts.

The investigation returned to the initial charges about a counter-revolutionary conspiracy in the leadership of the Moscow provincial NKVD. Its members had supposedly attempted to protect Trotskyist cadres. Their end goal was "to overturn the state through an armed uprising and take power."[158] Mass arrests of innocent people were supposed to turn the population against Soviet power. This phrase occurred frequently in the investigations of former NKVD workers as a means of removing responsibility from the true initiators of terror in 1937–38. At his final interrogations, Karetnikov named a memorized list of his former patrons, now cast as saboteurs and spies. The new wave of falsification differed little from the previous one.

Karetnikov's testimony figured into the investigation of one other Kuntsevo Chekist—Baglikov, arrested on January 8, 1939. The affair had come full circle for Baglikov, who had first informed superiors about the apartment affair of the ultimate insider. In contrast to Karetnikov and Kuznetsov, Baglikov did not face torture. He told the investigator frankly that he had been "arrested automatically" and that he knew he was one of the center's scapegoats whose punishment would absolve the leadership of responsibility. After the investigation transformed the charges against him from the typical "counterrevolutionary conspiracy" to the more convoluted "official offenses and workplace appropriation," it reached a dead end. Central authorities returned the case to investigators several times for additional work until the judgement was made in November 1939 "to end the criminal investigation of Baglikov, limiting punishment to his dismissal from the NKVD."[159]

Kuznetsov and Karetnikov met a different fate. On February 26, 1939, the Military Collegium of the Supreme Court of the USSR convened to hear Kuznetsov's case. The accused recanted his testimony and declared that it had been extracted under torture. "I did not make up the 'phony' cases. I only carried out arrests with the approval of the provincial administration." Nonetheless, the court sentenced him to execution. Karetnikov went before the same court on March 2 and received the death sentence as well. The sentences were carried out the following day. The executions marked the end of the story of these two men—NKVD officers whose careers peaked during the Great Terror. Its momentum carried away not only its victims but also its agents.

The Kuntsevo NKVD under Investigation

In the fall of 1938, the other workers of the Kuntsevo NKVD could only guess the fates of Kuznetsov and Karetnikov. By that time, the former district bosses had both become prisoners in Lubianka, hostages in a battle between clans at the highest echelons of Soviet power. The new chief of the district was Lieutenant of State Security A. F. Senenkov, who was sent from one of the capital's municipal districts to maintain order. The provincial administration reassigned an additional helper, A. G. Leonov, from Kolomna district of Moscow province. A year later Leonov would become head of Kuntsevo's NKVD when Senenkov moved into the provincial NKVD administration.

The new leadership found itself confronted with a large number of investigations that the provincial administration had sent back as "flawed." Orders from above slowed the pace of repression, but inertia on the ground carried the operations forward. According to the testimony of Vlasov, an officer in Voskresensk district (Moscow province), "In May we had 45–50 cases for espionage returned to us for further investigation. At the same time we received an order from Taganka prison not to free anyone, and if the case for espionage falls apart, get evidence of anti-Soviet activity."[160]

Kuntsevo's NKVD was caught in a similar situation until the arrests of Kuznetsov and Karetnikov. At that point, the provincial leadership suspended the district's cases but left the accused in Moscow prisons without proceeding with their investigations. After Beria replaced Ezhov, work in the NKVD began to return to normalcy. Kuntsevo's investigators hoped that they would find sympathetic ears among their new superiors and emerge from the mass operations unharmed. In the building on Zagorskii Street, they changed the portrait of the people's commissar and went about their business quietly. But they failed to bury the past.

Complaints from the accused and their relatives were endless and they drew inspectors from Moscow to Kuntsevo. On December 7, 1938, a provincial NKVD worker named Bulkin from the second department (operations) sent a report about the Kuntsevo office to V. P. Zhuravlev, the head of the Moscow provincial NKVD. Bulkin had reviewed thirty-seven unfinished investigations and in almost every case there was a violation of the criminal-procedural code. He proposed that Senenkov carry out new investigations immediately and prepare the cases for transfer to court.[161]

The provincial leadership made workers at the district office involved in the mass operations write reports about the supposed sabotage their former bosses had carried out. Without these documents it would be impossible to present such a full picture of the terror. Post-Soviet Russian document collections on the terror frequently publish these kinds of materials because of the insight they provide into the NKVD.[162] Nonetheless, historians must treat them with caution. Their authors did not fearlessly report the events of the mass operations, but above all attempted to justify their own actions.

In composing the reports, any act of defiance against the district leadership was priceless, a guarantee of rehabilitation. Officers wrote in everyday language, full of emotion and understated offense, rather than in the typical bureaucratese. Naturally, all the authors placed blame for what had happened on the leadership, particularly on Karetnikov. One worker said, "[Karetnikov] did not occupy himself with investigative work but was constantly setting up some kind of illicit deal for himself or for the former provincial leadership."[163] Each of the NKVD workers walked the razor's edge. They had to acknowledge the misconduct in the district without questioning the legality of the mass operations on the whole.

The officers absolved their own guilt with references to pressure from the district or provincial leadership. Tsyganov wrote, "We carried out arrests by list without authorization or incriminating evidence. In the materials provided this is clear from the marks written in Kuznetsov's handwriting. 'Order' meant we should write an order for arrest, that is, a fake order without incriminating evidence just because the person was a Pole or a German."[164] Rukodanov put his own slant on the events of spring 1938: "Beatings were one method of interrogation, again instigated by Karetnikov, because he had come from the province [the Moscow NKVD]. He said that they beat arrestees there, that Zakovskii had ordered it and himself beat arrestees at interrogations. When I tried to get out of it, Karetnikov said, chiding me, 'You, Rukodanov, don't know how to interrogate.' It made me feel as though I was suspected of being especially merciful toward the enemy."[165]

A few of the investigators wrote that they had informed the NKVD's leadership about the horrors committed in the district. The office's party organization announced that it had opposed Karetnikov's membership in the party. Materials from investigation files provided evidence of other attempts to oppose the terror. Kuntsevo's police department effectively sabotaged the leadership's demand to eradicate the "kulak town" in the ravine near the government highway; a review showed that there were no kulaks among the poor inhabitants of the shantytown, to Kuznetsov's chagrin.[166]

Kuznetsov and Karetnikov's removal was the consequence of numerous written signals about illegal acts committed in Kuntsevo. The authors of these letters were victims themselves or their relatives—often simple peasants—who usually addressed their pleas to NKVD chief Ezhov or procurator Vyshinsky. They sent letters to others as well, sometimes sending one letter to multiple recipients. Workers at the district office also participated in the letter writing. In August 1938, the party committee of Moscow province received an anonymous letter painting a vivid picture of Karetnikov's degeneracy and the travesties that occurred under his leadership. The letter concluded that his arrest would only be a half measure: "We need to see if it's only him or if someone else needs to answer for the dirty deeds perpetrated in Kuntsevo."[167] The investigation of Baglikov also had its basis in accusations about his time in Kuntsevo, made by former underlings whom he had fired. During the peak of the mass operations, such letters did not receive attention. However, by the end of the summer of 1938, they became the foundation for the purge of the state security apparatus.[168]

On December 30, 1938, inspectors assembled the evidence from the investigation in Kuntsevo, including the reports of district operatives, for Moscow NKVD head Zhuravlev. The report alerted the NKVD leader that seventy-three people were still under investigation after being arrested in late 1937 and early 1938. Fifty-five of them had been detained in the "national operations." "Under further questioning a number of arrestees maintain that they are Russians, Ukrainian, or Jews [rather than targeted national groups]. They were listed in their signed confessions as members and leaders of counterrevolutionary groups or organizations that they do not know of or know only through a shared workplace or living space." Graphologists determined that there were instances of falsified signatures in the case files.[169]

As the leadership of the provincial NKVD hastened to wrap up its investigation in the district, a new storm of activity began on Zagorskii Street. In 1939 the new year began with an unwanted present from the assistant military prosecutor of the Moscow military district to the Kuntsevo NKVD—an order to finish the investigation of the counterrevolutionary organization at Factory 46 in three days, by January 5, 1939.[170] Senenkov made frequent reports to Zhuravlev about the review of cases and the Moscow chief decided their fate. Leonov wrote that of the forty-eight people who had been under investigation, twenty-seven were released, "of whom 6 or 9 were released by the order of the commissar [of the NKVD]."[171]

A tragicomic meeting occurred during the feverish work of re-questioning arrestees for the review of cases in December 1938. A. I. Kudriavtsev found himself face to face with Rukodanov, the same person who had made him into the leader of an underground SR organization earlier that year in March. Rukodanov did not hesitate to ask the accused to explain his false testimony from earlier that year and had no scruples about writing down the answer, "harsh prison conditions."[172] When Rukodanov met another one of his supposed SR leaders, the teacher Zverev, the Kuntsevo investigator accused him of slander.[173]

NKVD leaders allowed a review of complaints by arrestees and their families in late 1938, initiating a final, intense wave of reevaluations of cases in the districts. The Kuntsevo office received orders from both the procuracy and the Moscow NKVD to reexamine its verdicts. In spite of the threatening language and harsh deadline given in these resolutions, the review dragged on for several months. It seems that confusion over jurisdiction in higher echelons allowed workers in the provinces to sort the review out among themselves without fear.

Although a military tribunal had convicted Kuntsevo's NKVD leaders, the only punishment rank-and-file operatives faced was transfer to new assignments or reprimands. Rukodanov, who had thrice received official warnings for falsification of investigatory materials, was fired from the NKVD with "no possibility of further employment." He attempted to contest the decision, writing a letter to the party's Central Committee, but received a reply to "go quietly."[174] Efremov and Dikii were also prosecuted, a process that ended with the young operatives receiving a scare but no more.[175] A. V. Solov'ev received a sentence of just ten days arrest for falsification of witness testimony because "his actions did not display malicious intent."[176] Another newcomer to the office, A. A. Tsyganov, continued to work in the NKVD until he died in 1943 on the Voronezh front in World War II.[177]

The proceedings in Kuntsevo reflect what occurred in lower-level NKVD offices throughout the USSR. Provincial NKVD administrations began to send albums of cases back for further investigation and workers at city and district offices had to release arrestees. In particularly odious cases, special investigators from the central NKVD apparatus arrived in the provinces. The material from their inspections made its way into orders for the arrest of NKVD workers from the lower and middle ranks.[178] According to the author's data, over half of the NKVD district chiefs in Moscow province were repressed in 1939 and evidence exists about similar purges in other provinces.[179] One or two underlings who had especially distinguished themselves during the period of mass terror usually fell alongside their chief at the military tribunal. When Germany invaded the Soviet Union, though, many of those who had received sentences to forced labor were pardoned and returned to work in state security.[180]

Executors or Executioners? A Psychological Portrait

It is almost impossible to believe that the mountains of investigation files, the mass graves at Butovo, and the thousands of ruined lives were all the work of a single cell of the NKVD, of some ten people. Indisputably, there were high-ranking leaders who devised the mass operations and there were executioners in the commandant's office who pulled the triggers at Butovo. All the same, the false accusations came from the desks of investigators in the dacha town of Kuntsevo, who under different circumstances might have been mere rural detectives. Can an ordinary person willingly become a part of such mass operations, taking on the role of judge and executioner? How could that person maintain their sanity after all they had seen and done?

The case of the Kuntsevo NKVD cannot provide a universal answer to these questions. Nonetheless, a picture of the rural executors of the mass operations emerges from the district, echoing to some degree what is already known about the leaders of the NKVD.[181] The majority of officers had less than a secondary education and rose up from the peasantry during the civil war. They gave absolute loyalty to patrons among their immediate superiors. They were shrewd and had picked up habits of military discipline in the Red Army, attributes that helped them make their careers in Stalin's regime. At the same time, the rapid rise of rural NKVD cadres occurred under a regime whose ideology they did not always understand. Their confusion about the particulars of Marxism-Leninism made them insecure. With one false step, they might lose the material comforts and privileges they had gained. As a defense mechanism, they developed hierarchical, informal groups— clans. Belonging to one of these groups proved more effective than moving through official bureaucratic channels.

Operatives, above all those at the lowest levels, adopted customs similar to the criminal world that they vowed to fight. These customs included fear-induced submission to authority, the presence of an honor code, mutual assurances, ritual division of spoils, and the use of coded language. Under the conditions of mass terror, these practices emerged in the monstrous form of disciplined atrocities. The quotas for arrests of "enemies of the people" in 1937 were the same kind of absurdity as plans to uncover a certain number of crimes that the police in Russia had to fulfill until recently.

Did provincial NKVD operatives believe that their victims—people from the district seat and the surrounding countryside—were really spies and saboteurs? It is hard to imagine that they did. Of course, they had to convince themselves and their colleagues of the logic of these baseless accusations. Many of those who ended up in the camps later wrote that investigators in Kuntsevo had misled them about the outcome of their investigation. When conducting interrogations, investigators talked about deportation from the greater Moscow area or a few years of exile, pointing to the temporary nature of repression. Some even said it reflected the flowering of "Stalinist democracy." A victim who was later released, Iu. S. Drobik, wrote, "When I was summoned to [investigator] Solov'ev in Kuntsevo after my arrest, I asked why they had taken me. He answered that they needed to deport me. I asked why they needed to arrest me for that because they deported the kulaks and their families without arrest. He explained that the Constitution does not allow that [administrative exile] now."[182]

Although they beat arrestees during investigations, Kuntsevo's agents do not seem to have been sadists. Perhaps they derived pleasure from mocking those who had just yesterday been among the powerful—the head of the district executive council, the director of a local factory or the chair of a collective farm. However, it appears that Kuntsevo's NKVD officers consciously turned off their feelings to fulfill the orders of the head of the district NKVD. Beating arrestees was just part of the party's mission. It was not pleasant but it had to be done. The faster the procession of arrestees moved through Kuntsevo in the mass operations, the less the NKVD men could distinguish between individuals. Ultimately, victims' real culpability did not play a role in their ceremonial sacrifice. Of the officers, perhaps only Karetnikov took pleasure in flogging innocent people into admitting their participation in spy networks he had fabricated. Even so, his chosen implement of torture—the phone book *All Moscow*—seems naïve compared to the specially made rubber clubs and marble paperweights his senior comrades at Lubianka used.[183]

Official zeal accompanied and induced terror among state security agents who feared that they themselves might face arrest. Practically all those arrested after Ezhov's downfall spoke of "the danger of being unmasked" as a motivating factor. These testimonies were collected during the purge of Ezhov's appointees, of course, and reflected the needs of that campaign. Nonetheless, they provide a window into the mindset of the executors of mass repression. These men justified themselves by arguing that they were mere pawns in a big game. They had scrambled for the chance to remain on the chessboard, even at the expense of their colleagues. In Karetnikov's testimony from February 9, 1939, he related a conversation with his patron Sorokin on the eve of the latter's departure for the Far East. Revealing the role of mutual protection in their clan, Sorokin said:

> Conscientious workers in the Moscow provincial NKVD have begun to talk about you and Kuznetsov, to say things about the work of the Kuntsevo district office that are unfavorable for us [the clan]. It was easy to mask your affairs when Zakovskii was the Moscow NKVD head. He presented Kuntsevo as a model to others, distracting the suspicions of honest workers and clamping their mouths shut. After they arrested Zakovskii and Karutskii shot himself, it is possible that someone among us will be arrested. If that happens, the conspiratorial organization cannot be let down no matter what and evidence against it cannot be given under any circumstances. If they arrest you, Viktor, don't give evidence about the conspiracy. If you have to, confess to misappropriations but not to participation in a conspiracy. If you do, then all of us, including you, will be shot.[184]

Sorokin's last phrase was no less than open blackmail.

The psychological state of Karetnikov and Kuznetsov differed little from that of thousands of their colleagues across the Soviet Union. They knew better than most how thin the line between prison and freedom was and their fear was appropriate. P. K. Filikhin was an operative in the Ul'ianovsk city NKVD who had taken part in mass executions. In the summer of 1939, he wrote a letter on the eve of his own arrest to party Central Committee secretary Andrei Zhdanov: "As I went about my work like everyone else, I expected them [internal investigators] to disarm me at any moment, to arrest me and to take me to the basement [to be shot]. . . . I experience an inhuman strain on my nerves all the time (from anticipation of arrest, [and participation in] the executions). I used the same methods as everyone else. Many old rank-and-file Chekists did the same. And according to rumor, many of them were taken to the basement. Now those methods of work, even the execution of convicted people, are incriminating."[185]

State security workers' real fear of being taken to the basement—to be executed—is comparable to the terror experienced by Orwell's Winston Smith in *1984* as he faced the rat cage placed on his head. Their reactions to this stress ranged from stoic depression to mental illness to suicide attempts. The inaccessible medical cards of NKVD workers for 1937–38 could speak volumes. But even without the statistics of "professional illnesses," it is not difficult to imagine how participation in criminal activity under the cover of the state's authority could break a person's psyche. The very same Filikhin wrote of himself, "I am now a mentally ill man who sometimes forgets his native language." Another NKVD operative, E. F. Bogomolov from Nizhnyi Novgorod province, began working in early 1938 and in less than six months was diagnosed with epilepsy.[186]

Moscow NKVD chief Karutskii and Kuntsevo investigator Smirnov were not the only suicides among state security employees. Executioners among state security workers accounted for a series of suicides. Prelov, of the NKVD in Mytishchi district, shot himself while being arrested.[187] Serpukhov district investigator Khvatov killed himself in Taganka prison on September 21, 1939.[188] Present-day legal writers rightfully talk about the "professional mutilation" of the minds of political police who participated in repression. The authors of one study write, "In the end, several workers turned into open sadists, at times mentally disabled; others attempted to forget through drinking and debauchery; still others became ill or committed suicide. All of them sooner or later experienced a profound disintegration of their identity."[189]

Nonetheless, these men were the organizers and executors of repression, not its victims. Perestroika-era arguments asserted that the system of repression did not spare its own and that a larger proportion of NKVD workers were executed relative to other parts the population. These assertions require serious revision. Although employees of the secret police became victims of the terror directed at the Stalinist *nomenklatura* as a whole, the situation in the Moscow provincial NKVD shows that rank-and-file operatives in state security faced arrest only in rare cases during the height of repression.[190] The shuffling of cadres in the NKVD accompanied by reprimands and arrests only began in the summer of 1938. Leaders at all levels attempted to create alibis for themselves, shifting responsibility to others—higher-ups blamed their underlings and vice versa.

Ordinary NKVD workers not only realized that they were committing crimes but also that punishment awaited them. When they found themselves under arrest, they recognized the truth of their situation. Filikhin wrote in a petition, "Now the bureau of the provincial party committee and the provincial NKVD are looking for concrete perpetrators who violated revolutionary legality. They want to find a scapegoat for someone else's sins. . . . We should not prosecute those who used accepted methods [torture] in their investigative work. It would be necessary to prosecute all those who worked in the NKVD without exception."[191]

When investigators arrested Radzivilovskii, Iakubovich, Sorokin, and other leaders of the Moscow provincial NKVD who were linked through mutual protection and unofficial relationships, the charges were not for the real crimes they had committed. These masters of political and criminal falsification became the victims of their own arts. However, there is no reason to talk about their innocence or even political rehabilitation, although one Kuntsevo promotee, Berg, received rehabilitation posthumously.[192] Did he deserve this dubious honor, having organized the executions in Butovo as head of the Moscow NKVD's administrative-economic department?

The stories examined in this book will not reveal why mass repression occurred in 1937–38. However, they do show the collateral damage that resulted from Stalin's orders. Fearing a major war, Stalin put his agents of state security to the test. After twenty years of Soviet rule, he wanted to see what lengths they would go to in order to fulfill his commands. They passed the test, to his horror—fulfilling the directives of the mass operations better than even he desired. Dissatisfied though he was with his agents at the end of the mass terror, he was reliant on these operatives to carry out work that no one else could. The Great Terror marked a major transformation in the country as Stalin broke clans from the district to the national level, making fear the principle motive for productivity. The Stalinist model of modernization was doomed to lose its energy and stagnate without similar bloodlettings. Those losses, experienced above and below, were coolly taken into consideration. According to Bolshevik logic, new cadres should have been better than the old cadres they replaced.

The conclusion of this story raises questions of morality. How did these people live afterward? Were they haunted by nightmares of their innocent victims? There were no cases where NKVD workers at any level voluntarily confessed to their role in the repressions of 1937–38. The majority chased away their memories of those years, although the past followed them at every step. Rukodanov continued to live in the house for personnel on the grounds of the Kuntsevo NKVD office—the same place where he condemned dozens of innocent people to death. Before Khrushchev's Thaw, he led the cadres section of the Kuntsevo town council, where he may have had dealings with his victims. When called to give testimony during rehabilitation hearings in the 1950s, he did not deny his actions but he continued to assert they were the product of pressure from above, saying, "All the cases concluded from August 1937 to April 1938 were violations of socialist legality. My explanation for these incidents is that our superiors demanded this work, telling us that it was our mission to carry out a ruthless struggle with the representatives of a fifth column. At the same time, they pointed out that we were Chekists above all and only after that members of the party. The system was such that if a man came from a socially alien background then he was an enemy of the Soviet government."[193] This system only ended when the Soviet government itself ended. However, society continues to be reluctant to remember the dark pages of its past, and post-Soviet state security agencies still resist attempts to reveal the truth about them. The terror on a district level, in Kuntsevo and in many other places, is only a small fragment of a larger tragedy that Russia suffered during the peak of Stalinism.

Part II: Patterns of Victimization

Social Collaboration in Repression

The lopsided balance of power between Soviet society and the state following the Great Turn of 1929 created a collective psychosis at the start of 1937. Regime-sanctioned repression gave people the chance to settle old scores and awakened in them the instinct to hunt cornered prey. Campaign after campaign in the press against Trotskyists, spies, and saboteurs drew a response from the public. In investigation files, "former people" (the upper layers of prerevolutionary society) reacted with poorly concealed gloating that "the situation must be bad if they've gone after their own." Yet people of lower social status understood what was happening as leadership in action. The torrent of denunciatory signals to institutions large and small—from the party's Central Committee to local trade unions—grew exponentially. Their authors' motives are difficult to generalize. Every situation arose from a different set of emotions and aims. There were earnest attempts to "save the beloved leader" as well as self-serving attempts at retribution.

A typical letter is that of a certain Goncharov, a truck driver at the provincial cropping station. The letter, dated March 24, 1937, shows the influence of newspaper articles about unmasked spies and saboteurs: "As soon as I read the article in the newspaper, I suddenly got an idea in my head about terrorism [against the state] that I could not get rid of. I kept the article and can think only about it."[1] His chain of thought led to two startling conclusions: first, the leadership of the station must have invited leaders of the party and government to a banquet in order to kill them; second, the station was using damaged vehicles and it was only a matter of time before one of those vehicles hit Stalin's limousine on the government highway. After these accusations, Goncharov, who was on probation for prior convictions, concluded with the request that his labor record book be returned to him.

All this could be written off as paranoid nonsense if similar conjecture a few months later had not turned into official accusations against thousands and thousands of people. Investigators painstakingly verified any material concerning the safety of Stalin and recorded the case in the operative archives of the NKVD in case it would be needed later. The file on the cropping station contains a series of denunciations against K. A. Pozdniakov. The author of the letters, a distant relative of Pozdniakov, wrote, "I'm asking that you arrest him in twenty-four hours. . . . Arrest him and put a bullet in his head. He's an irredeemable bastard, I know him." The writer said that if authorities did not arrest Pozdniakov he would commit suicide. The author received a sentence for slander in 1936 but this punishment did not stop his denunciations. Soon he wrote directly to Stalin, "By the time you receive my letter I will already be dead, I will lie my grave. But Comrade Stalin, I am very happy that you will stay alive. You are beloved in our society. You are the leader of the world's proletariat."[2]

The author of those lines, as one might suspect, turned out to be a patient at a psychiatric hospital. Nonetheless, the Kuntsevo NKVD verified each of the letters and deposited them in a case file. In the end, Pozdniakov received ten years in the camps because of the letter of a politicized maniac. Hypervigilance that crossed the line into insanity was a mass occurrence and a popular diagnosis. During the procuracy's review of cases in 1939, inspectors had to call in a psychiatrist to examine several victims in Kuntsevo district who had been arrested for slander against party and state leaders. In these cases, common sense alone would have been enough to give the correct diagnosis. These people fell victim to the propaganda of revolutionary violence. Over the first decades of the Bolshevik dictatorship, this syndrome seeped into Soviet people, then penetrated the top of the country's political hierarchy and turned upon society to exact irretrievable losses.

A considerable number of denunciations reflected economic dissatisfaction in the district. The denunciations' authors understood their situation in different ways. Some pointed to the drunkenness of collective farm chairs and the corruption of the district leadership, the embezzlement of "socialist property," and the crops left to rot in the fields. Others understood the apathy of leaders and ordinary workers about the results of their work as a sign of intentional damage. Failing to cover up a stockpile of beets or to turn a screw well when repairing a motor became sabotage. It is likely that if the authors had known that the investigations would turn into Gulag or death sentences, many of these letters would never have been written.

A different category of denunciation grew out of the extreme conditions of 1937, reflecting both pragmatism and the suppressed animosity of have-nots. Many inhabitants of the district continued to engage in entrepreneurial activities: various teams of disabled and otherwise housebound people produced goods that had widespread demand; peasant gardens fed all of Moscow with crisp greens; women took fresh milk to the train station for sale. According to letters that the district NKVD received, a few of these peasants had plots as big as a hectare and used them to make astounding profits while refusing to work for the greater good of society.[3]

In addition to these marketers, Kuntsevo had turned into a place where various exiles from the capital could settle. The livelihood of many depended on petty trade, understood by authorities as "speculation." The town and surrounding villages were filled with the descendants of noble families and entrepreneurial circles of prerevolutionary Russia, who maintained their caste-like insularity. Kuntsevo was a "regime" district—within a hundred kilometers of Moscow and therefore with official restrictions on who could live within its borders. Nonetheless, people whom authorities had exiled from the district frequently returned and lived with relatives illegally. These residents occupied a central place in the denunciations of vigilant citizens.

In many denunciations, the authors condemned a person's background rather than any concrete crime. The main point of reference in these denunciations was repression associated with collectivization— exile, confiscation of property, individual punitive taxes, and other punishments. Even while denouncing their neighbors, the authors of these letters did not hide their fear that local kulaks who had returned from exile might seek retribution. As Sheila Fitzpatrick writes, "Dekulakization, which victimized some peasants and enabled others to profit from their misfortune, added enormously to the sum of village grievance," leading to a frequency of complaints in the 1930s that was "without precedence."[4]

Enthusiasm for work in the fresh air of a household plot often took a fatal turn for those spending a summer evening outdoors. A standard formulation in witness testimony in Kuntsevo went: "Walking nearby the terrace of the neighboring dacha in the evening, I saw a counterrevolutionary gathering" or "heard anti-Soviet conversations." Reviews of cases in 1939 occasionally cited the layout of the local grounds and demonstrated that at a distance of ten meters, as well as with a fence in between, it was impossible to overhear the substance of a neighbor's conversation.[5]

A significant number of denunciations grew out of hostile relationships between relatives. Of course, investigators compelled arrested relatives to give testimony for ongoing investigations and in these cases witnesses hardly had a choice about providing condemning evidence. However, there were also voluntary denunciations that prompted investigations. Kuntsevo even had its own version of Pavlik Morozov, the child-martyr whom relatives killed after he denounced his family to local police, according to Soviet mythology. A Komsomol member from Kuntsevo wrote to his youth organization, "The sordid past of my father, as well as his current suspicious activity, makes me believe that he is an *enemy of the people*."[6] Most frequently the victims were not blood relatives but in-laws, above all mothers-in-law like Ul'iana Poda and Evdokiia Studenova. In the case of the latter, Rukodanov even asked the village council if the denunciation was connected to the hostility between mother and son-in-law.[7]

The most common authors of denunciations were neighbors. Crowded living conditions, social disorder, and the desire to improve one's own circumstances at the expense of those nearby—these factors all encouraged denouncers to take up the pen. Even Kuntsevo's dachas, divided by room or even by corner into closet-sized proportions, became the objects of fierce arguments over the partition of property. The state witness Shchadenko, a worker at Kuntsevo's NKVD garage, was also the neighborhood inspector of his village of Bakovka. In this role, he waged class war against neighbors from his building, "former people" who had once owned the entire property. The battle ended in victory for the representative of Soviet power. His neighbors, the brothers Selin and the wife of one of the brothers, were repressed.[8]

Many of the victims had no doubts that matters of real estate had ruined their lives.[9] V. M. Chuprik, a worker at a railroad station buffet who received ten years in the camps, described her November 1937 arrest: "It is possible that the building manager, who lived in the same building as I, raised the case against me because he hoped to take over one of the rooms in my apartment after the arrest of my husband. Once, when he insistently asked me about the room and I refused [to give it to him], he replied threateningly, 'If you don't give me that room, I'll give you a free apartment.' After my arrest, the building manager took the room in my apartment."[10]

The final victim of the mass operations in Kuntsevo, according to the date of the arrest, was Kh. A. Avramovich, a Montenegrin by nationality. He worked in the district court as a member of the collegium of lawyers, frequently defending "former peoples" in cases involving their property. Avramovich took on the case of the former owner of the building where he himself rented a corner of a room. The former owner, who apparently still owned at least part of the property, sued to evict an unwanted lodger, a police inspector. After the inspector won the case—a witness in Avramovich's own case recounted the scandalous trial in detail—he took aim at Avramovich, organizing witnesses to give the necessary testimony. The lawyer was arrested on April 12, 1938, and workers from the criminal police in the district carried out the investigation.[11]

Denunciations from the end of the mass repressions often had a personal subtext. In early investigations, though, signals from workplaces played a significant role. Their authors were workers who were not members of the director's clan and felt excluded. In these testimonies it is difficult to separate personal score settling from demonstrations of party loyalty. Nonetheless, it is clear that political accusations were far more frequent than denunciations about professional incompetence. For directors, a mistake on the "ideological front" could be more costly than the breakdown of their plant.

In the spring of 1937, a resident of Nemchinovka wrote to *Pravda*: "At a meeting called to discuss the trial of the counterrevolutionary band of Trotskyists including Piatakov, Radek, and company, the director of the provincial cropping station N. P. Nikolaev announced that if the USSR went to war with Japan and Germany, it was unclear who would win, them or us. . . . Characteristically, not a single party member contradicted Nikolaev's counterrevolutionary statement."[12] The lack of response was unsurprising. In official ideology, the prospect of socialism's lasting survival was linked to the country's ability to repel a foreign intervention.

It is apparent that the author was filled with doubt about his denunciation. At first he signed the letter, then erased his name and left only "a worker of the cropping station." Finally, he wrote an "addition" and gave his full address. In the postscript, his accusations against the director's clan went much further: "As you see, there is a system of collective responsibility. They support each other because they are all conducting counterrevolutionary activity together."[13] The letter of this vigilant party member took the usual path: the editors of *Pravda* sent it to the province's NKVD and the province then forwarded it to Kuznetsov, who had just received clearance to begin work in Kuntsevo by the head of the Moscow provincial NKVD, S. F. Redens.

Alongside the case of the cropping station, the new leadership of the district NKVD tested its strength against the director of the KIM factory, N. I. Lazarev, a notable in Kuntsevo. In denunciations against their director, workers described his lavish lifestyle—Lazarev had his own car—and suspicious contacts with foreigners. One visitor had brought him a typewriter as a gift. Indeed, the sewing needle factory was full of new German technology, and Lazarev himself had been to Germany several times on business. Sensing the threat of arrest, he attempted to protect himself, arranging for the district NKVD's buildings to be repaired. His graciousness would not spare him, though.

The case against Lazarev began in the party. On May 10, 1937, Morozov, the party secretary in Kuntsevo district, wrote to Ezhov reporting the compromising materials he had collected on Lazarev. Deputy NKVD Commissar Mikhail Frinovskii forwarded the letter to the Moscow provincial NKVD with a note that Lazarev may have been recruited as a spy in Germany. Clearly the district party committee also learned of this development and expelled the factory director from the party. After five days, on June 11, 1937, he was arrested.[14]

Until that point, only the provincial NKVD had handled cases like Lazarev's, where espionage was the charge and the accused was a visible member of the *nomenklatura*. That Radzivilovskii allowed the Kuntsevo NKVD to undertake the Lazarev investigation from start to finish demonstrated his particular trust in his client Kuznetsov and the increasing accent on political repression at the local level. The signal was not misunderstood.

The district NKVD began to use state and party institutions to find scapegoats for the underfulfillment of economic plans, failure to meet plans for construction, and damage of equipment. Responsibility for workers' general disinterest in their labor fell upon the shoulders of individuals accused of sabotage. M. M. Avdeenko, the chief mechanic of an ammunition factory that was constantly in a state of disarray, was removed from his position in June 1937. However, his file had a trail of denunciations from the preceding two years. Undoubtedly, many authors had written about real problems at the factory and lapses in the production process. Usually the letter went to the party committee and from there arrived at the district NKVD, although a number of authors immediately sent it to the police, writing "copy sent to the organs of the NKVD."

In the hopes of writing more persuasive denunciations, Avdeenko's accusers did not limit themselves to describing disruptions at the factory. Instead, they developed the supposed political motivations behind them. Propaganda campaigns from above, as well as personal experience, helped them formulate these accusations. In the spring of 1937, a colleague of the chief mechanic wrote, "I began to watch Avdeenko. Having some experience in the area of surveillance, because I worked in the NKVD, I was forced to the conclusion that Avdeenko clearly has an anti-Soviet disposition. Even though he hides it, it is clear all the same."[15]

The Avdeenko investigation ended with his execution. However, concrete instances of supposed sabotage were only of secondary importance and investigators did not check their accuracy. Instead, the most important factors were that he had lived in Harbin before the revolution and "had counterrevolutionary ties." The beginning of the mass operations eliminated the need for state security agencies to check the veracity of signals on the ground, turning the NKVD into an apparatus of terror with far greater authority than just the investigation and punishment of political criminals. This authority was no secret in society and people used it to get at enemies and to conceal their own mistakes.

Risk Groups and the Reign of Social Data

The popular notion that anyone could become a victim of repression in Stalin's regime is only partially correct. There were categories of the population who not only could be repressed but that the mass operations specifically targeted. The operational orders of the NKVD in 1937–38 named various groups: they included various "former people" and anti-Soviet elements—those who had previously faced political repression, former members of non-Bolshevik political parties, and those who had participated in various intraparty oppositions. Special operations targeted foreigners and those who had spent time abroad. These foreign travelers even included people taken prisoner in the First World War and the Polish-Soviet War. The category also included those who had worked outside the country, for instance the *kharbintsy* (people from the Chinese city of Harbin, a prominent settlement for Russians along

the Trans-Siberian Railroad) on the China Eastern Railway. The list of
those repressed in Kuntsevo shows that people who had arrived recently
were at far greater risk than those who were from the district.[16]

The first victims of the mass operations were people already under
investigation. They were important members of the *nomenklatura* at
the needle factory, as well as its foreign specialists and their circle of
acquaintances. Others under investigation were people whose lifestyle
neighbors considered suspicious—those who had loud parties, expressed their displeasure with the state of affairs under Stalin, or told
anti-Soviet jokes.[17] Local criminal police conducted these investigations
in their first stages. These officers had to do considerable work to translate ordinary nonconformity into political crime, but the mass operations
soon came to their aid. Theft of alcohol could now become embezzlement of explosive materials. A joke about Stalin could become the begin-
nings of an assassination plot.

The number of individuals under investigation in Kuntsevo district
was no more than twenty before July 1937. Those who had been held the
longest were the brothers Mikhail and Maksim Artsimen'ev, detained
since October 1936.[18] During the mass operations, the NKVD could
not afford to do investigatory work with informants and through surveillance. Instead, they had to select victims in a way that could realize
widespread terror—by working with documents. These documents included not only those from the operational archive of the NKVD but
from the personnel departments of local enterprises and institutions,
from the registration office, and even from the directory bureau. Officers
created lists of candidates for arrest based on ordinary biographical
data. The most important categories were nationality (or more accurately
a foreign-sounding name), place of birth, social origin, previous convictions or administrative punishments, and relatives who lived abroad.

Previous work for the Chekists did not save people from the threat
of arrest. Zhan Miklau, a Latvian, was the model of a dedicated revolutionary. He had joined the Bolshevik Party in 1914 at eighteen years old.
In November 1917, he participated in the seizure of power in Moscow.
As a member of the Latvian Riflemen, he defended the Kremlin and
served in the civil war as a commissar in the First Cavalry Army. After
the conflict ended, he worked for the Cheka and the OGPU. Twenty
years following the revolution, when he was the head of the important
chemical industry trust, he complained to a former underling from
his time in the Cheka, "Even if a person is innocent, they make him
confess."[19] The consequences of his frank statement came almost

immediately—a denunciation, expulsion from the party, arrest, and conviction for supposed participation in a conspiracy of Latvians. The only worker of the Kuntsevo NKVD who faced arrest at the hands of his colleagues was P. I. Viglei. He was an inspector of the local bureau of correctional labor and a descendent of Volga Germans. Viglei confessed, "I was made to hire people in the Kuntsevo NKVD who were our [i.e., German] protégés."[20]

One secret informant at the district office underwent a particularly difficult trial. This agent, code named "Snow White," had earlier provided information to Berg and in 1937 became an informant for the central NKVD apparatus. Snow White later wrote about a conversation she had with Karetnikov, who summoned her to his office and demanded to know why she had stopped providing information to Kuntsevo. "I responded to this ambush by saying that he had not been interested in the material I was bringing him so I passed it along to Moscow." Using the informer's Latvian background as a pretext, Karetnikov arrested Snow White and convinced her to sign a fabricated confession. He told her it was necessary to unmask a spy ring. "I believed him blindly because he was a representative of the NKVD and I stupidly fell into his net." Karetnikov ignored her requests that he inform her handlers in the central NKVD about what had happened and Snow White received a standard ten years in the camps.[21]

Arrested NKVD workers and their associates were the exceptions rather than the rule in the Great Terror. The largest and most easily uncovered at-risk group was dekulakized peasants who had been exiled from their villages at the beginning of the 1930s.[22] The majority of those who completed their terms of exile or received a pardon returned to their homes. A typical biography of a Kuntsevo resident shot at Butovo was of V. A. Tikhonov: "Approximately 35 years old, born in the village Barvikha, was a peasant and cobbler, had four houses, withheld taxes, disenfranchised, in 1931 deported with family: wife and two children. In 1933 was rehabilitated and returned to Barvikha, sold two houses before exile, one home given to son-in-law, remaining property confiscated. Now he has bought a storage shed covered with boards from M. S. Makarova and lives there."[23]

Even after they lost all their property and could no longer run an independent farm, dekulakized peasants retained authority and influence among their fellow villagers. Some peasants who returned from exile even managed to attain leadership positions in Kuntsevo's collective farms, as the district NKVD's "Creepers" case demonstrated.

However, the majority of returning peasants did not hide their hostility toward Soviet order in their village and took every concession the regime made as a sign of its weakness. The operational archive of Kuntsevo's NKVD was filled with denunciations from these peasants' adversaries in the village about their "kulak propaganda" and "secret meetings." The desire among the dekulakized for revenge kept Soviet authorities— in the Kremlin and in the village councils—in a state of constant fear. Order 00447 was the result of this fear, reflecting the typical Bolshevik logic that problems must be resolved once and forever. The children of exiled peasants, forever marked with the stigma of their parents' exile, also fell under the operations' purview. Usually these offspring had their own households or left to work in Moscow. Nonetheless, the regime continued to consider them socially hostile elements.[24]

As they carried out the "kulak order," police found considerable numbers of weapons in the villages. Usually these were small caliber Berdan rifles or the famous Nagant revolver—souvenirs of the civil war. However, they also took exotic items like a sword that was used by peasants as a spit, probably a leftover from past wars. In the town of Kuntsevo, police found hardly any weapons. However, they found ammunition—evidence that workplace theft existed even at Factory 46, a local arms enterprise.

Every confiscated gun led to the indictment of its owner for "terrorist intent." The police then usually included the weapon's owner in a larger group, allowing the use of the charge in several other arrests. F. P. Pech- nikov had a revolver with an expired license. Although he had only been a "sympathizer" in the SR party in school in 1902, he became a member of the "SR underground" in Kuntsevo.[25] Of course, the owners of these weapons did not keep them for terrorist activities. It seems likely that these arms were insurance against the possibility of dark times in the future. They allowed their owners to sleep soundly despite rumors of impending war and the nearing end of Soviet power.

Another easy target of mass repression was the clergy, whose alleged role was to "spread hostile ideology" among the population. The NKVD sent informants to watch virtually every member of the clergy. Judging by the denunciations against D. I. Ostroumov, a priest of the church in the village of Fedos'evo, no fewer than five secret informants followed him. Their agent names—"Customized," "Vigilant," "Binoculars"— testified to the fantasies of NKVD workers. Under constant watch, the priest of Fedos'evo nonetheless managed to mobilize his fellow villagers against outside incursions for a year before his arrest. The police described his action in the indictment: "Ostroumov in 1936 undertook the organization of a rebellion of believers. He sent two old churchgoers around the village to provoke the population into believing that Soviet power wanted to close the church. As a result, a large group of believers barged into the village council to demand an explanation."[26]

From August 8 to 20, 1937, the district NKVD conducted mass arrests among "church goers." Among those arrested was Elisei Shtol'der. If the indictment can be believed, the charges against him show that he was an exemplar of resistance to official atheism. As a priest of the church in Nemchinovka, he opposed its closure and, after moving to Romashkovo, continued to proclaim, "Soon the end of Soviet power will come and the church will return all the same."[27] A priest named Aleksei Sokolov worked at the same church. According to witnesses, he prophesized to a passersby, "We have to make our peace for now, but some day the churches will reopen, and indeed there will be more and people will support us. Then Stalin and his helpers will be but a memory."[28] Groups of the faithful did not hide their feelings about the "godless" and demanded that local authorities honor their constitutional rights. Repression in 1937 resolved the smoldering conflict between authorities in town and village soviets and the faithful in favor of the former. To fill out the ranks in the NKVD's indictments, conspiracies also included former nobles, church elders, choir singers, and even those who had given money for the construction or restoration of churches.

Local religious workers and their supporters were not the only ones who fell into the net of the NKVD. A nun from the Vsekhsviatskii Nunnery in the town Bolkhov, born Aleksandra Borodina, received her first sentence in 1931. In the Baikal-Amur Camp in the Far East, she became a housekeeper for a doctor and his family. She then accompanied the family when the doctor moved to the construction site of the Moscow-Volga canal. The final section of the canal went through Kuntsevo district, near Khoroshevskii Highway. Adjusting to the new location, Borodina began attending a local church. The doctor's wife took offense and wrote a notice to the local police, concluding, "Please inform me about your decision so that I can hire another worker in advance." At her interrogations with Karetnikov, Borodina confessed, "I am a religious person." However, she categorically denied conducting counter-revolutionary agitation. She was executed on September 14, 1937.[29]

Repression did not pass by people from non-Orthodox confessions. P. S. Gutkin conducted "illegal Jewish prayer meetings" and received a death sentence for counterrevolutionary agitation.[30] The danger of

repression was especially great for members of religious sects that received special mention in Order 00447. Members of these sects illegally
gathered in the apartments of their coreligionists and had discussions
about faith with their relatives and neighbors. A society of Baptist-
Evangelists at Nemchinovka station and nearby villages had tried several times to receive official authorization but without success. On
September 5, 1937, nine Baptists, including five women, were arrested.
During the investigation, the Baptists defended their religious beliefs,
including refusal to serve in the army, but would not acknowledge
them as counterrevolutionary.[31] Another two Baptist elders, attempting
to hide from repression on the outskirts of Moscow, chose a profession
that NKVD workers believed had given them a singular opening for
religious propaganda. P. I. Polegen'ko and P. K. Kordon, both Ukrainians, had become mail carriers in the village Ochakovo where vigilant
citizens denounced them. Before converting, one of the Baptists had
been a priest in the Ukrainian Autocephalous Orthodox Church.[32]

Prerevolutionary elites ("former people") were also a group the
NKVD pursued, although state security agencies did not have concrete
instructions for their repression. Occasionally investigation files contain
excerpts from a parish book about a person's noble origins. The NKVD
searched for certificates showing that suspects had property before
1917 or tax data showing entrepreneurial activity during the years of
the New Economic Policy (NEP, the semimarket economy of the 1920s).
These records were supposedly incontestable evidence that investigators' targets were members of prerevolutionary high society. Through
materials from the terror in Kuntsevo, one can follow the history of entre-
preneurship in the district: G. P. Petrov was the owner of the district's
first cinema, called "Record"; I. M. Zanegin delivered lumber and coal
to the city; M. K. Volkov was a local toy maker.[33] The repression of the
district's "former people" also included figures of national significance:
I. A. Maevskii was a member of the Ukrainian National Rada from the
Left Socialist Revolutionary Party. N. S. Chenykaev was the governor
of Kaluga province before the revolution.[34]

The line for the arrestee's "social origin" in the arrest file left an
open field for the fantasies of the investigator. The most important goal
was to frame arrestees' origins in a way that would allow the possibility
of their illegal thoughts or actions. Small workshops turned into factories, farmers into estate holders, and local police into agents of the
tsarist Okhrana (secret police). "Use of hired labor" or having been
nobility was effectively a criminal indictment. Participation in the First

World War became "service in the tsar's army." However, it was enough to collect witness testimony that the accused acted like a "social alien element" for the NKVD to send the case to the troika.

The NKVD paid particular attention to past members of "anti-Soviet" political parties—that is, any non-Bolshevik party. People with prerevolutionary political experience conducted themselves more steadfastly than younger arrestees. V. M. Odinokov, a member of the SR Party at the beginning of the century, constantly commented during the investigation. On the resolution stating the repressive measures to be taken against him, Odinokov wrote that he had not undertaken any counterrevolutionary activity. On the resolution concluding the case, he wrote, "I was made familiar with the materials in this case through the investigator because I was not given my glasses."[35] NKVD workers preferred not to deal with the ill and weak. A group of believers under investigation included V. E. Egorov, written into the indictment as a member of the Union of the Archangel Michael (a right-wing nationalist group of the Russian Empire). On September 23, 1937, Karetnikov wrote a resolution postponing the arrest of Egorov, sick with terminal cancer, "until his recovery."[36]

Former managers in the party, government, or industry who were unable to keep their positions were also a kind of "former people." Many were not even marked as members of oppositionist organizations. Yet their dismissal from ranking positions, especially if they received an official reprimand from the party, drew the attention of NKVD workers. Their ranks included many foreigners—political immigrants or former functionaries of foreign communist parties or the Comintern. Some were victims of factionalism and infighting among clans in party leadership circles in their countries. In Russia as "strangers among friends," foreign communists depended entirely on the Comintern, which tried to arrange for them to work in Moscow or in the surrounding area.

Several people with revolutionary biographies settled in Kuntsevo district. Bulgarian P. D. Dimova, arrested on February 20, 1938, had hidden an entire communist printing office in her house in Pleven. After police found the print house, she and her husband fled to the Soviet Union. Dimova had no ties to the leadership of the Communist Party of Bulgaria and life in her new motherland was no paradise. She received work at the daycare at Factory 95 and housing at the workers' settlement nearby. In order to obtain a death sentence for Dimova, investigator Solov'ev quoted her as confessing to a conspiracy worthy of a spy-training textbook: "Knowing the weakness of every mother, I attempted to praise the child of one mother whom I wanted to engage. In doing so, I befriended the worker, made conversation with her, and thus learned all I needed to know about Factory 95."[37]

Korean San-Tagi Kim, whose apartment was later occupied by district chief Kuznetsov, traveled home to Korea on a mission from the eastern office of the Comintern in 1925–26. Others arrested in Kuntsevo included former members of the communist parties of the United States, Yugoslavia, Poland, and other countries. All of them could tell their share of real stories about illegal work in the name of world revolution. Instead, all signed fake confessions that they had been recruited ten or even twenty years earlier in their own countries. They had come to the Soviet Union supposedly to conduct covert activities as spies and saboteurs.

All people with foreign citizenship were targets in the "national operations" of 1937–38, although many had been citizens of the Russian Empire before 1917. After the countries on the empire's borderlands gained independence, their citizens—Poles, Finns, and Baltic peoples— transformed in the minds of Soviet leaders into a potential "fifth column." The recruitment of specialists from abroad in the five-year plans and political emigration facilitated the influx of foreigners. Those who remained in the mid-1930s were forced to accept Soviet citizenship or lose their right to work and state benefits.[38] The majority of Soviet citizens from "hostile nationalities" in the published lists of Kuntsevo's victims were Poles, followed by equal numbers of Latvians and Germans. Rarer victims included a Slovenian, Montenegrin, Croatian, Persian, and a few Koreans and Greeks.

Locals who had contact with foreigners were also at risk. In a district next door to the capital—moreover one known for its dachas—these contacts were relatively frequent and police tracked them carefully. The case of the Greek spy ring in Kuntsevo began when a relative working in the Greek embassy visited local resident Elena Kostaki. According to Karetnikov, the head of this ring was Dmitrii Isakov, a Russian worker who lived next door to the Kostaki family.[39] N. A. Pavlenkovich, a ranger living in Bakovka, rented his dacha to a diplomat from Lithuania. The indictment accused him of "close connections with the secretary of the Lithuanian embassy."[40] The Krys'ev family from the village Krylatskoe developed a close relationship with their summer lodgers, the family of the secretary of the German embassy Fritz Werth. The peasants paid the diplomats visits and the Krys'evs' daughter brought them a gift from their small garden plot. This relationship led to the arrest of head of the family Timofei even before the beginning of the mass operations.[41] A disproportionate number of the residents of the picturesque village of Krylatskoe were indicted for participation in espionage. Foreign correspondence also provided a pretext for arrest. The receipt of packages from abroad was especially suspicious, even if those packages were from close relatives.[42]

The categories of Soviet citizens who could come under the suspicion of the NKVD were many. Naturally, after the arrest of the main suspect, relatives and acquaintances also faced the threat of arrest. Despite the existence of categories of repression, even those who were far from the risk groups were never fully safe from repression. Finding the balance between rational and irrational practices in the Great Terror remains a challenge for scholars and public historians.

Counterrevolutionary Agitation or Public Opinion?

One of the most common accusations against victims was that they had undertaken "counterrevolutionary agitation." Although it is tempting to reject these "anti-Soviet statements" as fabrications, they should not be dismissed as complete fantasies of Ezhov's men. The mass terror of 1937–38 had no parallels in the past that would have caused the disaffected to hide their emotions. Although open and sharp condemnation would seem unbelievable under Stalin's regime, the unprecedented nature of the terror made yet unfazed citizens willing to make strong criticisms. NKVD officers could not have invented all the evidence that appears in interrogation records. Poetry, couplets, and jokes are particularly good examples because officers would hardly have had time to create them. NKVD investigations took these examples of anti-totalitarian public opinion and transformed them into anti-Soviet crimes like "agitation." In many cases, the true authors of these compositions were not even the accused. Rumors and folk poetry were the collective products of conversations in taverns at collective farms and in train stations, in lines and during smoke breaks.

Most often witnesses testified about anti-Soviet statements after overhearing them in lines, where people shared news from high politics to local gossip. The second most common place where witnesses recorded these conversations was on the job, where people expressed the broader grievances of society. A number of cases began with a drunk suspect whom police arrested for "debauchery" but at the station then charged with "counterrevolutionary declarations."[43] Kuntsevo's police detained more than ten citizens from Kuntsevo and nearby areas who, apparently unable to contain their emotions while waiting for the train, made compromising statements. The fifty-fourth department of the Moscow city police oversaw these cases and more than one resulted in a death sentence.[44] Witness testimony is full of phrases like "overheard the conversation at the railroad buffet" or "was nearby in the corridor of the train," although in the latter case the witness could have hardly heard the victim, even if they were speaking directly to one another.

Overheard phrases recorded in Kuntsevo's case files included classics of urban legend. One person declared that "party cards serve as bread tickets for communists."[45] Another person gave a toast "for the ships that perished at the hands of the Fascist pirates in Spain." Scenes from rural life that became fodder for prosecutions are no less striking. Elizaveta Selina yelled to her husband who was mending their fence, "Come here and eat. Why are you even trying? The Soviet bandits will take it all the same."[46] In some cases, simple complaints about local authorities' abuse of power became the basis for a conviction, for example, "Soviet power is based entirely on bribes and you won't get anything done honestly."[47]

Are there criteria for testing the authenticity of these quotes? It may only be possible to verify them when there is a substantial collection of examples of "counterrevolutionary propaganda." However, it seems clear that the more an anti-Soviet statement differed from a generic accusation (e.g., "the accused cursed Comrade Stalin"), the greater the chance that it happened and was then merely adapted for the purposes of NKVD workers. State security workers treated this kind of material with the greatest care. In a number of case files, the jokes a suspect told were written on a scrap of paper and sealed in an envelope. Investigators replaced Stalin's name with ellipses and curses against communists were made general (e.g., "antisemitism" or "vulgarity").

The case files in this study only include examples of spoken "agitation" that came from witnesses' testimony or the denunciations of informants. The only exception to this rule is a letter written in the spring of 1937 by a resident of the village Ramenskoe, Nikolai Remizov, to his uncle Vasilii. In the letter, Remizov informed his uncle about the death of his father in a camp for special settlers. These lines hardly demand analysis. It is incredible that an ordinary young peasant could so clearly and graphically describe his feelings at that moment:

> Goodbye father! You died far from your home, sent by the whims of fortune into the deep debris of Siberia. Your terrible

destiny, your terrible fate you shared with millions of people, people driven away into the terrifying jaws of famine, deprivation and forced labor, where they disappeared. Who doomed you to this slow, tortuous fate? O, how many canals were opened, how many impenetrable forests were felled and railroads built by your labors! Your skulls pave the canals you opened. Instead of railroad ties, your bones glisten. Your bodies have filled an impassible swamp drained on the path to an imaginary goal that cannot be achieved in our time. On your bones we are building our vision of socialism. And all this [horror] hides behind a thick wall of lies and falsehoods. Screws that were tightened long ago are tightening more still but everything has its limit. Bolts can break if the screws do not give slack. The truth is suffocating everywhere, but there will come a time when a brave person will step forward and reveal the truth. Its bareness will be horrible to all, and those who are at fault for these horrors will be stunned and turn away.[48]

According to the recollections of his neighbors, the twenty-two year old was a leading figure in the village. He was well-read and managed to work while studying in a journalism department and writing for the district newspaper *Bolshevik*. The operations department of the camp where Vasilii Remizov was located intercepted the letter and sent it to Kuntsevo, where it started an investigation. Five Remizovs were arrested in the summer of 1937 in the case. Along with the letter, the case file included the poetry of Nikolai, the youngest Remizov arrested, and his caricature depicting the chair of the Ramenskoe collective farm as he overslept weeding duty. Every sheet of paper turned into a separate point in the indictment.[49] The thoughts that Nikolai Remizov committed to his letter, published in 1991, were raised constantly, although they come to us only through their retelling by investigators of the Kuntsevo district NKVD. "Soviet power doesn't allow the agricultural economy to grow. It boasts about how much it has done but kulaks or exiled villagers do it all," said one dekulakized resident of the village of Troitse-Golenishchevo, V. V. Pyl'nov.[50]

Only one person refused to reject his criticisms of the Soviet order when cases were reopened in 1939. He was the oldest of those arrested in Kuntsevo, the guard of Ochakovo state farm Karl Kotsin. An ethnic German, Kotsin continued to maintain that "landowners were better managers of estates than state farms" and "for every worker there is one administrator." After a year in prison, the Special Counsel of the NKVD freed Kotsin and said that his year of preliminary confinement had been sufficient. The reason for this lenient punishment—the only such sentence among the repressed in Kuntsevo—was not Kotsin's honesty but a more pragmatic motivation. The labor camps had no need for dependents. The Special Counsel adopted the procurator's assessment: "After examination of the case, we must take into account that the medical examiner has declared Kotsin unfit for labor at seventy-four years old."[51]

The opinions recorded in these case files of "counterrevolutionary agitation" do not just reflect popular attitudes, of course. NKVD investigators selected these statements for their own purposes. The majority of cases involved contemporary issues—the "fraudulent" constitution and elections, unabashed lies in the press, lack of goods in stores, and incompetence of leaders. The accusations placed the blame for these problems on the communists, who usurped power in the country and were unable to create a stable existence for citizens. From a straightforward set of complaints, investigators created the skeleton of an accusation fleshed out by the general atmosphere in the country.

The sharpest critics were those people who were able to compare the current situation in the country either to prerevolutionary life or to the situation in other countries. V. M. Shtybor was an ethnic Pole born in Germany who spent his youth in the United States before moving to the Soviet Union in 1932. In the protocol of his interrogation, he made the characteristic opposition of "us and them": "Was this an election of the entire nation? It is entirely clear that they [Soviet leaders] bind themselves to the people they need and not to workers. They have just one goal in mind—if the representatives of workers had power, then all their labor would go toward their [workers'] benefit. Now it all goes to the military."[52]

The complaints of dekulakized peasants typically featured an understandable bitterness. One stated, "This [Soviet] power ruined my entire life. They kicked me out of my home in my old age and, if that was not enough, did so for my possessions, which they stole and then criticized and arrested me for."[53] Besides their bitterness, these statements reflected an expectation of an imminent war that would spell the end of the regime. This rumor was one of the most durable of the 1930s and its persistence in popular opinion among peasants is apparent from other sources.[54] The entrance of foreign armies (usually German, Polish, or Japanese) into Russia was supposed to lead to the disintegration of collective farms and the death of all communists.

The wealth of these bellicose declarations in the interrogation protocols of 1937 fit into the orders that local NKVD workers received from Lubianka to uncover and liquidate the country's "fifth column." These threats, born of a feeling of personal impotence, became the "programs of the terrorists." V. E. Letuchev, an exiled former villager of Troitse-Golenishchevo, said of the Bolsheviks, "We'll wait a little longer and then we'll dispose of them. They won't exile me twenty times but for exiling me twice I'll get my revenge and dispose of them."[55] Perhaps the most interesting aspect of Letuchev's statement is that he believed, like many dekulakized peasants, that his situation could not get worse. They did not understand that authorities could take from them one last thing—their lives.

Many peasants raised analogies from the past, trying to find parallels with the country's current troubles. One arrestee's interrogation protocol expressed a common opinion: "When the Romanovs were overthrown, war played a big role. We need to be ready for the approaching war so we can destroy those (insult) communists and not leave any prisoners."[56] An even more popular contrast was of the 1920s with the 1930s. One arrestee said, "Soviet power and the collective farms turned the peasantry into shirkers. They drove the good workers away to the corners of the Soviet Union, some they exiled and some ran away. When Lenin was alive he had different policies. He created NEP, and if he had lived until that time [collectivization] it would have stayed the same. Instead he trusted Stalin who drove away the peasantry."[57]

People from the upper ranks of prerevolutionary society openly gloated about the failures of Soviet power, believing that the new regime would eventually ask them for help. "Voroshilov created so many colonels but none of any worth, far less than the old colonels. When there is a war, they will surely call for us and then we old patriots will live well."[58] Victims expressed particular joy at the show trials of Old Bolsheviks, saying things such as, "Soon we will settle scores with you and we won't leave one of you alive. You've already begun to shoot your own and you will all meet the same fate";[59] or, "They've begun to shoot those close to Stalin. It's clear that they will get to Stalin soon and that will be the end of Soviet power."[60]

Antisemitic declarations occurred frequently in cases about "counter-revolutionary agitation." According to one witness's testimony, the former owner of a samovar factory in Tula, N. E. Batashev, said, "I wait and wait for a return to my old way of life when I felt free and lived with honor. Now I live in trembling fear. It is all because those (antisemitism) Jews and (insult) communists sit in power."[61] The NKVD categorized antisemitism as an aggravating circumstance even in cases where the offender was drunk.[62] The use of antisemitism as an accusation is an argument against the interpretation of the Great Terror as a forerunner to the later purge of Jews from the *nomenklatura* in the postwar period.[63] At the same time, not all the victims expressed antisemitic sentiments. Many professed their certainty that life would be better if Leon Trotsky or Grigory Zinov'ev—Jewish Bolsheviks—were in power: "If Trotsky was in power, we wouldn't have permanent forced labor."[64]

Evidence in the case files shows that the scope and the targets of the Great Terror were no secret. One victim stated, "In its attempt to avoid war, Soviet power, headed by those (insult) communists has begun to jail all former peoples, especially former officers, but you can't jail everyone. There are still a few of them left among us in the Soviet Union and they will continue their activities. Soon there will be a war, Hitler will come to the USSR and we will help him here. We'll make hell for the communists. We'll avenge all our insults."[65] Citizens often explained the purge of the country's leadership as a result of increasing tensions between Soviet chiefs. Others explained the broader terror through the old proverb "when the lords fight, the servants suffer." One of the accused in Kuntsevo expressed his confidence that "Tukhachevskii, Gamarnik and others are completely innocent but Voroshilov wanted to destroy them and he did. Now a horrible terror rages among us. Many innocent people will waste away in prison."[66] Had the phrase about the terror's masses of victims been the work of the investigator, he could have faced charges of disclosing state secrets, so close was the accusation to the actual unfolding of events in 1937–38.

Protests occurred not only in private conversations but also at campaign events for the 1937 elections to the Supreme Soviet of the USSR, the new legislative body created by the Stalin constitution. In these instances, public complaints were similar to private outbursts. A resident of the village of Tatarovo, M. G. Bushinov, engaged the speaker at one of the campaign meetings, commenting: "You say that our constitution is the most democratic in the world but according to our constitution you can't say a single word. If you do say something and wound our leaders, then they pick you up by the scruff of your neck and throw you in jail. That's democracy for you. It would be better if we didn't have that kind of democracy." It was typical for authorities to put forward grandees as candidates in regions where they had little or no connection. In Tatarovo K. Galeev refused to vote for the official candidate, editor of *Pravda* Lev Mekhlis, saying, "Can't there be any good people left in

Kuntsevo?" He proposed himself as a candidate.[67] According to a number of accounts, local priests offered themselves as candidates for election in December 1937. Party leaders' fear of these potential alternative candidates grew until they decided to forgo the entire process of free elections.[68]

Another popular anti-Soviet statement was to declare approval for the December 1934 murder of party leader Sergei Kirov, accepting the official story that the assassination was counterrevolutionary terror.[69] Endorsement of the murder allowed investigators to assume that victims would replicate the crime and charge them with "terrorist intentions." This offense ranked higher in the hierarchy of political crime than simple counterrevolutionary declarations. Investigators claimed that T. P. Ivanovskaia, an elderly woman from a landholding family, had pronounced the bloodthirsty phrase, "It would be good to do what they did in Leningrad. We need to act decisively, to find weapons, to go to the Mozhaisk Highway. There, waiting for government cars, we will throw ourselves under them while others kill the passengers."[70]

The enormous number of investigations about attempts on Stalin's life raised laughter even among NKVD workers. The acting head of the Moscow NKVD's third department (counterespionage), A. O. Postel', admitted under questioning, "If you analyze the interrogation protocols and case files of punished 'terrorists' . . . we get the unbelievable picture that the parade columns on Red Square [during revolutionary holidays] were filled with dozens or hundreds of 'terrorists' who supposedly wanted to shoot [at party leaders] as they marched by the mausoleum. Then they were supposedly hindered for various reasons. Or [we get the idea] that on the Mozhaisk Highway various groups of terrorists were keeping guard on summer days, waiting to shoot state cars when they passed by. These terrorists were not even aware that state cars were there. They, too, failed because of reasons concocted to make the evidence seem credible."[71]

The puzzlement of the NKVD officer raises an important question: Why did the NKVD not find a single real terrorist among a mass of fabricated fiends? Despite the many examples of political terror in Russian history, no real terrorism occurred in Kuntsevo or anywhere else. This statement is not meant as an expression of regret but an entry into the broader problem of resistance. Historians working within the totalitarian model claimed that in the years of mass repression, Soviet society saw the danger in Stalin's regime but it was incapable of resisting the dictatorship. It is worth using the example of the terror in a single district to add to this point. Although the capital loomed large in Kuntsevo's economy, villages retained elements of self-sufficiency characteristic of traditional societies. One could love or hate the Bolshevik party, but it was a link between the various socio-geographical centers of the country. Alternatives to the Bolsheviks did not appear in the case files except as acts of external aggression or the revenge of figures like Trotsky or Zinov'ev. The experience of two civil wars—the Russian Civil War of 1917-21 and the collectivization campaign of 1930-32— sapped the real potential for a popular uprising after those conflicts broke the back of the peasantry. Even the strongest villagers, those who had held out and saved their property, served no political purpose higher than sharing anti-Soviet jokes.

It is no coincidence that Rukodanov made recent arrivals (e.g., collective farms chairs, teachers, veterinarians) into the leaders of "insurgent groups" in various villages. If the regime had not arrested practically the entire priesthood in the preceding years, clergy could have also served in this role. Kuntsevo's case files contain evidence that priests maintained their authority in the villages of the 1930s. During the census of 1937, an appeal spread among the population that "all believers should say they are believers. If there are too few of us [on the census], Soviet power will exile us and torment us. If we declare our belief as an entire village, then [Soviet] power will be afraid to touch us."[72] Only the wives of arrestees in the passion of the moment engaged in acts of defiance.[73] The chair of the Bakovka village council, Uzunov, complained to the district NKVD that the wife of B. I. Selin, Elizaveta, "terrorized the population against Soviet power," threatening to exact violent revenge on him and Shchadenko, the local inspector and staff witness.[74]

The Terrorists from Nemchinovka

The chair of the village council of Nemchinovka, I. V. Kulikov, had long been the target of written attacks by his fellow villagers. The main charge against him was his supposed defense of "former people." Above all these "former people" were property owners who had somehow managed to keep at least part of their holdings, often registering real estate under the names of relatives and friends. The have-nots who lived in these buildings felt ill at ease under the spiteful gaze of the former haves. These tenants demanded the removal of the landowners, a move that would have undoubtedly also improved their own living situation. It seems that Kulikov kept these sentiments in check, perhaps in exchange for a reward from the "former people" of Nemchinovka. No matter the reason, he came under the fixed stare of the Kuntsevo NKVD.[75]

Indeed, the NKVD was not only watching Kulikov but the entire village. It was located next to the dachas of a number of high-ranking leaders, including famed cavalry commander and Stalin ally Semen Budennyi. Moreover, the village was also near the railroad crossing, where all vehicles, even those of government officials, had to stop. There was no better place for a terrorist attack. It is unknown whether locals discussed this possibility, but attempts on Stalin's life were the first accusation in the list of indictments against residents.[76] The investigators planned to make Kulikov the head of the village's terrorist organization but he disappeared after arrests began. It is possible that "his people" in the district NKVD warned him ahead of time. After two weeks on the run, Kulikov committed suicide. Investigators had to reassign the roles in the conspiracy on the fly. Standing out among those detained in the first round of arrests on October 28, 1937, was P. A. Domninskii, a former landowner and officer of the tsarist army. Searching his person, police found a ticket to the previous Congress of the Soviets (the predecessor of the Supreme Soviet), which Stalin had attended. Domninskii became the chief organizer of the conspiracy.[77]

Only one of the arrestees, an accountant from the Commissariat of Machine Construction, D. P. Sal'nikov, agreed to give the investigators testimony immediately upon arrest. Karetnikov interrogated him, apparently convincing Sal'nikov that his testimony "was needed for the sake of the motherland." Sal'nikov signed the interrogation protocol at the end of the page and not after every answer, perhaps an indication that this was a prepared protocol. The protocol for November 5 ended with the standard question asking the accused to confirm his answers from the interrogation. The answer read, "They are plausible, reflect reality and are written in my own words accurately."[78] The mistake of writing "plausible" (*pravdopodobnyi*) rather than "truthful" (*pravdivyi*) demonstrates that Karetnikov had not yet perfected his art. Nonetheless, the case would become an important step in his career in Kuntsevo.

The confession of Sal'nikov, an outsider in the village, was clearly insufficient as the basis for a case, so the district office sent a rookie investigator named Aleksandr Nikitin to Nemchinovka. Armed with instructions from Rukodanov, a model for witness testimony, and a list of suspects, he approached the chair of the Novo-Ivanovskii village council, S. F. Zhirnov. Threatening Zhirnov with arrest on charges of counterrevolutionary activity, Nikitin received not only Zhirnov's denunciations of arrested residents from Nemchinovka but also his continued partnership. Questioned in January 1940, Zhirnov admitted that the investigator left him a list of names and an outline of an interrogation. "From this outline I wrote witnesses' testimony and then had them [people on the list] sign."[79] During his frequent trips to the village, Nikitin worked over those witnesses who refused to be a part of the charade with Zhirnov.

The brazen gathering of large numbers of denunciations threw Nemchinovka into a state of civil war. The NKVD agent became a symbol of colossal evil. One disabled witness later recounted at a questioning that Nikitin forced him to sign two witness protocols. Nikitin said that no one would harm a disabled person like him. "I signed no more [protocols] and I avoided him because people in the village learned that I gave testimony and began to think of me as a liar. There was even an incident when they beat me. I told Nikitin and he asked me to collect testimony about a girl who he was chasing after. I refused and he wanted to arrest me. He took me to the train station but then let me go."[80] The incident could be the basis for a novel. In 1937 even affairs of the heart demanded a Chekist's techniques—the collection of compromising information and the blackmail of one's beloved.

According to Zhirnov, they collected more than thirty denunciations, giving the massive volume of cases in the Nemchinovka affair the necessary solidity. Indeed, the testimonies later became evidence in new arrests.[81] Unsure at first of how the provincial NKVD would react to such a large conspiracy, the investigators split the twelve arrestees into three groups of four. Their fear was unfounded. The case passed through the Moscow troika without incident, except that would-be terrorist Vladimir Shnaidruk received only eight years. Shnaidruk was just seventeen and for those who reviewed the case at the provincial level, this factor perhaps influenced the lightened sentence. The case of the "terrorists from Nemchinovka" became the blueprint for large-scale conspiracies in 1938. Within two years, the case would go under review and be terminated for lack of evidence.

The Muralov Affair

Sergei Muralov had been the head of the Kuntsevo district council since 1933. His immaculate biography had not once come under suspicion even though party leaders in Moscow in those years consistently

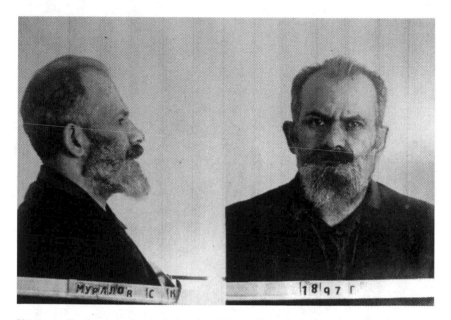

Kuntsevo district executive committee head Sergei Muralov under arrest. (GARF, f. 10035, op. 1, d. 25777)

demanded "self-criticism," a euphemistic call to attack local leaders. The son of workers, Muralov fought through the entire civil war, serving as the commissar for a regiment in the First Cavalry Army and receiving the Order of the Red Banner for his participation in the suppression of the Kronstadt rebellion. It seemed that the only thing that could go wrong for Muralov was if someone mistakenly thought he was a relative of Nikolai Muralov, one of Trotsky's most famous and loyal associates.[82]

To shield himself from his foes, Muralov had kept friendly ties with then head of the district NKVD Baglikov, providing him with various favors. However, Baglikov moved to another position and this friendship of necessity had not yielded the fruits Muralov had expected. Dark clouds began to gather over Muralov's head in the spring of 1937. The former commander of his regiment suddenly remembered that as commissar, Muralov had shown Trotskyist leanings in 1923. It is a mystery why this person, a resident of faraway Irkutsk province, decided after so many years to write a denunciation to the Party Control Commission of the Communist Party. That document became the first in a voluminous case file—the result of a secret investigation that began in the district party organization. Party officials kept the evidence under lock and key, waiting for the moment when they could use it as a sign of their vigilance.

That moment came quickly. Muralov entered into a protracted conflict with the leadership of the Moscow provincial land administration, which was responsible for various agricultural issues, and clearly overestimated his own strength. A commission from the land administration arrived in the district and denounced the "infiltration of social-alien elements in the leadership." The commission claimed they were main reason for all of Kuntsevo's problems—lowered crop yield, the death of cattle, and even "sabotaged crop rotation." The commission shifted from the sphere of agriculture to political crime, concluding, "In Kuntsevo district there is organized sabotage aimed at the destruction of collective farms. It is necessary to give this material to investigatory organs to bring the guilty to justice."

In the USSR then and later, the district's party committee took the credit for every success while its administration bore the burden for every problem. Typical of this dynamic, Muralov lost his position rather than the district party secretary. He appealed his termination to the Moscow provincial party committee where he received an audience with the secretary. Muralov later remembered the secretary's words: "No one takes a dead man back into the building." What the secretary meant would become clear in the upcoming months.

In December 1937, the chair of the Moscow provincial administration, N. A. Filatov, was arrested. All his subordinates automatically fell under suspicion for their "connection with an enemy of the people." The Kuntsevo party committee sent the provincial procurator an overflowing file on Muralov with three accusations: his Trotskyist wavering in 1923; his suppression of democracy on collective farms; and degeneracy. Each of those points was enough to justify arrest. But the military background of the First Cavalry Army commissar served him one last time. He received an appointment to a large factory in Leningrad. However, the post was not for long. At the end of January 1938, arrests began at the Kuntsevo district land administration. Muralov himself had not so long ago conducted a purge of cadres in Kuntsevo—one that had apparently missed many "enemies." A better candidate than Muralov was hard to find for a conspiracy on the scale of the whole district.

Coming home to his family on March 11, Muralov was arrested on the platform of Leningrad Station in Moscow. His family had no idea what had happened to him until Karetnikov appeared at their door to search the apartment. Muralov's wife Ekaterina described the search in a letter to Ezhov: "The search found absolutely no materials that compromised my husband. At the end of the search, Karetnikov phoned to report that he found nothing. Then Karetnikov warned me that I should move into a single room with my son because they would probably take the other two rooms. With that he sealed them shut. After a day, Karetnikov told me that the case did not look good for Muralov, that I should look for work." The belated search was related to the detainee's refusal to give evidence. The investigators hoped that information about the sad state of his family including personal details might convince him to "cooperate with the investigation." Karetnikov took documents, personal correspondence, and even Muralov's Order of the Red Banner. Later, it turned out that Karetnikov had not placed the order into storage at the district office but simply stole it. A week after Muralov's arrest, Ekaterina wrote her first letter to Nikolai Ezhov—dozens would follow—and emphasized, "I am writing you not as a wife but as a Soviet citizen. I declare that I would have the courage to tell the NKVD if over the last twenty years I had noticed anything anti-party in my husband." The atmosphere of the years of terror can raise no doubts about the sincerity of her plea.

After his arrest, Muralov himself stayed in the preliminary holding cell of the district office for several days. The devastation that overtakes arrested people who know they are innocent is difficult to put into words. For this reason, "fresh" detainees immediately went to be interrogated while still in shock so that investigators could wrest the needed confession from them. Muralov gave his first confession on March 14, just three days after his arrest. When he returned after eight years in the camps at Kolyma in the Far East, Muralov continued naïvely to believe that his sad lot was the fault of the party line being twisted at the local level. In one of his letters to Stalin, Muralov wrote, "I consider myself guilty. After having been in the party for twenty years and having gone through its militant schooling, I am guilty of being weak willed and giving in to the physical force and tricks of the investigators, who made me write the most odious slanders about myself. 'If you love the party, you must sign the investigation protocol.' 'Our country now needs this kind of confession.'"

The protocol of the first interrogation of Muralov begins with the question that was the trademark of the Kuntsevo investigators: "What are your political views?" The first sentence of the answer was just as standard: "My political views on the existing regime and the party are negative." After this sentence the arrestee gave a more specific answer, in Muralov's case the following: "In 1923 I did not support the politics of the party but instead I was for the platform of the Right-Trotskyist elements (Bukharin, Rykov, Trotsky). I formally masked myself as a member of the party, carrying out double-dealing, treacherous politics within it." Muralov's confession should raise the hairs of historians. In 1923 Trotsky was a leftist who favored forced-pace industrialization. Bukharin had stood with Stalin against Trotsky, favoring gradual industrialization with a limited market economy. This stance brought Bukharin into conflict with Stalin's increasingly radical policies in the late 1920s. Muralov's ahistorical confession had its basis in the current trials of Stalin's opponents. On March 13, 1938, the third Moscow show trial lumped Bukharin and other rightists together with Trotsky as supposed co-conspirators. How could district investigators construct historically accurate accusations when they had been raised on the propaganda of the show trials?

From Muralov's confession onward, the case took its cues from the front-page editorials of *Pravda*. In the show trial, former commissar of agriculture Mikhail Chernov was sentenced to execution based on charges that he carried out sabotage in agriculture, even intentionally sowing weeds. Newspapers published the sentence the same day that investigators made Muralov sign the first protocol. For NKVD workers in a rural district, agricultural affairs were near and dear, and the investigation continued along those lines.

The materials the party had compiled on Muralov played an essential role when they were added to the investigation on March 15. A significant section of the investigation file was made up of denunciations by a truly Gogolesque figure—an inspector in the administration of agricultural accounting whose last name was Gogol. Like the famed writer, the inspector was also a voluminous author of sorts. Although he started by sending denunciations to the district party committee, he quickly learned who needed his denunciations of saboteurs. Poor Rukodanov had to pour over his voluntary assistant's spreadsheets and calculations of cattle fertility. The conclusion was forgone: Hidden enemies had undermined the district's agriculture and threatened the capital's supply of food. The only unsettled matter was to choose the "staff" of Muralov's organization and to determine the roles among its members.

A script under the heading "Testimony of Muralov, March 14–16, 1938" appeared in several dozen case files. The scenario for the conspiracy was that Muralov headed an underground organization throughout the entire district, "a multibranch counterrevolutionary organization of saboteurs covering all areas of the economy." This underground group then connected to the provincial level of the national "Right-Trotskyist Center." At the local level, *nomenklatura* workers commanded cells of the organization. In the villages of Romashkovo and Kamennaia Plotina, for example, the supposed conspirators were the heads of local collective farms. At Rasskazovo, Odintsovo, and Mnevniki, they were the heads of village councils.[83]

In addition to these counterrevolutionary cells, the investigation asserted that there were affiliated groups in the agricultural economy. These groups included workers from the machine-tractor station, the land department of the district administration, and plenipotentiaries from central agencies responsible for statistics, grain requisitions, and the like. Kuntsevo's veterinarians made up a special group, arrested nearly in their entirety. During collectivization peasants had slaughtered their cattle in large numbers, feasting rather than allowing their property to be assimilated by the collective farm. In 1937–38 livestock was still at precarious levels, a situation that provided mountains of material for accusations of wrecking against veterinarians. Rukodanov and his underlings asserted that the veterinarians had intentionally sabotaged livestock breeding. "They kept breeding bulls on a leash, used artificial stimulation on them and quickly wore them out" at a time when infertility among cattle was 30 percent.[84] The main accusation against the veterinarian saboteurs was that they consciously infected herds with hoof and mouth disease. When the case was reopened in the spring of 1939, it emerged that bulls were supposed to be kept on a leash, not in the herd, and that intentional infection was a common technique. However, none of the veterinarians or zoologists received political rehabilitation.

Incorporating the elderly former members of "counterrevolutionary parties" arrested during the last push of March 1938 presented a bigger challenge than the other members of the affair. Only by including them in the conspiracy of "rightists" was Rukodanov able to create a sufficient case for indicting them. With this goal in mind, investigators wrote in the summary of Muralov's testimony: "In its directives about the expansion and strengthening of counterrevolutionary organizations in the localities, the provincial troika of rightists resolved not only to expand the organization's ranks with rightist cadres but also with SRs, Mensheviks, and other hostile elements. They attempted not only to protect them but to promote them into the state administration." This phrase preceded a list of names of those who would then become the leaders in district committees of "counterrevolutionary parties."

In their attempts to create a plausible conspiracy of "rightists," Kuntsevo's investigators tested the constraints of the rational. One of the arrestees was supposedly the "tally clerk of the terrorist organization." It was apparently his responsibility to count the number of murdered members of the party-state. The alphabetically organized inventory of the Muralov conspiracy's subversive activities ended on the eighteenth letter, "r," a sign of the comprehensiveness of the accusations. The implementation of just a few of the points of the counterrevolutionary program would have turned the lives of Kuntsevo's peaceful citizens into a living hell.

The investigators did not succeed in bringing the Muralov affair under the umbrella of the mass operations and the investigation continued for more than a year. None of its victims received death sentences. In contrast to the "national operations," though, the NKVD did not take any measures to rehabilitate the group's innocent members after Beria replaced Ezhov. When Baglikov was arrested in January 1939, he faced the charge that he maintained a "connection to the enemy of the people Muralov."[85] Even at that time, the former chair of the district committee was still being kept as a potential witness in case another wave of repression occurred. After investigators worked him over in March 1938, Muralov had no interrogations for the next nine months. Only on May 29, 1939, did he receive a sentence of eight years in the camps from the Special Counsel of the NKVD.

The Presnov Affair and the "Family Method"

The small village of Krylatskoe, located on the steep banks of the Moscow River, did not have named streets but instead its houses simply had numbers. Nearly half of the village's inhabitants shared the last name Presnov. The center of the extended family was the large peasant household living in house 127. After the death of her husband, Ekaterina Presnova raised her four children alone. The eldest, Vasilii, turned thirty-eight in 1937 and the youngest, Nikolai, turned twenty-two. The proximity of the capital and a large household garden allowed the Presnovs to survive the hungry years of the early 1930s. During collectivization they had been forced to give their family's plot to the nearby collective farm, "Free Labor." The brothers frequently traveled to

Moscow to take jobs. Their sister Varvara took orders to mend clothes at home. Their lives settled down. Vasilii and Ivan began their own families.[86]

Soon their good fortune came to an end. A worker from the German embassy, Ernst Schule, appeared in the picturesque village. The diplomat rented a room from the hospitable peasant family, paying 1,500 rubles for the season—a large sum for those times. In all likelihood, Schule not only wanted to enjoy the countryside's natural beauty but also to study the mysterious Russian soul by living in a genuine village just a dozen kilometers from the Kremlin. It seems that the German liked it there. He continued to visit the Presnovs after the end of dacha season, giving the village boys a demonstration in downhill skiing on the famous Krylatskoe hills. This idyllic life in 1937 could not continue long. The embassy car stood out on the village paths and one of the Presnovs' vigilant neighbors wrote a denunciation to the district NKVD. If the Presnovs had known how their short-lived acquaintance with the Western diplomat would end, they would never had let him near their door. On January 22, 1938, NKVD operatives appeared at the house and emptied it of inhabitants. On a single arrest order they took everyone they found: Vasilii, Nikolai, Varvara, Ivan, and his wife Tat'iana. Additionally, the operatives took a second Ivan Presnov, a cousin who lived next door.

Their acquaintance with the German diplomat was the starting point for a spy group that supposedly operated from the village. But what kinds of secrets could simple workers—a construction laborer, a dockworker, a fitter, and a freelance clothes mender—give to foreigners? The first interrogation of each of the Presnovs only contained basic biographical details and an admission of their acquaintance with Schule. However, the fabricated protocols they signed later included a significant sentence: "The main goal of the spy group that I and the others I listed joined was to destroy the military capacity of the Soviet Union by systematically gathering information on locations of military importance." The main military objects in the case were a food warehouse, the House of Leisure (the Comintern's Moscow vacation house), and the collective farm "Free Labor."

The creation of these unbelievable stories was half of the investigators' work, but they then had to make the arrestees sign those lies. A week passed between the first and second documented interrogations of the six Presnovs. Investigators typically did not keep records of the period of "intense cultivation" of arrestees—the period where they

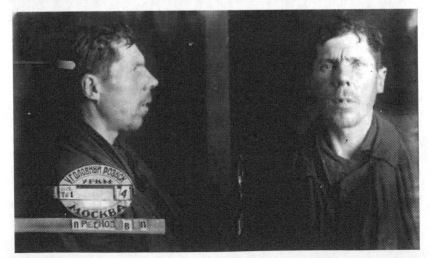

Tat'iana and Ivan Presnov, wife and husband, under arrest, later executed. (GARF, f. 10035, op. 1, d. p-60958; d. p-60959)

Top 4 left: Cousins Nikolai and Ivan Presnov under arrest, later executed. (GARF, f. 10035, op. 1, d. p-60960; d. p-60952)

Bottom 2 left: Vasilii Presnov under arrest, later executed. (GARF, f. 10035, op. 1, d. p-60951)

refused to sign confessions. One can only guess what methods convinced the semiliterate peasants to confess to crimes they had not committed. Tat'iana was the first to surrender. On February 2, she signed the interrogation protocol confessing to espionage. Over the following two days, investigators obtained similar confessions from the other Presnovs. Each of the two-page, typed protocols was as indistinguishable as drops of water from one another. Even the signatures of the peasants were similar—and possibly were also the work of the investigator. On February 20, 1938, the provincial dvoika sentenced all six Presnovs to execution. A few days later they fell at the firing range at Butovo. The case that brought an ordinary peasant family to its fateful end would be the last achievement of NKVD sergeant B. D. Smirnov. On February 26, he committed suicide in his office.

The tragic story of the Presnov family had an unexpected continuation. After the arrests, the sole proprietor of the large peasant home was Ivan and Tat'iana's six-year-old son Vitia, left to the care of his grandfather. The house remained sealed until the beginning of dacha season when a new inhabitant took up residence—Karetnikov. The new dacha lodger was not planning to pay for renting the house and did not allow the child and his guardian to visit. Grandfather Pavel Morozov was not afraid to write a petition to the courts and even forwarded a copy to Ezhov. The arrest of Karetnikov effectively resolved the conflict in favor of the last of the Presnovs.[87]

The family from Krylatskoe was far from an exception. The NKVD frequently conducted arrests using the "family method." In a rural district, this method was highly expedient. Besides the time that operatives saved in conducting group arrests and searches, they did not have to invent connections between the arrestees. Incomplete data from July 1937 to March 1938 shows that Kuntsevo's NKVD fabricated more than forty cases that involved close relatives. On January 26, 1938, operatives arrested father and son-in-law Semen Kozlov and Aleksandr Shuvalov in their village of Teplyi Stan. A month later, NKVD workers delivered the father and son of the Skladnov family from their village of Troparevo to the building on Zagorskii.[88] Together with other arrestees, authorities drove them to Butovo. Perhaps they had enough time to share parting words with one another before the revolver shot. On August 16, 1938, authorities executed three brothers, Ivan, Iosif, and Bronislav Etminus. All three were among the top workers at Kuntsevo's needle factory. What brought them to the attention of the NKVD was their Polish background, even though the brothers were born within the borders of the Russian Empire.[89] The same spy group included a brother and sister Boltrukovich and a father and son Tsikhotskii. A father and son named Brevdo, workers at the ammunition factory, were arrested separately but ended up in the same cell at Taganka prison.[90]

Entire families of *kharbintsy*, people who had lived in Manchuria and worked on the China Eastern Railway, faced repression under NKVD Order 00593. On November 20, 1937, Evdokiia Balykova and her son Vasilii were arrested in Kuntsevo. The following day, Vasilii's twin brother Petr, a student at a Moscow university, returned home to an empty apartment. (Their father had been arrested earlier.) He immediately set off for the district office of the NKVD to ascertain his mother and brother's fate. His mission ended in predictable tragedy. After speaking with Karetnikov, the NKVD arrested Petr as well. The twins received ten years in the camps while their mother was sentenced to death.[91] The sisters Evdokiia and Ul'iana Poda plus the husband and son of one of the sisters moved to Kuntsevo after the China Eastern Railway became the property of China. They were all arrested.[92] A former Harbin resident, Vera Chuprik, first saw her son and husband arrested but later police followed up by arresting her brother and Vera herself.[93]

It is not always possible to determine the relationship of the people in the list of Kuntsevo's victims. In the countryside in particular, nearly everyone was related to some degree. The seven Remizovs from the village Amin'evo, including the student-poet Nikolai, were brothers, uncles, sons, and nephews to one another. Beyond those Remizovs repressed during the mass operations, an equal number had faced political charges in other campaigns. They all had been deemed kulaks for resisting forced collectivization. Mikhail and Ivan Remizov had spent three years in exile from 1932. Ivan's brother Nikolai, the chair of the Amin'evo village council, made it until 1935 before being exiled. On the eve of the July 1937 issuance of Order 00447, Aleksandr Remizov received a prison sentence for counterrevolutionary agitation. Kuntsevo's specialist on class war in the countryside Rukodanov conducted all these cases. Perhaps the NKVD found especially fertile ground in the ancient village of Amin'evo. Or perhaps it was simply a convenient target, just a stone's throw from the district office.[94]

The German Colony and the Feyerherd Affair

Kuntsevo district became the new home for many German communists. A list of Germans among Stalin's victims recorded ten members of the

Communist Party of Germany (KPD) who were repressed in Kuntsevo.[95] After the rise of Hitler, they became political émigrés in Soviet Russia, their revolutionary pasts bringing them to the district. Although their émigré status in the mid-1930s would become an unshakeable stigma, at first it had been a boon for them. During the NEP years, the Soviet Communist Party's cult of "our people abroad" had implied that foreign class brothers living under capitalist persecution would be met warmly and receive the protection of the USSR. This pact of friendship gradually gave way to a fear of "strangers among us," including even foreign communists.

Those who had been arrested or incarcerated before arriving in the Soviet Union automatically fell under suspicion of having been "recruited by the class enemy" while in prison. An intensive verification of political émigrés led to a sharp decline in their ranks. The growing gap between Soviet realities and the ideals that the foreigners had imagined existing in the first socialist country led to psychological breakdowns, even suicide. Awaiting those who managed to adjust and become "Soviet people" was a final test—the Great Terror of 1937–38. Just like in the case of the Presnovs, the "family method" was the primary way the NKVD conducted arrests among the foreign communists.

The most visible of the German political émigrés in Kuntsevo were Luise and Wilhelm Hadrossek. According to his Comintern autobiography, Wilhelm grew up in a family of left social democrats and participated in the German November Revolution of 1918 at age seventeen. Later he became a member of the military-political apparatus of the KPD and helped prepare an attempted revolution, the so-called "German October" of fall 1923. After its failure, police began to track him and he emigrated to the USSR, where he worked in the Volga German Republic. Three years later he returned to Germany and stayed until 1932, formally working as a clerk at the Soviet trade office but in fact acting as the contact between the KPD and the Comintern.[96]

Luise Hadrossek also grew up in a revolutionary environment. Her father Kurt Steinbrecher was a founding member of the KPD and six of her siblings shared her radical leftist views. In March 1921, Luise acted as a courier during the communist uprising in central Germany and spent several months in jail in Halle after its suppression. After her release, comrades would hide the young woman in Berlin, where she worked in the German party's Central Committee under the assumed name Rosa Stiller. Later she worked as a typist in the Soviet trade office.

Luise Hadrossek. (GARF, f. 10035, op. 1, d. 25777)

In 1932 the Hadrossek family arrived in Kuntsevo, where Wilhelm began to work as the technical director of the needle factory. Although he experienced a slight delay in his transfer to the Soviet Communist Party, the career of the young engineer was quite successful. The factory used modern machinery from Germany and Hadrossek accompanied the factory's director Lazarev on several business trips there, serving as advisor and translator. While raising her son Heinz, Luise attempted to play the role of den mother for the German colony at the factory, arranging communal breakfasts for them. In spite of the seeming model lifestyle Kuntsevo's political émigrés lived, the cadres department of the Comintern received multiple inquiries from the NKVD asking for negative information about them. For a long period, the NKVD received a standard reply: "No compromising material exists."

On October 15, 1936, one of Wilhelm's colleagues wrote an absurd denunciation about him. The colleague did not hide the motivation of his letter, a recent falling out between his family and the Hadrosseks. Although officials at the Comintern did not believe the letter writer, they sent it to the "corresponding organization" in charge of these issues, Stalin-era jargon for state security agencies. On November 11, the central NKVD arrested Wilhelm. In April he received a relatively light sentence of five years. However, after a year at Dalstroi, the chain of labor camps in the Far East, he fell under the gaze of punitive organs again and was executed.

Luise entered into a cocoon after the arrest of her husband. Her old friends did not want to draw attention to themselves by socializing with the suspect foreigner. The local press used information from the district NKVD to create a suffocating atmosphere of total suspicion. The district newspaper *Bolshevik* wrote in a front-page editorial, "Separating himself from the party organization through lies and hypocrisy, Lazarev surrounded himself with lackeys who were happy to carry out any dirty deed. In this atmosphere, enemies were able to arm themselves over a long period of time, in particular the German spy Hidrossek [*sic*], formerly one of the closest to Lazarev."[97]

The colony of German communists in Kuntsevo grew smaller by the day. Luise Hadrossek found herself at the district office on Zagorskii Street on October 25, 1937. When Wilhelm was arrested, investigators confiscated his German-made motorcycle, which mysteriously disappeared. When the NKVD arrested Luise, their remaining belongings, moved from Germany, vanished as well. Attempts to recover the lost items in the 1950s turned up nothing. When questioned twenty years later, investigator S. K. Efremov from the Kuntsevo district NKVD explained, "Workers at the district office carried out the inventory and delivery of arrestees' property to the state on their own."[98] However, the case files from Kuntsevo contain no paperwork that shows this process occurred. The archive of the Kuntsevo NKVD's finance department might have shed light on the fate of repressed people's property, but these files were destroyed during World War II.

More than even the loss of her freedom, the forced separation from her son was the most significant consequence of arrest for Luise Hadrossek. The ten-year-old boy went to Danilovskii house, an orphanage for children of "enemies of the people." Heinz's was the only case of its kind in the Kuntsevo NKVD. To avoid unnecessary trouble, offspring of victims typically went to live with relatives who, fortunately for the children, were numerous in the countryside. Luise and Wilhelm's son received a new name, the Russian version of his given name. After a standard investigation ending with a falsified interrogation protocol, Luise's case went before the Special Counsel of the NKVD. The ten years it gave her for supposed counterrevolutionary agitation among Kuntsevo's residents was fodder for a joke. When Hadrossek appealed to Ezhov and Soviet procurator Andrei Vyshinsky, she only wrote in German. How could she have spread propaganda among Kuntsevo's Russian-speaking inhabitants?[99]

The criteria for the selection of the remaining members of the "Hadrossek group" was the same as other groups—foreigners and family connections. In January 1938, the NKVD arrested Latvian Karl Burhard and Germans Erika Huebner, Tatyana Sommerfeld, and her father.[100] Margarita Guenther, who had kept her German citizenship, escaped with relative ease. Investigators merely took away her exit visa. After a year and a half of dealing with the modest hairdresser, the NKVD stopped pursuing her indictment on charges of espionage.[101]

However, German citizenship did not save Wilhelm Steinitz (given name Arthur Kovalevsky) from execution. Steinitz joined the KPD in 1920 and was a member of the Alliance of Red Front-Fighters, effectively a functionary of the militarized wing of the party. On New Year's Eve 1932, Steinitz carried out an audacious operation. At Troisdorf, near Cologne, he stole more than two hundred kilograms of dynamite and eight thousand detonators and fuses. The communists needed the explosives in the event of an armed uprising. As Steinitz told the investigators, "I sent half to Berlin and half to local organizations." But the armed uprising would not be and instead the Nazis came to power.[102]

Steinitz and his assistant Peter Zirt went underground after their exploit and in May 1933 the party sent them to the USSR.[103] Both set down roots in Kuntsevo and began to work at the needle factory. Steinitz lost no time in spoiling his relationship with German colleagues and the factory administration. He constantly complained about his small salary and "voluntary" contributions to bond campaigns. During a typical campaign in May 1935, Steinitz refused to pay for the bond, the size of a monthly salary, and quit. According to Wilhelm Hadrossek's message to a KPD representative, Steinitz "did not conduct himself like a communist" and "deserted the factory." Nonetheless, the German party obtained a pension for the veteran of the movement through the International Red Aid (MOPR) organization.

The personal discord in Steinitz's life grew. First, his wife Kristina left for Germany to be with their children. The communist refused to take Soviet citizenship and began to search for peace at the bottom of a bottle. Kuntsevo's police detained him several times for drunkenness. After the leadership of the KPD learned that he had tried to leave for the United States, it expelled him from the party.

The dangerous signs around Steinitz increased persistently. In April 1937, the NKVD arrested his circle of Russian acquaintances, including the Mikhailova sisters and G. I. Belousov.[104] They gave investigators the necessary compromising information on Steinitz. But the arrest of foreign citizens still required the sanction of higher authorities. NKVD Order 00439 (the German operation) approved the arrest of German citizens working in weapons factories and untied the hands of Kuntsevo's NKVD. To include Steinitz in the scope of the order, investigators made him the head of a mythical spy network at Factory 46, an armaments factory where he had never worked. Because Wilhelm Steinitz lived in the USSR under an assumed name, investigators hardly had to treat him like a foreign citizen. The German embassy could barely find him and would not have interceded anyway on the behalf of someone with his past. In Arthur Kovalevsky's homeland, the Gestapo was waiting to throw him into a concentration camp. Instead, Kuntsevo's NKVD sent Wilhelm Steinitz to the execution pit at Butovo.

His conspiratorial group included German communist émigrés Friedrich Grietsche and Ernst Meier.[105] The latter lived with Steinitz. It is likely that Meier had followed his roommate's advice when he went to the police on the eve of his arrest to gather forms to apply for Soviet citizenship. At his interrogation, he explained his motives, "First, my wife left for Germany on July 17, 1937, and I didn't want to live without her. Second, I knew that I was going to be arrested here all the same."[106] His visit to the police was followed by a speedy arrest. The third department (counterespionage) of the Moscow NKVD led the investigation that resulted in Meier's execution.

Two others joined the Steinitz group—Karl and Gertrude Geflikh, the rivals of the Hadrossek family for unofficial leadership of Kuntsevo's German colony.[107] Karl, whose given name was Georg Helei, was one of the chief actors in the Hungarian Revolution of 1919, and the leader of the Military-Revolutionary Tribunal in Budapest. After the fall of the Hungarian Soviet Republic, he fled to Germany and organized the financing of newspapers for the central administration of the KPD. Later, Karl and Gertrude Geflikh worked in the Soviet school in Berlin and emigrated to the USSR in March 1933.[108]

Even after Karl Geflikh's arrest, the KPD's secretary for transferring émigrés to the Soviet party, Walter Ditbender, vouched for the prisoner. Ditbender's act was a rarity in 1937. Even the closest of friends usually cut ties with the NKVD's victims. Ditbender's courage in questioning the motto that "Chekists do not make mistakes" deserves respect. However, soon after the NKVD would arrest Ditbender himself and his interrogations would reveal the close connection between his office and the organs of state security.[109]

Steinitz's accomplice in the explosives caper also changed his last name, becoming Peter Funk. In contrast to his sullen partner from the KPD's military branch, Funk found his place in Kuntsevo. Funk-Zirt became one of the leading producers at the needle factory and in November 1935 took Soviet citizenship. A year before that his wife Katy Lorsheid joined him in the USSR, having spent several months in a concentration camp after the Nazis took power.[110] The young couple had a daughter named Tat'iana in 1936. Funk-Zirt's personnel file, maintained at the Moscow office of the KPD, did not include a single negative remark. The lack of compromising materials probably explains why the only accusation against Funk-Zirt was his "contact with arrested spies." However, the limited charges against him were enough to obtain a death sentence.[111]

After the needle factory, the second highest concentration of German political émigrés in Kuntsevo district was at Station 1 of the Comintern's department of international connections, located near the village of Sukovo. The station housed secret couriers from foreign communist parties, where they underwent training and held conspiratorial meetings with the leaders of the Comintern's executive committee. Additionally, Station 1 was also the location of the House of Leisure. The house was the summer vacation home for Comintern employees, and its farm was a source of fresh food for the cafeteria at the Comintern executive committee. Its founding in 1932 came at a time when food shortages in the country led to the Comintern's disassociation with Insnab (foreign provisioning), the institution that supplied diplomatic missions in Moscow. The situation forced the Comintern's leadership to undertake serious measures to supply itself, including the founding of a pig farm.[112]

The history of the supplemental farm at Kuntsevo's House of Leisure is worth exploring briefly. Its first director was a German, Adolf Stange. He came to Russia as a prisoner of war and from 1918 worked for the German Council of Workers and Soldiers Deputies, which appropriated the functions of the German embassy in the capital of Soviet Russia. After the embassy building on Denezhnyi Lane became the property of the Comintern, Stange began to work as a courier for that organization.

Sent to the countryside with a propaganda brigade in the early 1920s, he found a charming location not far from the rail station Nemchinovka. The village Soviet gave him the land and building of the former proprietor of Sukovo. The German settler created a model property, raising flowers and strawberries. He played the role of propagandist among the local population, raising their envy and spite. Villagers said, "A new proprietor has appeared, and even worse he is from the Comintern." Stange began to rent out his house during the summer and sell milk and berries, sometimes even in the building of the Comintern. His actions did not go unnoticed. In the party's membership purge of 1929, his peers demanded his expulsion from the party as a speculator. Only the intervention of Otto Kuusinen, the secretary of the Comintern executive committee, saved him. As Kuusinen's wife remembered, "Otto did not risk anything in defending the German communist. Moreover, he loved strawberries."[113] The reprimand Stange received for his "economic fouling" was the first link in a chain of problems. The final blow to his "farming business" (according to purge documents) was collectivization. To avoid losing the property, Stange came up with a brilliant idea. He would surrender it to the Comintern in exchange for considerable compensation and become the director of the supplemental farm.

Four hectares of land and a former manor house, now the House of Leisure for thirty people, did not solve the Comintern's problems in provisioning or the organization of summer recreation. However, the property became the object of extensive wrangling during the party purge of 1933. Stange stood accused of mismanagement and bribery, having given oats and potatoes to the leaders of the local collective farm. Above all, his comrades in the party were frustrated that they themselves had to go to Nemchinovka to weed the property. The famous

Bolshevik jurist, A. A. Sol'ts, at a meeting of the Party Control Commission, of which he was a member, read the party's sentence for Stange, "He lives on your [the Comintern's] property and at the same time you allow him to develop his own operation there. In this situation, the business will inevitably become a kulak operation."[114] Feeling the weight of these political accusations, Stange returned to work at the Comintern executive committee. Instead of his own house, he received a corner of a room from authorities in Kuntsevo, where he, his wife, and six daughters had to adapt to their cozy conditions. In August 1937, the Comintern cut its staff and fired Stange. Kuntsevo's NKVD workers arrested Stange in January 1938 and included him in a group of Soviet German spies. In this imagined conspiracy, Stange did not even receive the honor of being its leader.[115]

Stange's successor as the director of the Comintern's dacha was another German, Arthur Golke. In the 1920s he was the member of the German party's Central Committee in charge of its finances. As a deputy of the Prussian Landtag, Golke was famous for his fistfights with representatives from rightist parties. After a conflict within the KPD led to his removal from its leadership, he immigrated to the Soviet Union. He received the protection of Ia. Abramov-Mirov, head of the department of international connections of the Comintern's executive committee, who procured Golke his post. The indiscriminate arrests of workers at the department led to Golke's dismissal from the Comintern apparatus for his "connection with enemies of the people."[116]

Analogous accusations were the prelude to arrest for many of the political émigrés in the Soviet Union in 1937. Naïvely trying to wait out the wave of repression, they left Moscow for villages outside the capital or in nearby construction sites, but there, too, repression awaited them. An entire community of German émigrés, independent of the group at the needle factory, gathered at the House of Leisure near Kuntsevo, recently renamed Station 1. Besides Golke, its residents included Inga Felker, and three Feyerherd siblings—Berta, Lidia, and Alexander.

The sad story of Feyerherd brothers and sisters, six in total, deserves special attention. The family had lived in Chisinau at the start of the First World War, where authorities interned the brothers. After the Brest-Litovsk Treaty, the Feyerherds moved to Germany one by one. In Berlin in the 1920s, the siblings worked first at the Soviet embassy, in the Comintern and for Soviet intelligence. On the recommendation of Spartacus League organizer Leo Jogiches, in December 1918 the eldest Feyerherd brother Fritz had become a courier for Soviet emissaries in

Berlin supporting the German revolution. Later, he opened a store that sold appliances and became one of the most reliable sources of income for the KPD.[117]

The Berlin office of the *reichskommisar* (state commissioner) for social order had a file on all the members of the Feyerherd family. However, the greatest objects of interest for German counterintelligence were Fritz and the Feyerherds' cousin Paul. Fritz had become the secretary for the Soviet representative in Berlin, N. N. Krestinskii, while Paul worked as a diplomatic messenger who often carried valuables that were sold to finance communist propaganda. According to a report from July 23, 1927, Paul smuggled a box of diamonds worth two million marks from Moscow to Germany.[118] Another Feyerherd, Wilhelm, spent the years of the civil war in Russia and was mobilized into the forces of General Anton Denikin. He arrived in Berlin via Turkey where he began to serve in the Soviet embassy. His brothers, Franz and Alexander, worked as chauffeurs there and his sister, Berta, was a typist. When Hitler came to power, they moved to the USSR.[119]

The first of the siblings to face repression in the Soviet Union was Fritz, who was then working for military intelligence in the Red Army. The NKVD arrested him on August 13, 1937, as part of the "anti-Comintern affair," a campaign that was part of a planned fourth show trial.[120] On November 5, a week after Fritz's execution, the NKVD arrested Paul. He, along with the others the Military Collegium sentenced to death, was interred at the former dacha of NKVD chief Iagoda.[121] The house was not far from the Butovo firing range, where the NKVD would execute Wilhelm Feyerherd on May 28, 1938.[122]

The three surviving Feyerherds had long been suspects of the Kuntsevo NKVD. After the death of their father in 1935, their mother Rosina Ettinger and the two sisters moved from Berlin to Moscow. Rosina died a month after her arrival in the USSR and Berta took on the role of head of the household. She arranged to work at the Comintern's department of international connections while her sister Lidia continued her studies. Finding housing proved nearly impossible so the women settled in the Comintern's dacha. The village on the outskirts of Moscow could not compare to their lives in Berlin, especially in winter. The arrest of two brothers and Berta's dismissal from her work at the Comintern were the final blows. In this hopeless situation, Berta decided to take a desperate step—to apply for a visa at the German embassy.

The next day, January 26, 1938, the NKVD arrested her. Operatives took her sister at the same time. Although they arrived at the NKVD

Alexander Feyerherd. (RGASPI, f. 495, op. 205, d. 5625)

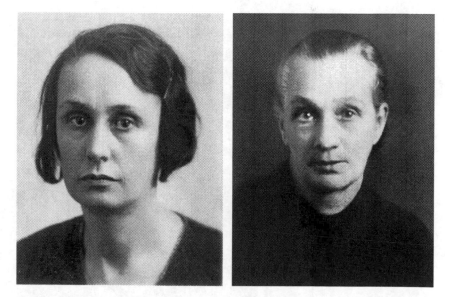

Berta Feyerherd, before and after arrest. (RGASPI, f. 495, op. 205, d. 912; GARF, f. 10035, op. 1, d. p-23478)

Wilhelm Feyerherd. (RGASPI, f. 495, op. 205, d. 5625)

Friedrich Feyerherd. (RGASPI, f. 495, op. 205, d. 3163)

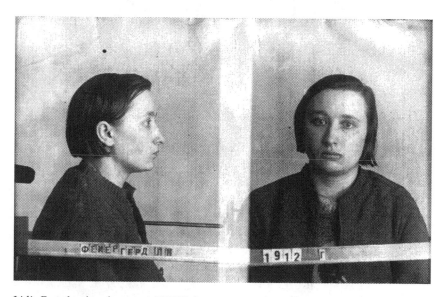

Lidia Feyerherd under arrest. (GARF, f. 10035, op. 2, d. 30515)

building in one car, the investigation claimed that Lidia was arrested based on evidence her sister had given. Investigators had little trouble obtaining a confession to acts of espionage from the terrified young women. A short excerpt from Lidia's interrogation provides an intriguing insight into the construction of these accusations:

> Question: Living in the village Sukovo, did you know that an airfield
>   was located there?
> Answer: Living in the village Sukovo, I knew that an airfield was
>   located there and saw how planes landed and that tents
>   were located there.
> Question: Have you ever been on the territory of the airfield and
>   why?
> Answer: I have never been on the territory of the airfield at the
>   village Sukovo and have had no reason to go there.
> Question: The investigation has established that you frequently
>   took walks in the area around the Sukovo airfield. Who did
>   you take walks with and what was the goal of your walks?
> Answer: Yes, it is true that I frequently walked in the area near
>   the Sukovo airfield in my free time and on the weekends
>   with my sister Berta Karlovna Feyerherd and also with my

brothers, Alexander, Wilhelm, Friedrich, and their wives and
children. . . . The goal was to spend our time in a pleasant
way, since it was a dacha town.[123]

Investigators pieced together a strong enough indictment from this
dialogue to send the case to extrajudicial organs. The story was that the
girls befriended pilots at the airfield on their strolls, gaining secret information from the young and inexperienced trainees. The testimony
of Berta and Lidia set off a chain reaction of arrests among all their
acquaintances whose biographies fit the mold of "enemy of the people."
The leader of the conspiracy was Arthur Golke. On the night of March
14, 1938, as investigators pried the first testimony from Sergei Muralov, the district NKVD undertook an operation for the "disarming of
a national-espionage group" that included the unemployed Golke,
chauffer Alexander Feyerherd, pensioners, two cooks, an accountant
from "Glavsakhar" (the committee of the Soviet sugar industry) and a
firefighter. In total the arrests numbered eight—all Germans, Poles, or
Latvians.[124]

The protocols of the interrogations claimed that as a chauffeur,
Alexander Feyerherd had sent Berlin "information about the condition
of highways of Moscow province."[125] In the event of war, the cooks
were ready to provoke an anti-Soviet rebellion among their clients.
Apparently, they planned to cut the amount of food put into dishes
they prepared. The indictment accused the sugar accountant of dis-
rupting supplies to the capital. All the accusations had the makings of a
bad joke, except they led to executions.

Kuntsevo's investigators had to labor the most over the interrogation
protocols of the pensioners, housewives, and the unemployed. One of
their most creative confessions concerned V. V. Kolbut, a Pole who was
placed in Golke's group for lack of Germans. His confession read, "I am
well acquainted with Kuntsevo district and have a great deal of free
time because I do not work. I had the chance to take long walks and
learned at that time about the state of highways in the district and the
location of important military objects. I gave that information to Alexander Feyerherd. After I received seeds of weed grass from him, I planted
them among collective farm fields in order to lower the harvest and
create discontent among collective farmers."[126]

In contrast to the majority of spy cases in the Kuntsevo NKVD, investigators summoned additional witnesses to give testimony against Golke
from his subordinates at Station 1. However, they could not give specific

examples of their boss's espionage and instead signed the investigator's formulaic accusations that Golke "imposed a Fascist system of running affairs" and "related to Russian workers with suspicion and intentionally did not study the Russian language." It is possible that the one honest accusation was that the German had confiscated alcohol from workers at the entrance and sent drunks to the basement for the night until they sobered up.[127]

The main argument in the indictment of Golke was his friendship with B. N. Mel'nikov (Muller), executed in 1937 along with other workers from the Comintern's department of international connections. However, the search for a link between spy conspiracies fabricated in Moscow at Lubianka and those at the lower levels of the NKVD led to a dead end. Foreign specialists planning to return home, embassy workers who had diplomatic immunity, and those foreigners who were already executed in the terror were unavailable to give testimony for the investigation. These factors precluded a deeper investigation into the cases. Paradoxically, though, investigators could thus ascribe the lack of evidence to unavoidable obstacles. In August 1938, three members of the "Golke group" were executed while the rest went to labor camps.

The story of the Feyerherds would not be complete without turning to the lone survivor of the six siblings, Franz. Compared to his siblings, he had the good fortune of working in the Soviet embassy in Vienna during the union of Germany and Austria in 1938. The Nazi regime sent him to the Ravensbruck concentration camp. Why Franz Feyerherd was unable to flee to the Soviet Union before his arrest is an open question. It is possible that he learned about his relatives' fate and was reluctant to repeat it. He survived life in the concentration camps and in the 1950s worked as a diplomatic courier in East Germany.[128]

The National-Workplace Principle as Practice in Repression

The case of sabotage at the Moscow provincial cropping station, headed by its director Nikolaev, was the first where the NKVD used the workplace principle in the selection of its victims. In Kuntsevo's factories, the only group to face repression before the beginning of 1938 was the eight workers and clerks arrested at the Odintsovo lumber-tar plant.[129] When the district NKVD became involved in the "national operations," how officers falsified cases changed. They used the national-workplace principle to create spy groups. As a result, repression shifted from the countryside to the factories.

February 28, 1938, was unexpectedly busy at the Butovo firing range. Amid the frost, the commandant's group had to complete the remainder of its monthly quota. By the end of the day, they had carried out 562 executions—a horrifying record for Butovo. The mass murder occurred as the term of NKVD Order 00447 was nearing its end. *Nonetheless*, the mass operations would continue, but with different categories of victims, those from the "national operations." Among the last victims of the "kulak operation" were the first test cases of the new campaign, Kuntsevo residents Roman Kliat and Eduard Tsikhotskii. Investigators sent them to their deaths after gathering the testimony that would allow them to uncover a supposed spy conspiracy at arms Factory 95.

As the "resident" of the spy group, Karetnikov chose Evgeniia Babushkina. A more suitable person would have been hard to find. Babushkina was a research associate at the Academy of Sciences who had at one time worked at the factory and whose mother had worked as a cleaner at the Polish embassy. Babushkina's group included five people, each of whom had a separate case file. Even before these five could go to the dvoika, another rash of arrests occurred at Factory 95. On February 22 and March 12, investigators arrested eighteen people from the factory, all Poles according to their biographical data. In order to process the surge of new arrests, Karetnikov's primarily technique was to force arrestees to sign interrogation protocols created in advance. According to a handwriting expert, Kuntsevo registration bureau worker Metelkina wrote M. M. Anikovich's interrogation protocol.[130]

The spy conspiracy expanded into other enterprises in Kuntsevo through family connections. Mechislav Tsikhotskii had been in prison for a week when executioners killed his son. According to the victims' case files, the father and son did not know of each other's espionage even though both were supposed to have worked for Polish intelligence.[131] Mechislav Tsikhotskii was the deputy chief accountant at the needle factory. Because of his position, he was an excellent candidate for the role of chief in a "national terrorist-insurgent, wrecking-diversionary and spy group," as it appeared in all the indictments.[132] For ordinary members of the spy group, the factory's personnel department effectively filled the ranks of the conspiracy by supplying the police with data on Polish employees. The factory's administration claimed later that police demanded incriminating materials on thirteen arrestees. Factory director D. M. Chistov described this practice: "Workers from the Kuntsevo district NKVD always stressed that they had significant evidence against arrested people. In doing so, they indicated the kind of evidence we needed to provide about factory workers. If I gave objective assessments, they sent them back. When the police returned them, they hinted to me that I was placing myself under suspicion with those kinds of evaluations about enemies of the people."[133]

The arrestees were primarily from the factory's higher ranks—heads of workshops and engineers—but there were also ordinary workers. Because the factory produced simple sewing needles, it was difficult to accuse a worker of spying. Investigator Solov'ev found a way out of this conundrum, inserting a phrase into interrogation protocols, "If we jammed up the factory, we would put the army's supply of clothing in jeopardy and threaten soldiers' morale."[134] Ten of the thirteen members of the "counterrevolutionary Polish organization" were executed. The needle factory fell into shambles after the NKVD deprived it so quickly of a large part of its leadership. Elsewhere in the modest industrial zone of the town, Karetnikov and his underlings "cleansed" it of its Polish and Latvian nationals. When they could not find real Poles and Latvians, the operation included Ukrainians, Belarusians, Jews, Lithuanians, and Estonians.

Beyond the factories, Karetnikov invented more and more exotic webs of spies in Kuntsevo. After investigator Smirnov's suicide, Karetnikov inherited the investigation of two Greeks, whose files described them as unemployed. One declared himself innocent but the other, G. Kh. Iliadis, signed a protocol stating he was the "resident for German intelligence in charge of a counterrevolutionary-spy group of Greeks."[135] More accurately, Iliadis became the head of an espionage ring of Greek women, for Iliadis was the only male member of the conspiracy. Typically espionage was considered a man's profession in the Soviet Union and the Kuntsevo NKVD had not included women in these groups previously. However, it seems that the population of men with suitable biographies had dried up. Or perhaps NKVD officers had an easier time scaring women into signing the protocols. During the March peak of repression, investigators may have chosen to conserve their time and energy by picking easier targets. Investigators did not mind that the Greek women were all homemakers or minor traders with no access to military secrets. In two days of interrogation on March 3 and 5, Karetnikov obtained eight confessions to espionage. The Greek women supposedly seduced workers at military factories to extract secret information from them. With confessions to this crime, the NKVD and procurator determined that each would receive eight or ten years of forced labor.[136] The arrest of the unemployed Greek women demonstrates that information about "hostile nationalities" came from sources other than the passport registrars and factory administrations. The criminal police must have also contributed information about "nationals" and in doing so made themselves participants in a statewide campaign of repression. With the help of the police, a German language teacher could turn into a German, and spies could come from people without a known workplace, as in the case of the Greeks.

Kuntsevo's investigators created conspiracies with victims connected by nationality or a common workplace, with a few exceptions. From March 14 to 16, investigators Dikii and Solov'ev created an entire spy group from participants who, according to Solov'ev's testimony in 1940, "only met one another in the holding cell."[137] Investigators made textile plant turner V. F. Danich into the group's leader. Its twelve members included five women. The accusations against them were rather weak. A German language teacher, G. G. Ferapontova, had "preached the advantages of the Fascist system among schoolchildren." Homemakers in the group were supposed to have spread anti-Soviet rumors. Despite their group's alleged connection with Polish intelligence, its members were Latvians, Germans, and Jews. Masking the blatant fabrication in the case was not possible, even during the "March peak." The investigation only managed to send Danich and R. K. Neiman their deaths. The other members of the group would see their cases reviewed.[138]

The failure of the case (the provincial NKVD sent the investigation back for "reworking") only reinforced the reliability of the workplace principle of repression. The largest concentration of victims in the mass operations in Kuntsevo was at arms Factory 46, a producer of small caliber ammunition. For various reasons, the factory was fertile ground to uncover spy conspiracies. Explosive materials, turnover in personnel, and apathy led to constant accidents, although accidents were hardly unusual against the backdrop of rapid Stalinist industrialization. Although factory director Plotkin committed suicide, he should be counted among the factory's first victims. His suicide was likely in advance of imminent arrest. The chief mechanic of the factory, M. M. Avdeenko, was arrested in October 1937. Its chief engineer D. V. Novikov and commercial director S. A. Martkovich were arrested in November.[139]

At the end of January 1938, officers stopped arresting individual saboteurs and began to target entire spy collectives. The first of the "residents," Latvian Karl Ozolin, was imported from the capital.

Investigators from Moscow's Sokolniki municipal district had arrested him on January 28. Neither in Ozolin's indictment, nor in his interrogation did the Latvian mention Factory 46 or his future "spy group" in Kuntsevo.[140] After being sentenced to death, though, Ozolin returned from the grave as an absentee witness who would allow investigators to begin a new series of arrests. It is likely that colleagues at Sokolniki informed Kuntsevo's investigators that Ozolin had connections with Latvian workers at Factory 46. Based on this information, operatives Smirnov and Solov'ev conducted an investigation that lasted just a week. In the end, ten of the twelve members of the "Latvian spy group" at the ammunition factory, including Novikov and Martkovich, received death sentences. Soon it became clear that this case was just the start of the operation at the factory. It would be the largest campaign in Kuntsevo during the mass operations and the last of Karetnikov's career. To save time conducting arrests, Karetnikov and an operative group went to the factory themselves.[141] Over the course of a few days in March, operatives arrested roughly fifty factory workers, of whom a third were women. More than half of them were categorized on arrest forms as Poles, followed by a number of Germans and Latvians, and then other national groups.

Karetnikov based the conspiracy on a report the factory's chief engineer sent to the Kuntsevo NKVD listing the enterprise's most vulnerable locations.[142] The places the engineer named were literally all over the factory—from its power station to the powder warehouse, from the firefighting water tanks to the service roads. All Karetnikov had to do was fill in the locations with arrested workers to create a spy group. Interrogations of the factory's workers occurred at crushing speed. Of thirty interrogation protocols created in two weeks, Karetnikov signed fourteen, registry bureau inspector V. F. Petushkov signed ten, and head of the firefighters A. S. Zhivov signed six. It is worth noting that Petushkov and Zhivov only copied interrogation protocols that Karetnikov had fabricated and forced arrestees to sign. The absurdity of the accusations is hard to comprehend. As soon as war broke out, no fewer than ten people were supposed to destroy each of the factory's workshops—each saboteur working independently. Nonetheless, after Karetnikov's arrest he faced charges that he had missed spies at Kuntsevo's factories. He allegedly left more than a hundred people with suspicious biographies untouched. If the Politburo had not set the end date of the "national operations" for April 15, 1938, the second purge of the ammunition factory would not have been its last.[143]

Even after the grey cardinal of the district's NKVD was gone, the machinery he created continued to swallow new victims. New arrests ceased but investigations continued to go to trial before the dvoika. The factory's status as a defense enterprise gave the cases added significance. Six female workers from Factory 46 were sentenced to death on July 29, 1938. Days later, on August 13, authorities issued a resolution referring the cases to extrajudicial organs for review. But by that day, Aleksandra Shpakova, one of those sentenced, was already buried at the Butovo firing range. The remaining women had to wait two more weeks for their ominous hour.

The Consequences of the Mass Operations in Kuntsevo

According to incomplete evidence, the Kuntsevo district NKVD arrested more than 560 people in the nine months of the mass operations. Of those, more than half received death sentences. The most common prison term the troika or dvoika gave was ten years. One arrestee, S. G. Dulin, a member of the mythical organization "Our Cause," received the maximum term of fifteen years.[144] Although the cases of SRs usually went before the Special Counsel of the NKVD, Dulin went before the Military Collegium of the Supreme Court. Clearly, his misfortune was due to his acquaintance with high-ranking oppositionists. One of Dulin's associates was Mikhail Tomskii, the former head of the trade unions and Bukharin ally who committed suicide in August 1936 when it appeared certain he would face arrest following the first Moscow show trial. Lawlessness continued after extrajudicial organs made their decision. Victims often went to their execution without hearing their sentence.[145] Those who received forced labor sentences only learned the length of their term when they arrived at the Gulag.[146]

The suffering that family and friends experienced is immeasurable. They quit their jobs and went to Moscow's jails every day. Often they received the standard announcement that the prisoner has "ten years without the right of correspondence." Many family members faced eviction on flimsy pretexts. After losing their home, the wife and two young children of arrestee A. A. Gailesh found themselves in new lodgings—an unheated veranda just five square meters in size.[147] Peasant families lost their main wage earners, pushing them to the brink of starvation. After the arrest of Ivan Diuchkov, the village of Tereshkovo found nine children without a father in its midst. The youngest, a newborn boy, died when his mother went into a state of nervous shock and could not feed him.[148] Victims' relatives bore the stigma of being an "accomplice of an enemy of the people." They had to erase their relatives, friends, and coworkers from their memory.

When Beria replaced Ezhov, authorities took only half measures to understand what had happened in the terror. No one pretended to dig into its motivations or to rehabilitate its victims. Roughly a hundred detainees from Kuntsevo continued to languish in holding cells, including in Kuntsevo itself. The majority of them had already confessed to crimes they had not committed. In a report on December 26, 1938, Tsyganov noted, "A few people were jailed before their cases were completed. Therefore we are currently making progress on their investigations."[149] After New Year's 1939, several operatives from neighboring Krasnogorsk and Istra districts came to work at Kuntsevo. The district NKVD quickly put the investigations into order, conducting new interrogations in these cases. Open falsification no longer occurred but the inertia of the mass operations was hard to resist. Many accused protested that they had been coerced into making confessions in March 1938 and these protests became part of new interrogation protocols. However, their earlier confessions also continued to appear in indictments from the first half of 1939.

Witnesses called to testify in this round knew exactly what evidence they had to give. Although standard accusations about diversionary activities and wrecking disappeared, new formulas like "slanders against the collective farm system" arose. Operatives still demanded compromising documents and character assessments from the administrators of Kuntsevo's factories. A year after her arrest in 1938, warehouse worker Bronislava Boltrukovich faced new accusations of "extreme neglect of the warehouse and confusing organization."[150] In accordance with statute 206 of the criminal-procedural code of the USSR, investigators began to inform the accused when their investigations had closed. Accusations of spying and terrorism gave way to counterrevolutionary agitation. In a number of cases, a formulaic statement appears in the case file: "In the process of the investigation, the participation of <NAME> in a counterrevolutionary SR-Menshevik organization proved unsubstantiated but the investigation received information that <NAME> engaged in counterrevolutionary agitation."[151] The accused went before the Special Counsel of the NKVD where they received three to eight years in the camps.

Only in January 1939 did the first movement begin toward freeing the victims of the mass operations in Kuntsevo. The first released were twelve workers from Factory 46, where twenty-seven workers would eventually receive reprieves. During additional questioning, it became clear that T. S. Kokhanskaia was Ukrainian and I. Ia. Red'ko Belorussian, not Polish as investigators had earlier written in both forms.[152] Several Jews, many of whom had never been to Poland, also benefitted from the revision of their nationality. However, the files of reviewed cases contain no information about the coercion Karetnikov and his underlings used during the investigation. Even those Kuntsevo residents who received their freedom experienced emotional trauma that would last their whole lives. Many victims' health suffered from the year they spent languishing in the insufferable tedium of jail. M. S. Golengrin, arrested on March 13, 1938, during her fifth month of pregnancy, gave birth in Novinskaia women's prison, located on the current site of Moscow's city hall.[153] Although Kuntsevo's NKVD received orders to restore the housing of those released, fulfilling this order was impossible. Losing their jobs and friends, released arrestees found themselves alienated from society.

On December 26, 1938, joint NKVD and procuracy directive 2709 ordered state security agencies to review any grievance about the decisions made by the troikas or dvoikas.[154] However, the review of written grievances was usually a formality. Only in the best of cases were witnesses requestioned during reviews. The majority of the reviews end with the words "the sentence does not demand revision." A few lucky people were exceptions. Vladimir Shnaidruk, the last survivor of the twelve "terrorists" from Nemchinovka, wrote a polished complaint to the procurator in 1939. The investigatory section of the Moscow NKVD reviewed the case and determined that it was entirely fabricated—from the witnesses' testimony to the indictment. The investigatory section also demanded that criminal charges be filed against the two main culprits in the Nemchinovka case: the investigator Aleksandr Nikitin and his assistant in procuring witness testimony, Zhirnov, the head of the village Soviet.[155]

Besides the appeals of victims and their relatives, petitions arose from other sources. Collective letters were atypical but occurred. In one case, forty-two members of the collective farm called "The Defense of Socialism" protested arrests to Kuntsevo's deputy to the Supreme Soviet and editor of *Pravda* Lev Mekhlis. He forwarded the letter to Beria who initiated a review at the highest level. However, when the review returned no revision of the sentence, the collective farm's chair received a reprimand from the party.[156] In 1939 the Greek embassy sent the

Commissariat of Foreign Affairs a request to review the cases of the women whom Karetnikov had written into the "Greek spy organization." As it happened, two of the victims were relatives of an embassy worker, his brother and mother. Both were residents of Bakovka and had kept their Greek citizenship. Beria took personal control over the situation. The review found that two witnesses who had been instrumental in constructing the case simply did not exist.[157] Incidentally, the review also uncovered that E. E. Kostaki and L. E. Papakhristodulo had not received sentences and remained in detention as suspects at Novinskaia prison. During questioning, both of the women spoke of their battles with psychological trauma that made them sign false confessions. At the end of 1939, authorities closed the case as based on unsubstantiated accusations.[158]

The case of the informant Snow White, arrested by Karetnikov without the approval of her handler in the central NKVD, came to a less happy conclusion. In a letter she sent from the camps, she complained of the arbitrariness of Kuntsevo's investigators. It seems the letter reached the right target. In February 1939, first deputy NKVD commissar Vsevolod Merkulov issued a threatening directive about the case: "The head of the NKVD of Moscow province will create a commission to review cases in Kuntsevo District NKVD for the time that Karetnikov and Kuznetsov (arrested) worked. Its goal is to discover all cases where the investigation was led incorrectly." This directive was only good on paper, though. On several occasions, investigators from the Moscow NKVD attempted to review the case of the former secret informant but met with insurmountable bureaucratic obstacles. All attempts ceased in April 1941. Snow White herself died in the camps just a few months before the end of her ten-year sentence.

Relatives selflessly fought for their loved ones who had gone to the camps. No sooner was Iosif Iliukovich cleared of charges in January 1939 than he began to search for relatives arrested not long before him.[159] In his petitions, he described the injustices that had occurred in the Kuntsevo NKVD. Case files are full of appeals that relatives sent through all probable and improbable channels. Occasionally, these petitions had the power to move the unwilling machinery of Stalinist justice. The three sons of grade school teacher G. G. Ferapontova used a variety of new facts and arguments in each of their letters to authorities. The letters are especially notable because they demonstrate how well informed residents of the town were about affairs in the local NKVD. In the sons' petition from June 11, 1940, they emphasized that "a short

while after the arrest of mother, many of the officers, including investigator Dikii, were removed from their posts and arrested." Ferapontova
was eventually freed on January 4, 1941.[160] A review of Vasilii Ugletskii's
case began in March 1939 after his three children wrote to Lev Mekhlis.
In the letter, the Young Pioneers assured their benevolent "uncle" of
the innocence of their father. The review closed quietly a half-year later
when investigators learned that Ugletskii had died in Sevvostlag (the
camp system in the northeast of the country) on December 10, 1938.[161]

In 1939 Soviet legal organs finally escaped their paralysis, too. Even
the secretariat of the Special Counsel of the NKVD occasionally refused
to pronounce a sentence, instead sending a case for judgment to the
criminal courts.[162] The Moscow provincial court pronounced peasant
S. A. Shushunov from the village Mnevniki innocent after witnesses
refused to confirm their testimony when called to the court.[163] The
provincial procurator also sent several cases of Kuntsevo residents
arrested during the mass operations back to the NKVD for further
investigation.[164]

The rehabilitation of victims under Beria did not last long, though.
As the influx of petitions grew ever larger, the NKVD and procuracy
issued joint directive 0165 in April 1940. The new order retracted the
previous directive that had called for mandatory reviews when the
accused petitioned. This reversal also had a retroactive effect. A prisoner
at the Baikal-Amur camp, A. I. Zaitsev, who had received permission
for release just days before the issue of directive 0165, was not freed.[165]
On five occasions from 1939 to 1946, authorities reviewed the case of
five workers from the swineherding state farm "Five-Year Plan," whose
land bordered the Fili aviation factory. Each time the review ended
differently. One reversed the sentence entirely, another lowered it to
the period already served, while another left the original sentence intact.
Because of this bureaucratic muddle, none of the swineherds left the
camps before the end of their initial sentences. Two finished the full
term, two died in the camps, and one was executed in 1937.[166] Nearly
all the petitions by victims of repression in Kuntsevo mentioned the
threats and physical coercion that made them sign falsified interrogation
protocols. Nonetheless, Rukodanov, fired from his position in the NKVD
and starting a job as head of the special section in Kuntsevo district's
commercial office, continued to insist in March 1941 that he "used no
coercion or physical measures against the accused. We used only their
words when we wrote interrogation protocols and they signed without

any pressure."[167] His testimony was one reason that the majority of sentences from 1937–38 went without review.

None of those from Kuntsevo's German colony were among those rehabilitated on the eve of the German invasion. Berta Feyerherd could not survive the harsh conditions of the Soviet north and died in the camps. Her younger sister was one of those aboard the infamous train of German political émigrés sent to Germany at the end of 1939—a gift to the Gestapo. She met a man on that train who would become her husband but who soon after perished on the Eastern Front. Authorities also exiled the wife of Alexander Feyerherd to Germany, but she committed suicide on the border with Poland. With the help of the Red Cross, relatives sent their orphaned son to Germany.[168]

Luise Hadrossek found herself in the naked steppe of Kazakhstan in Karlag near Karaganda. There, she wrote for help to KPD leader Wilhelm Pieck, whom she knew personally from her time working in the apparatus of the German party's Central Committee. Written on the letter are notes by the secretary of the Comintern's executive committee Georgi Dimitrov, who ordered the Russian translation of the text sent to the "corresponding organization"—the NKVD. No materials suggest that Luise Hadrossek's comrades in the KPD stood up for her.[169] The procuracy was the first to review her case, then the Moscow provincial NKVD. The result was a resolution signed by Merkulov on September 9, 1940. The deputy commissar refused to review the case because "Hadrossek is an extremely suspicious case of spying."[170] Despite being in a foreign country with poor command of the language, Hadrossek never lost her spirit even under the inhuman conditions of Stalinist labor camps. In her letter to Pieck, she wrote, "[I am employed] in construction work in the manufacture of bricks. . . . The work is satisfactory to me, although it is difficult. You feel yourself a valuable member of society after a long time [of preliminary detention in jail]. . . . In June I will receive my first earnings so I can buy a little something. The climate here is raw, windy and fickle. All that surrounds us is the bare steppe and hills. I suffer tremendously from the changes in the weather because of my heart disease but I need to bear it because nothing else is left."[171] Luise survived all of it—the silence of her former comrades, ten years in the camps, exile to a special settlement after the Gulag, and a battle for rehabilitation that she received only in 1961. Her son Heinz had taken the Russified name Gennadii Vasil'evich and only managed to find his mother through the Red Cross in February 1962. Luise received permission to move to East Germany in 1964 after submitting a formal request to the party Central Committee. However, authorities denied her son and his family permission to move with her.

The harsh conditions of the north, the hunger, and the backbreaking labor took their toll on prisoners. Of all Kuntsevo's victims who served sentences in labor camps, more than half did not survive. Statistics about their mortality rate, sometimes not recorded in the case files at all, reveal two peaks in 1939 and 1944. Those who survived remained in the camps until the end of the war. When they finished their sentences, many victims could not return to their homes even in cases when close relatives continued to live nearby. The district fell into the regime's infamous "restricted area"—a radius of one hundred kilometers around the capital where former convicts could not live. Returnees settled outside the zone along the Belorussian railway line out of Moscow, allowing them to visit relatives in the district secretly. Ekaterina Blinova, who received eight years in the labor camps for belonging to the Baptists, had seven sons who remained in Nemchinovka during her incarceration. By the time she left the camps in 1945, three of her sons had died on the Eastern Front. Nonetheless, authorities did not let the old woman live in her own home for another ten years. She was forced to visit her remaining sons secretly from Smolensk province.[172]

At the end of the 1940s, a new round of repression struck victims from the district. People who had finished forced labor sentences of eight or ten years and remained near the camps as free laborers faced renewed accusations for crimes they did not commit—often under the same statute as in 1938. Their case files have a second volume, filled with the same standard documents. Authorities made no exceptions for women or the elderly. Muralov, the former head of the district executive committee, finished his sentence and settled in Aleksandrov, just outside the restricted zone to the northeast of Moscow. In 1948 authorities sent him back to the camps and the second time he would not return.[173]

The mass rehabilitation of victims began only after the death of Stalin. Thin, greying people returned to Kuntsevo, which was now practically part of the growing capital, with documents confirming their release from the camps. To receive permission to live in the district, the victims had to return to the same building on Zagorskii Street that had set them on their tortuous path. If they were lucky, returnees had relatives in town willing to register them at their homes. The process of rehabilitation only began upon the petition of the victims or their relatives.

Military procuracy workers responsible for rehabilitation relied on materials from the investigations of Karetnikov and Kuznetsov. Information from the Kuntsevo officers' downfall were added to the files of their victims. In cases where witnesses still lived in the district, rehabilitation workers usually summoned them to comment on their testimony. Their comments made clear the practices of the mass operations. Cases of obfuscation and coercion came to the surface. Some witnesses claimed that they were semiliterate and had been unable to read the protocol they had signed. Others asserted that investigators had lied to them about the contents of the protocols or made them sign blank sheets. There were even cases where witnesses refused to recognize their signature on the protocol.

Despite these efforts, the rehabilitation and compensation of victims was far from complete. The relatives of those executed in the mass operations often received false information about their loved ones' deaths. Ekaterina Presnova heard no information about the fate of her children and other relatives for more than two decades. Only in the summer of 1958 did she dare to send the KGB a petition for information, written by neighbors for the illiterate women. Authorities lied, saying that the young Presnovs had all finished their long sentences in the Gulag but had died at different times after their release.[174] No one received compensation for the life and good health they lost in the half-hearted rehabilitation of the Khrushchev period. Victims' time in the camps appeared simply as any period of employment might in their labor records. Any grievances victims raised about confiscated property were only resolved in cases where NKVD workers had created a careful inventory. The typical amount returned was the equivalent of two or three months of pay. Victims who lost financial documents received no compensation whatsoever.

The last stage of rehabilitation only occurred in the 1990s. Relatives of those sentenced to execution finally learned the truth about their deaths. In 1993 authorities revealed the location where the majority of victims from Kuntsevo district died—Butovo firing range. Citizens have created a memorial there, and the Orthodox Church erected a sanctuary dedicated to Russian martyrs. It is worth noting that mass executions continued to occur at the firing range long after the mass operations.[175] After the fall of the USSR, victims and their relatives received the right to view their own case files. Countless tears fell at the offices of the Moscow province FSB and then at the reading room of the Russian State Archive. People saw everything: the last photographs of their loved ones, torture-wrenched confessions, and letters from incarceration. The files contained other materials that forced readers to brace themselves—the denunciations of neighbors, sometimes relatives, and the lies of witnesses who feared for their lives. Above all, they saw the remorselessness of the punitive machine that worried only about fulfilling orders from above. The case files contain only a fraction of the story about the mass operations. It seems hard to believe the assurances of today's FSB officials that other documents about the terror at the district level—office correspondence, orders from the provincial leadership, reports by ordinary perpetrators—were destroyed. The time will come when this evidence will also come to light.

Epilogue: New Kuntsevo Forgets the Past

Personal sentiment usually does not have a place in academic studies. In this case, however, the author will write a few words for himself. Archival findings from the cases of the terror's victims in Kuntsevo brought me no joy. On the contrary, I hoped that the river of human tragedy would run dry, that the stream of helpless victims would stop flowing in front of my eyes. When I opened investigation files, I looked into the faces of humans photographed days before execution and read the letters of loved ones who were completely unaware of their relatives' fate. My revulsion approached physical illness. There is no joy in calculating the magnitude of terror.

They say that time heals all wounds. Maybe for this reason it was fated that the Great Terror precede World War II. It was perhaps easy to forget the terror's victims in the midst of the death of tens of millions. After the Twentieth Party Congress and Khrushchev's "Secret Speech" in 1956, Soviet leaders undertook a halfhearted rehabilitation of victims but without punishment for their oppressors. Kuntsevo's collective farms felt Moscow's influence more and more strongly. The capital brought a new way of life to the district, a bulldozer destroying the recent past. At the bend of the Moscow River, where the villages Terekhovo and Mnevniki used to be, Soviet planners dreamed of building a giant theme park called Wonderland—the USSR's preemptive answer to the yet unbuilt Disneyland. The promises of the future seemed to excuse the twists and turns of Soviet history, a mentality encapsulated in the phrase, "the sacrifice of our victims was not in vain."

Bones found at the Butovo firing range.

Another four decades passed and time did its work. Those who might have told their children and grandchildren about the terror passed away. Many of them would never have broken the silence that they observed voluntarily or as part of agreements they signed upon release from prison or the camps. Ideological barriers have fallen away but historical amnesia in Russia has remained strong. This obliviousness feeds on the problems of today's Russia, where some only care about the unrestrained drive for wealth and many others struggle for subsistence. The territory of Kuntsevo district turned into the southwestern part of Russia's capital. The modest wooden houses of the district have given way to luxurious private residences and high-rise towers owned by "new Russians." A hint of the district's village past remains only in the titles of contemporary micro-districts—Matveevskoe, Davydkovo, Ochakovo, or Troparevo.

This book is a reminder of events that are difficult to imagine. The current residents and visitors in the district are executives and politicians living at villas at Barvikha or Nemchinovka. They are commuters who drive every day along the Amin'evo or Rublevka highways. The last survivors of the now exotic countryside live at Troitse-Lykovo. Commuters live in the bedroom communities of Strogino, Teplyi Stan, and Ramenki. Factory workers live in Solntsevo, Shchukinskaia, or

Memorial at the Butovo firing range. (from the author's collection)

Mnevniki. Children race down Krylatskoe's hills and play at Suvorov Park. All of these people should know that in 1937–38 these places were the scenes of pitiless state terror that took hundreds of lives. The only material traces of this past are the yellowing pages of archived case files and a few lines in post-Soviet martyrologies. When the victims were alive, there was no one who could stand up for them. Now they are dead but their shadows will cover us as long as the last of them is not remembered by name.

It is worth remembering another facet of the terror—that those who drove the machine of repression in the district were but a few people in an ordinary building on a quiet street in Kuntsevo. Young people in the clean uniforms of state security workers later swore that they were simply following orders. No, they agreed to perform the leading roles in a play written in the Kremlin and at Lubianka. Far from all of them read their lines with passion and inspiration. Some experienced disgust and raised timid protests. These objections also bear recollecting, but how can we remember these incidents without knowing the full story of the terror?

The most frightening aspect of Kuntsevo's experience of the terror is that it contained more of the typical than the unique. When we write about the Great Terror of 1937–38, we should not limit ourselves to the crimes of the central leaders in the party and the NKVD. The history of Kuntsevo's NKVD at 5 Zagorskii Street is just a small part of an immense tragedy that the country and its people endured at the apex of Stalinism. In the fairy tale of the snow queen, a kingdom fell into an age of darkness when a cursed mirror broke into myriad pieces, sowing frosty indifference among its people. As in this fable, the living fragments cast asunder in Soviet power's war against its people will weigh upon us until they are retrieved and placed into the light of day—to the very last person.

Notes

Foreword

1. Alexander Solzhenitsyn, The Gulag Archipelago, 1918-1956: An Experiment in Literary Investigation, vol. 1-2 (New York: Harper and Row, 1974), 68.

2. Robert Conquest, *The Great Terror: Stalin's Purge of the Thirties* (New York: Macmillan, 1968).

3. The population of the USSR in 1937 was 162 million and in 1953 was 187 million. The adult population was considerably smaller, approximately one hundred million people in 1937.

Introduction to the English-Language Edition

1. These are official figures calculated by the KGB, the Soviet secret police, under Khrushchev. Gosudarstvennyi arkhiv Rossiiskoi Federatsii (GARF), f. 9401, op. 1, d. 4157, ll. 201-5. (Artizov et al., *Reabilitatsiia—Kak eto bylo: Dokumenty TSK KPSS i drugie materialy*, vol. 1, *Mart 1953-fevral' 1956* [Moscow: Demokratiia, 2000], 77.)

2. *Agents of Terror* generally uses the term "Great Terror" as it captures the overlapping, interconnected whole of repression in this period. In contrast, "Great Purge" suggests repression against the party. *Ezhovshchina* places too much responsibility for the terror on Ezhov and too little on party leaders who monitored repression and NKVD operatives who implemented it.

3. Marc Jansen and Nikita Petrov, *Stalin's Loyal Executioner: People's Commissar Nikolai Ezhov, 1895-1940* (Stanford, CA: Hoover Institution Press, 2002), 70.

4. The outstanding book on perpetrators in the German case is Christopher Browning, *Ordinary Men: Reserve Police Battalion 101 and the Final Solution in Poland* (1992; repr., New York: Harper Collins, 1998).

5. Parts of the orders for the mass operations first appeared in public as "Rasstrel po raznariadke, ili kak eto delali bol'sheviki," *Trud*, June 4, 1992, 1–4.

6. Moshe Lewin, *The Making of the Soviet System: Essays in the Social History of Interwar Russia* (New York: Pantheon, 1985), 121–41; Lynne Viola, *Peasant Rebels under Stalin: Collectivization and the Culture of Peasant Resistance* (Oxford: Oxford University Press, 1996), 29–38.

7. Lynne Viola, *The Unknown Gulag: The Lost World of Stalin's Special Settlements* (Oxford: Oxford University Press, 2007).

8. David Shearer, *Policing Stalin's Socialism: Repression and Social Order in the Soviet Union, 1924–1953* (New Haven, CT: Yale University Press, 2009), 64–180.

9. A. I. Kokurin and N. V. Petrov, *Lubianka: VChK-OGPU-NKVD-NKGB-MGB-MVD-KGB, 1917–1960; Spravochnik* (Moscow: Demokratiia, 1997), 557.

10. Matthew Lenoe, *The Kirov Murder and Soviet History* (New Haven, CT: Yale University Press, 2010).

11. "Politicheskii arkhiv XX veka. Materialy Fevral'sko-martovskogo plenuma TsK VKP(b) 1937 goda," *Voprosy istorii*, no. 2 (1995): 16–17.

12. "Vzbesivshiikhsia sobak nado rasstrelit'!" *Pravda*, August 23, 1936.

13. Oleg Khlevniuk, *Khoziain: Stalin i utverzhdenie stalinskoi diktatury* (Moscow: Rosspen, 2010), 263–67.

14. David Shearer and Vladimir Khaustov, *Stalin and the Lubianka: A Documentary History of the Political Police and Security Organs in the Soviet Union, 1922–1953* (New Haven, CT: Yale University Press, 2014), 186–92.

15. Shearer, *Policing Stalin's Socialism*, 294.

16. On the military purge, see Roger Reese, *Red Commanders: A Social History of the Soviet Army Officer Corps, 1918–1991* (Lawrence: University Press of Kansas, 2005), 87–133. On the provincial purges, see J. Arch Getty, *Origins of the Great Purges: The Soviet Communist Party Reconsidered, 1933–1938* (Cambridge: Cambridge University Press, 1985).

17. I. V. Stalin, "O nedostatkakh partinnoi raboty i merakh likvidatsii trotskistskikh i inykh dvurushnikov," *Pravda*, March 29, 1937, 2.

18. Wendy Goldman, *Terror and Democracy in the Age of Stalin: The Social Dynamics of Repression* (Cambridge: Cambridge University Press, 2007).

19. Shearer, *Policing Stalin's Socialism*, 285–370.

20. J. Arch Getty and Oleg Naumov, *The Road to Terror: Stalin and the Self-Destruction of the Bolsheviks, 1932–1939* (New Haven, CT: Yale University Press, 1999), 501–12.

21. "Ob oshibkakh partiorganizatsii pri iskliuchenii kommunistov iz partii, o formal'no-biurokraticheskom otnoshenii k apelliatsiiam iskliuchennykh iz VKP(b) i o merakh po ustraneniiu etikh nedostatkov," *Pravda*, January 19, 1938, 1.

22. Shearer and Khaustov, *Stalin and the Lubianka*, 226–27 (citing Rossiiskii gosudarstvenni arkhiv sotsial'no-politicheskoi istorii [RGASPI], f. 558, op. 11, d. 58, l. 61).

23. Robert Conquest, *The Great Terror: Stalin's Purge of the 1930s* (New York: Macmillan, 1968).

24. Getty, *Origins of the Great Purges*, 6. See also Peter Solomon, "Local Political Power and Soviet Criminal Justice, 1922–1941," *Soviet Studies* 37, no. 3 (1985): 305–29; T .H. Rigby, "Was Stalin a Disloyal Patron?," *Soviet Studies* 38, no. 3 (1986): 311–24; Graeme Gill, *The Origins of the Stalinist Political System* (Cambridge: Cambridge University Press, 1990).

25. Perhaps the best estimate is by the human rights organization Memorial. It claims that in 1937–38 more than 1.7 million people were arrested and no fewer than 725,000 were executed. "Zhertvy politicheskogo terrora v SSSR," *Memorial*, http://lists.memo.ru/index.htm.

26. Michael Ellman, "Soviet Repression Statistics: Some Comments," *Europe-Asia Studies* 54, no. 7 (2002): 1151–72, estimates the total deaths at 1–1.2 million including those who died in the Gulag.

27. See Robert Conquest, "Victims of Stalinism: A Comment," *Europe-Asia Studies* 49, no. 7 (1997): 1317–19.

28. Shearer, *Policing Stalin's Socialism*; Paul Hagenloh, *Stalin's Police: Public Order and Mass Repression in the USSR, 1926–1941* (Washington, DC: Woodrow Wilson Center Press, 2009).

29. Oleg Khlevniuk, "The Reasons for the Great Terror: The Foreign-Political Aspect," in *Russia in the Age of Wars, 1914–1945*, ed. Silvio Pons and Andrea Romano (Florence: Feltrinelli, 2000), 159–73.

30. Felix Chuev, *Molotov Remembers: Inside Kremlin Politics* (Chicago, IL: Ivan R. Dee, 1991), 254.

31. William Chase, *Enemies within the Gates? The Comintern and the Stalinist Repression, 1934–1939* (New Haven, CT: Yale University Press, 2001), 196–97.

32. Shearer, *Policing Stalin's Socialism*, 299–302.

33. Rolf Binner and Marc Junge, *Kak terror stal bol'shim: Sekretnyi prikaz No. 00447 i tekhnologiia ego ispolneniia* (Moscow: Airo XX, 2003).

34. J. Arch Getty, "Pre-Election Fever: The Origins of the 1937 Mass Operations," in *The Anatomy of Terror: Political Violence under Stalin*, ed. James Harris (Oxford: Oxford University Press, 2013), 229–30. For an early version of this argument, see Getty, "'Excesses are not permitted': Mass Terror and Stalinist Governance in the Late 1930s," *Russian Review* 61, no. 1 (2002): 113–38.

35. For information about the limits as quotas see below, pages 43–44.

36. Ian Kershaw, "'Working Towards the Führer': Reflections on the Nature of the Hitler Dictatorship," *Contemporary European History* 2, no. 2 (1993): 103–18.

37. Jan Gross, *Revolution from Abroad: The Soviet Conquest of Poland's Western Ukraine and Western Belorussia*, expanded edition (Princeton, NJ: Princeton University Press, 2002), 120.

38. Sheila Fitzpatrick, "How the Mice Buried the Cat: Scenes from the Great Purges of 1937 in the Russian Provinces," *Russian Review* 52, no. 3 (1993): 299–320." Fitzpatrick, "A Response to Michael Ellman," *Europe-Asia Studies* 54, no. 3 (2002): 473–76.

39. See below, pages 58–61 and 82.

40. Goldman, *Terror and Democracy*; Goldman, *Inventing the Enemy: Denunciation and Terror in Stalin's Russia* (Cambridge: Cambridge University Press, 2011).

41. Gabor Rittersporn, *Anguish, Anger, and Folkways in Soviet Russia* (Pittsburgh, PA: University of Pittsburgh Press, 2014), 1–63.

42. Waitman Beorn, *Marching into Darkness: The Wehrmacht and the Holocaust in Belarus* (Cambridge, MA: Harvard University Press, 2014).

43. Wendy Goldman, "Comment: Twin Pyramids—Perpetrators and Victims," *Slavic Review* 72, no. 1 (2013): 24–27.

44. Lynne Viola, "The Question of the Perpetrator in Soviet History," *Slavic Review* 72, no. 1 (2013): 1–23.

45. Gerald Easter, *Reconstructing the State: Personal Networks and Elite Identity in Soviet Russia* (Cambridge: Cambridge University Press, 2000).

46. See below, pages 62–68.

47. See below, page 143.

48. Nanci Adler, "Reconciliation with—or Rehabilitation of—the Soviet Past?," *Memory Studies* 5, no. 3 (2012): 327–38.

Introduction: Why Kuntsevo? Setting the Stage

1. On collectivization, see Moshe Lewin, *Russian Peasants and Soviet Power: A Study of Collectivization* (1968; New York: Norton, 1975); Lynne Viola, *Peasant Rebels under Stalin: Collectivization and the Culture of Peasant Resistance* (Oxford: Oxford University Press, 1996).

2. The NKVD had many different functions. For the purposes of this book, the NKVD refers to its popular association with policing and state security functions. These functions were the responsibility at the national and provincial level of the NKVD's Chief Administration of State Security (GUGB), which inherited the state security functions of the United State Political Administration (OGPU). However, besides the GUGB, the NKVD was responsible for the criminal police, firefighters, internal security at railroads, and other functions. For information on the structures of Soviet policing agencies, see A. I. Kokurin and N. V. Petrov, *Lubianka: VChK-OGPU-NKVD-NKGB-MGB-MVD-KGB, 1917–1960; Spravochnik* (Moscow: Demokratiia, 1997).

3. Robert Conquest, *Inside Stalin's Secret Police: NKVD Politics, 1936–1939* (London: Macmillan, 1985); J. Arch Getty and Oleg Naumov, *The Road to Terror: Stalin and the Self-Destruction of the Bolsheviks, 1932–1939* (New Haven, CT: Yale University Press, 1999); David Shearer, *Policing Stalin's Socialism: Repression and Social Order in the Soviet Union, 1924–1953* (New Haven, CT: Yale University

Press, 2009); Paul Hagenloh, *Stalin's Police: Public Order and Mass Repression in the USSR, 1926–1941* (Washington, DC: Woodrow Wilson Center Press, 2009).

4. A. G. Tepliakov, "Personal i povsednevnost' Novosibirskogo UNKVD v 1936–1946," *Minuvshee: Istoricheskii al'manakh* 21 (1997): 240–93. An exception is Roberta Manning's work on the Great Terror in a region in Smolensk. However, as Manning acknowledges, the study examines the district party as the driving force in repression, while the archives of the police and NKVD were unavailable. Manning, "The Great Purges in a Rural District: Belyi Raion Revisited," *Russian Review* 16, nos. 2–4 (1989): 409–33.

5. Oleg Khlevniuk, *Politbiuro: Mekhanizmy politicheskoi vlasti v 1930-e gody* (Moscow: Rosspen, 1996), 188–90.

6. Moscow city's Commission for the Restoration of the Rights of Rehabilitated Victims of Political Repression funded the publication of an eight-volume commemorative series, *Butovskii poligon, 1937–1938 gody: Kniga Pamiati zhertv politicheskikh repressii*, ed. L. A. Golovkova (Moscow: Panorama, 1997–2007).

7. For example, Iu. M. Zolotov, ed., *Kniga pamiati zhertv politicheskikh repressii Ul'ianovskoi oblasti*, vols. 1–2 (Ul'ianovsk: Dom pechati, 1996).

8. An example is N. K. Bogdanov, the chief of the Luga district in Leningrad province, whose son wrote about him in Iu. N. Bogdanov, *Strogo sekretno: 30 let v OGPU-NKVD-MVD* (Moscow: Veche, 2002).

9. The biographies of NKVD leaders are available in N. V. Petrov and K. V. Skorkin, *Kto rukovodil NKVD, 1934–1941: Spravochnik* (Moscow: Zven'ia, 1999).

10. L. A. Golovkova, "Osobennosti prochteniia sledstvennykh del v svete kanonizatsii novomuchenikov i ispovednikov rossiiskikh," *Al'fa i omega*, no. 4 (2000): 214.

11. A. L. Litvin, "Sledstvennye dela sovetskikh politicheskikh protsessov kak istoricheskii istochnik," in *Problemy publikatsii dokumentov po istorii Rossii XX veka*, ed. A. D. Stepanskii (Moscow: Rosspen, 2001), 334.

12. For a debate about the use of Stalin-era secret police materials, see Jochen Hellbeck's criticism of the use of NKVD materials as popular opinion in "Speaking Out: Languages of Affirmation and Dissent in Stalinist Russia," *Kritika: Explorations in Russian and Eurasian History* 1, no. 1 (2000): 71–96; Sarah Davies and Hellbeck's exchange in "To the Editors," *Kritika: Explorations in Russian and Eurasian History* 1, no. 2 (2000): 437–40. Like Peter Holquist, "'Information Is the Alpha and Omega of Our Work': Bolshevik Surveillance in Its Pan-European Perspective," *Journal of Modern History* 69, no. 3 (1997): 415–50, Hellbeck argues that the secret police did not report the world as it was but as the regime wished it would be. Davies is more optimistic that NKVD and other official documents contain genuine popular opinion, although she acknowledged that these reports cannot reveal how representative reported opinions were.

13. Andrei Sakharov Center, *Martirolog zhertv politicheskikh repressii, rasstreliannykh i zakhoronennykh v Moskve i Moskovskoi oblasti v 1918–1953 gg.* Available online at http://www.sakharov-center.ru/asfcd/martirolog/.

14. Gosudarstvennyi arkhiv Rossiiskoi Federatsii (GARF), fond 10035, opis 1–2.

15. Barry McLoughlin, "'Vernichtung des Fremden': Der 'Große Terror' in der UdSSR 1937–38 im Lichte neuer russischer," *Jahrbuch für Historische Kommunismusforschung* 8 (2000–2001): 78.

Part I: Executors of Terror

1. Gosudarstvennyi arkhiv Rossiiskoi Federatsii (GARF), f. 10035, op. 1, d. p-7698.

2. GARF, f. 10035, op. 1, d. p-67528.

3. J. Arch Getty, *Origins of the Great Purges: The Soviet Communist Party Reconsidered, 1933–1938* (Cambridge: Cambridge University Press, 1985); Gerald Easter, *Reconstructing the State: Personal Networks and Elite Identity in Soviet Russia* (Cambridge: Cambridge University Press, 2000).

4. From the interrogation of Favorov, January 20, 1939. This archival file is now closed.

5. GARF, f. 10035, op. 1, d. p-7698.

6. GARF, f. 10035, op. 1, d. p-67528.

7. "Materialy fevral'sko-martovskogo plenuma TsK VKP(b) 1937 goda," *Voprosy istorii* (February 1995): 22–25.

8. N. V. Petrov and K. V. Skorkin, *Kto rukovodil NKVD, 1934–1941: Spravochnik* (Moscow: Zven'ia, 1999).

9. After former Siberian OGPU head Leonid Zakovskii became the head of the Moscow NKVD in January 1938, Siberian Chekists flocked to the province. A. G. Tepliakov, "Personal i povsednevnost' Novosibirskogo UNKVD v 1936–1946," *Minuvshee: Istoricheskii al'manakh* 21 (1997): 68–113. About professional clans among the leadership of the NKVD in Ukraine, see Sergei Belokon', "Massovyi terror kak metod gosudarstvennogo upravleniia v SSSR (1917–1941)" (PhD diss., Ukrainian National Academy of Sciences, Institute of Archeology and Source Criticism, Kiev, 1999).

10. GARF, f. 10035, op. 1, d. p-67528.

11. I. V. Stalin, *Sochineniia*, vol. 14, *Mart 1934–Iiun' 1941* (Moscow: Soiuz, 2007), 40.

12. Petrov and Skorkin, *Kto rukovodil NKVD*, 352, 390.

13. From the interrogation of Favorov, January 20, 1939.

14. From the interrogation of Karetnikov, February 5, 1939. This archival file is now closed.

15. GARF, f. 10035, op. 1, d. p-23556.

16. GARF, f. 10035, op. 1, d. p-67528.

17. On the reforms of the NKVD see Shearer, *Policing Stalin's Socialism: Repression and Social Order in the Soviet Union, 1924–1953* (New Haven, CT: Yale University Press, 2009), 94–129; Paul Hagenloh, *Stalin's Police: Public Order and*

Mass Repression in the USSR, 1926–1941 (Washington, DC: Woodrow Wilson Center Press, 2009).

18. Petrov and Skorkin, *Kto rukovodil NKVD*, 34–38.

19. GARF, f. 10035, op. 2, d. 23043. The group's leader, M. Iu. Ryvkin, was later sentenced to death by a troika.

20. Sergei Kudriavtsev, "Oglasheniiu ne podlezhit," in *Veroi i pravdoi: FSB, stranitsy istorii*, ed. Viachislav Pilipets (Iaroslavl': Niuans, 2001), 242.

21. Iu. N. Bogdanov, *Strogo sekretno: 30 let v OGPU-NKVD-MVD* (Moscow: Veche, 2002), 121.

22. See the case of German specialists working at a needle factory who were arrested along with their acquaintances in April 1937. GARF, f. 10035, op. 1, d. p-40549; op. 2, d. 27605; d. 27609; d. 28272; d. 28645. In this case, many of the indictments refer to NKVD Order 00439, which implied that all Germans working at armaments factories should be arrested. The order was also interpreted broadly. For example, a German woman, O. G. Rosenberg, fell victim to the order because her husband had worked at an armaments factory and had been arrested earlier. GARF, f. 10035, op. 1, d. p-57225.

23. See, for example, GARF, f. 10035, op. 1, d. p-25316.

24. GARF, f. 10035, op. 1, d. p-23556.

25. GARF, f. 10035, op. 1, d. p-50167.

26. GARF, f. 10035, op. 1, d. p-46577.

27. GARF, f. 10035, op. 1, d. p-26331 (Matveevskoe); d. p-61546 (Nemchinovka); d. p-47579 (Mnevniki); d. p-31299 (Orlovo). See similar groups of village investigations: d. p-52089 (Terekhovo); d. p-31357 (Dudkino); d. p-74993 (Troitse-Golenishchevo).

28. GARF, f. 10035, op. 1, d. p-26915.

29. GARF, f. 10035, op. 2, d. 23854; d. 23855; d. 23856; d. 23857.

30. Sheila Fitzpatrick, *Stalin's Peasants: Resistance and Survival in the Russian Village after Collectivization* (Oxford: Oxford University Press, 1996), 198.

31. GARF, f. 10035, op. 1, d. p-34643.

32. GARF, f. 10035, op. 1, d. p-61546.

33. Chernov built his home on a scenic plot of land where dekulakized peasant I. A. Tikhonov had lived. The latter was executed on September 14, 1937. GARF, f. 10035, op. 2, d. 21044.

34. Kudriavtsev, "Oglasheniiu ne podlezhit," 247.

35. "Repeated warnings were made that the troika would not take individual cases, that this was the result of poor investigation. One person could not carry out anti-Soviet activities. He had to have a group of sympathizers around him." Bogdanov, *Strogo sekretno*, 125.

36. Nikita Petrov and Arsenii Roginskii, "'Pol'skaia operatsiia' NKVD, 1937–1938 gg.," in *Repressii protiv poliakov i pol'skikh grazhdan*, ed. Aleksandr Gur'ianov (Moscow: Zven'ia, 1997), 28. The authors have in mind operatives in provincial administrations as well as district NKVD operatives.

37. GARF, f. 10035, op. 1, d. p-59771.

38. From the report of district operative G. N. Dikii from December 26, 1938. Tsyganov's testimony provided similar figures: "Kuznetsov and Karetnikov said: 'Today you must produce five interrogation records,' a physical impossibility." Both reports are available in GARF, f. 10035, op. 1, d. p-23556.

39. GARF, f. 10035, op. 1, d. p-20247.

40. GARF, f. 10035, op. 1, d. p-26549; d. p-37890; d. p-58333; d. p-32553; d. p-25639.

41. From the interrogation of Solov'ev from December 17, 1955. GARF, f. 10035, op. 1, d. p-26041.

42. From the report of Petushkov from December 28, 1938. Along with Petushkov, the office secretary and archivist at the registry bureau participated in the rewriting of protocols. *Butovskii poligon, 1937–1938 gody: Kniga Pamiati zhertv politicheskikh repressii* (Moscow: Panorama, 1997–2007), 5:353.

43. "Revolutionary legality" was the term given to the observance of legal norms in the early 1930s. See Peter Solomon, *Soviet Criminal Justice under Stalin* (Cambridge: Cambridge University Press, 1996), 158–61.

44. GARF, f. 10035, op. 1, d. p-47776.

45. From the petition of A.-R. P. Vizula. GARF, f. 10035, op. 1, d. p-51145.

46. From the petition of A. A. Gailesha from April 19, 1940. GARF, f. 10035, op. 1, d. p-51107.

47. Ibid.

48. GARF, f. 10035, op. 1, d. p-49562.

49. From the petition of Breivinskaia from February 26, 1939. GARF, f. 10035, op. 1, d. p-47883.

50. Petition of June 2, 1954, from exile, where Babushkina was sent after eight years in the Noril'sk camps. GARF, f. 10035, op. 1, d. p-21556.

51. GARF, f. 10035, op. 1, d. p-48708. Miklau was arrested on January 17, 1938.

52. GARF, f. 10035, op. 1, d. p-35561. During the NKVD's investigation of its abuses in December 1938, Rukodanov himself interrogated Konon-Kononov. When he asked for proof of beatings, the schoolteacher of thirty years modestly answered his all-too-recent interrogator: "There were no witnesses, and traces from the blows to my face of course did not last."

53. GARF, f. 10035, op. 1, d. p-48282.

54. Testimony of Sidiropulo, Ligeropulo, and Papakhristodulo about the methods of investigation during the review in 1939 of the case of the "Greek spy organization." GARF, f. 10035, op. 1, d. p-61785; d. p-48229; d. p-48224.

55. From the petition of A. P. Demidov from August 14, 1940. GARF, f. 10035, op. 1, d. p-25010.

56. From the petition of A. A. Gailesh from April 19, 1940. GARF, f. 10035, op. 1, d. p-51107.

57. From the petition of A.-R. P. Visul. GARF, f. 10035, op. 1, d. p-51145.

58. GARF, f. 10035, op. 1, d. p-25316.

59. GARF, f. 10035, op. 1, d. p-53465.

60. Galina Ivanova, "Kak i pochemu stal vozmozhen GULAG," in *GULAG: Ego stroiteli, obitateli i geroi*, ed. I. V. Dobrovolskii (Moscow: Mezhdunarodnoe obshchestvo prav cheloveka, 1998), 16.

61. On other regions, see Iu. N. Balakina, ed., *Rekviem: Knigi pamiati zhertv politicheskikh repressii na Orlovshchine* (Orel, 1994), 1:53.

62. The protocols listed a falsified place of work for Shchadenko. GARF, f. 10035, op. 1, d. p-20247.

63. GARF, f. 10035, op. 1, d. p-50029.

64. GARF, f. 10035, op. 1, d. p-20247.

65. GARF, f. 10035, op. 1, d. p-7934.

66. Rukodanov wrote, "We sought witnesses through the police and then left them at the district NKVD office with the officers leading an investigation. This is perhaps what happened with the witness Kozhevnikov. He was in all likelihood handed over to me by one of the police officers and I questioned him reflexively, without establishing his identity." GARF, f. 10035, op. 1, d. p-7934.

67. GARF, f. 10035, op. 1, d. p-48283.

68. GARF, f. 10035, op. 1, d. p-18431.

69. GARF, f. 10035, op. 1, d. p-52533.

70. GARF, f. 10035, op. 1, d. p-47776.

71. GARF, f. 10035, op. 2, d. 27651.

72. GARF, f. 10035, op. 1, d. p-24551.

73. The file contains an interesting document—a certification that Meier said during his interrogation, "I hate the organs [of state security] because those in the NKVD are not men but animals." Whether this outburst was a reaction to beatings and humiliation is not clear. GARF, f. 10035, op. 2, d. 28164.

74. GARF, f. 10035, op. 1, d. p-49816 through d. p-49828.

75. See Alexander Weissberg-Cybulski, *Im Verhör: Überlebender der stalinistischen Säuberungen berichtet* (Vienna: Europaverlag, 1993), 183.

76. From the report of Tsyganov of December 26, 1938. GARF, f. 10035, op. 1, d. p-23556.

77. Petrov and Roginskii, "'Pol'skaia operatsiia' NKVD," 28.

78. GARF, f. 10035, op. 1, d. p-52696. Capitalized in the original.

79. See "Govoriat byvshie palachi" in I. Osipova, comp., *"Khotelos' by vsekh poimenno nazvat'": Po materialam sledstvennykh del i lagernykh otchetov GULAGa* (Moscow: Mir i Progress, 1993), 11–12.

80. In the "Polish operation" roughly 150,000 people faced repression. In the "German operation" over 60,000 were repressed. See Petrov and Roginskii, "'Pol'skaia operatsiia' NKVD," 40. Nikita Okhotin and Arsenii Roginskii, "Iz istorii 'nemetskoi operatsii' NKVD 1937–1938 gg.," in *Nakazannyi narod: Po materialam konferentsii "Repressii protiv rossiiskikh nemtsev v Sovetskom Soiuze v kontekste sovetskoi natsional'noi politiki,"* ed. I. L. Shcherbakova (Moscow: Zven'ia, 1999), 63.

81. From the testimony of operative of the district office N. D. Petrov. GARF, f. 10035, op. 1, d. p-59771.

82. Bogdanov, *Strogo sekretno*, 123.

83. From the testimony of Kuznetsov from February 3, 1939. GARF, f. 10035, op. 1, d. p-23556.

84. Il'in sent his report on May 8, 1938. On May 13, Karutskii killed himself. GARF, f. 10035, op. 1, d. p-20635.

85. From Karetnikov's testimony of February 9, 1939. GARF, f. 10035, op. 1, d. p-23556.

86. From the report of Dikii on December 26, 1938. GARF, f. 10035, op. 1, d. p-23556.

87. From the report of Tsyganov of December 26, 1938. GARF, f. 10035, op. 1, d. p-23556.

88. From the report of Rukodanov of December 1938. GARF, f. 10035, op. 1, d. p-41234. Similar demands ("they gave a quota of 5–6 persons per work day") are found in other sources. See *Butovskii poligon*, 3:348.

89. Solov'ev wrote, "In order to realize the control figures of no fewer than 45–50 cases in a week, Karetnikov created an investigative team from people who had no connection to operative work (the head of the registry bureau, the head of the town fire department Zhivov, the district inspector). He took typists from almost all the enterprises of Kuntsevo district to type interrogation protocols and indictments." From the report of Solov'ev of December 29, 1938. GARF, f. 10035, op. 1, d. p-60184.

90. Balakina, *Rekviem*, 1:54.

91. GARF, f. 10035, op. 1, d. p-28856.

92. GARF, f. 10035, op. 1, d. p-59678.

93. From the testimony of Kuznetsov from February 3, 1939. GARF, f. 10035, op. 1, d. p-23556.

94. GARF, 10035, op. 1, d. p-50179.

95. For example, a foreign name like Mariia Ottovna Alkhimova. GARF, f. 10035, op. 1, d. p-21922.

96. In the indictment, the word "espionage" in the section characterizing the group was underlined with pen. GARF, f. 10035, op. 1, d. p-46735.

97. GARF, f. 10035, op. 2, d. 27491.

98. Ben Eklof, *Russian Peasant Schools: Officialdom, Village Culture, and Popular Pedagogy, 1861–1914* (Berkeley: University of California Press, 1986), 243.

99. GARF, f. 10035, op. 1, d. p-25714.

100. Ibid.

101. "The case of Muralov and others at first was one volume, a single general counterrevolutionary group, but when the indictment was written and sent for confirmation to the leadership of the NKVD of Moscow province, the case was proposed for separation into different cases." From the testimony of Rukodanov of June 8, 1940. GARF, f. 10035, op. 1, d. p-22114.

102. GARF, f. 10035, op. 1, d. p-27480.

103. GARF, f. 10035, op. 1, d. p-41234.

104. For dates and sentences from Kuntsevo's investigations, see the list of victims in the Russian version of this book, A. Iu. Vatlin, *Terror raionnogo masshtaba: "Massovye operatsii" NKVD v Kuntsevskom raione Moskovskoi oblasti 1938–1938 gg.* (Moscow: Rosspen, 2004), 216–47.

105. A representative work of the "traditionalist" perspective is Robert Conquest, *The Great Terror: Stalin's Purge of the 1930s* (New York: Macmillan, 1968).

106. Igal Halfin, *Stalinist Confessions: Messianism and Terror at the Leningrad Communist University* (Pittsburgh, PA: University of Pittsburgh Press, 2009); Gabor Rittersporn, *Anguish, Anger, and Folkways in Soviet Russia* (Pittsburgh, PA: University of Pittsburgh Press, 2014).

107. Getty, *Origins of the Great Purges* is the classic "revisionist" treatment of intraparty dynamics in the terror. Wendy Goldman, *Terror and Democracy in the Age of Stalin: The Social Dynamics of Repression* (Cambridge: Cambridge University Press, 2007).

108. See Bogdanov, *Strogo sekretno*, 115.

109. For example, in January 1937 the district office received a denunciation regarding a former member of the Socialist Party of the United States, M. M. Anikovich, who worked at Factory 95. It asserted that Anikovich was meeting with foreigners, received money from abroad, and had a few years earlier been at the dacha of Georgii Piatakov, one of the major figures accused in the second Moscow show trial. Further inspection did not confirm these accusations, but Anikovich was arrested nonetheless in February 1938. GARF, f. 10035, op. 1, d. p-27841.

110. Copy of the district party committee's resolution from April 5, 1937. GARF, f. 10035, op. 1, d. p-26944.

111. GARF, f. 10035, op. 2, d. 18853.

112. Manning, "The Great Purges in a Rural District: Belyi Raion Revisited," *Russian Review* 16, nos. 2–4 (1989): 409–33. This dichotomy of sources is true of Wendy Goldman's work on factory party committees. See Goldman, *Terror and Democracy.*

113. It is worth noting that materials from the party organization of Belskii region of Smolensk province also were not saved. This absence may be the consequence of the devastation that repression inflicted on the district party organization in the previous stage of repression. Manning, "The Great Purges," 66.

114. Otdel khraneniia dokumentov obshchestvenno-politicheskoi istorii Moskvy (OKhDOPIM), f. 113, op. 1, d. 52, l. 117.

115. The only accessible records of the Kuntsevo district party bureau are for January–March 1936. Among those victims of the mass operations excluded from the party during this period were V. I. Dvoretskii, A. A. Garkovik, and R. F. Karpilo.

116. OKhDOPIM, f. 113, op. 1, d. 52, ll. 90–91.

117. GARF, f. 10035, op. 1, d. p-25316, t. 1.

118. GARF, f. 10035, op. 1, d. p-26912.

119. Ibid.

120. GARF, f. 10035, op. 1, d. p-23240. See the second half of this book for an in-depth examination of the case of Muralov.

121. GARF, f. 10035, op. 1, d. p-31797.

122. "In March 1938, by request of the former head of the district office of the NKVD Kuznetsov, the city committee [of the party] discussed the case of Kokhov in connection with arrestee Muralov's assertion that Kokhov was supposedly in a hostile counterrevolutionary group. Because doubts were raised about this accusation, Kuznetsov insisted that Kokhov was already fully exposed and that the order for his arrest had already been received. Considering this fact, the bureau of the city committee accepted the resolution to expel Kokhov from the party." GARF, f. 10035, op. 1, d. p-22114.

123. Badaev and Kokhov wrote about their arrests in petitions from labor camps. GARF, f. 10035, op. 1, d. p-29451; d. p-22114.

124. GARF, f. 10035, op. 1, d. p-46577.

125. From the meeting of the party committee at Factory 46 on March 27, 1938: "Kokhanskaia displays open mistrust of the policies of the party, she sympathizes with enemies and spies and worries about whether they will be uprooted, including at our factory." "Seeing that they are unmasking enemies, she claims that supposedly in the Soviet Union they are arresting all foreigners." GARF, f. 10035, op. 1, d. p-33920.

126. GARF, f. 10035, op. 2, d. 42798.

127. OKhDOPIM, f. 113, op. 1, d. 59b, l. 271.

128. OKhDOPIM f. 113, op. 1, d. 57, l. 58.

129. From the testimony of Karetnikov from February 7, 1939. This archival file is now closed.

130. OKhDOPIM, f. 113, op. 1, d. 57, l. 40.

131. GARF, f. 10035, op. 1, d. p-46575.

132. From the case file for Gorbul'skii. GARF, f. 10035, op. 1, d. p-22682.

133. From the summary of the case file for V. I. Khvatov. GARF, f. 10035, op. 1, d. p-64568.

134. See Roberta Manning, "The Great Purges," 68. It is unclear, however, whether Vinogradov was arrested, fired from the NKVD, or given a promotion.

135. Elena Osokina, *Our Daily Bread: Socialist Distribution and the Art of Survival in Stalin's Russia, 1927–1941* (Armonk, NY: M. E. Sharpe, 2001).

136. For more on Soviet automobile culture, see Lewis Siegelbaum, *Cars for Comrades: The Life of the Soviet Automobile* (Ithaca, NY: Cornell University Press, 2008).

137. GARF, f. 10035, op. 1, d. p-25777.

138. GARF, f. 10035, op. 1, d. p-47575.

139. Ibid.

140. "I took fruits and vegetables from state farm [sovkhoz] 22 without paying. For example, in 1937 I took three boxes of apples and forty-five kilos of fruits from that sovkhoz for Radzivilovskii and Iakubovich. Iakubovich called on the telephone several times and demanded deliveries of fruits, vegetables, and so on." From the testimony of I. D. Berg. GARF, f. 10035, op. 1, d. p-67528.

141. Berg's investigation contains the testimony of a doctor, a secret informer, who claimed that he needed to carry a bottle of alcohol to meetings with agents. Ibid.

142. From the report of agent Iosifov to the head of the fourth department of the Moscow provincial NKVD Petrovskii from July 20, 1938. This archival file is now closed.

143. GARF, f. 10035, op. 1, d. p-39083.

144. GARF, f. 10035, op. 1, d. p-26549.

145. Manning, "The Great Purges," 99.

146. GARF, f. 10035, op. 1, d. p-7698.

147. See Iu. M. Zolotov, ed., *Kniga pamiati zhertv politicheskikh repressii Ul'ianovskoi oblasti* (Ul'ianovsk: Dom pechati, 1996), 1:876.

148. From the inquiry in the archive-investigatory file of V. I. Khvatov. GARF, f. 10035, op. 1, d. p-64568.

149. From the interrogation of Karetnikov from February 9, 1939. GARF, f. 10035, op. 1, d. p-23556.

150. GARF, f. 10035, op. 1, d. p-7698.

151. GARF, f. 10035, op. 1, d. p-4961.

152. GARF, f. 10035, op. 1, d. p-25482.

153. From the testimony of Karetnikov, February 7, 1939.

154. GARF, f. 10035, op. 1, d. p-4961.

155. Conditions for guards in the Gulag, though never as bad as those of prisoners, were not enviable. Work in the labor camp system was an undesirable assignment. See Galina Ivanova, *Labor Camp Socialism: The Gulag in the Soviet Totalitarian System* (Armonk, NY: M. E. Sharpe, 2000); Alan Barenberg, *Gulag Town, Company Town: Forced Labor and Its Legacy in Vorkuta* (New Haven, CT: Yale University Press, 2014); Fyodor Vasilevich Mochulsky, *Gulag Boss: A Soviet Memoir*, ed. and trans. Deborah Kaple (Oxford: Oxford University Press, 2011).

156. "Titel'man called me in for questioning and asked for testimony not about counterrevolutionary activity but rather convinced me to confess to abuses [of authority]. I said that I stole money, that I was a thief and not a counterrevolutionary. I illegally bought furniture for Zakovskii and so on. I categorically denied my guilt in appropriation of money, but Titel'man said that if you confess to that, you will go to work in the camps, but otherwise they would make you into a Trotskyist and then you would answer for a counterrevolutionary conspiracy." From the interrogation of Berg from December 29, 1938. GARF, f. 10035, op. 1, d. p-67528. Titel'man recognized the delicacy of the

situation and tried to limit punishments, knowing that his prisoner could someday be free or even back in the ranks of the NKVD. Later he himself was arrested for "participation in a counterrevolutionary conspiracy."

157. On a carbon copy of the denunciation Tsesarskii made a note dated August 28: "Petrovskii should check and report." This archival file is now closed.

158. From the testimony of Karetnikov, February 5, 1939.

159. GARF, f. 10035, op. 1, d. p-7698.

160. Vlasov's testimony is in GARF, f. 10035, op. 1, d. p-40802.

161. On the report, Zhuralev wrote, "Use Gubochkin for the investigation. Send two operatives to help. Report on results. December 8." This archival file is now closed.

162. See *Volia: Zhurnal uznikov totalitarnykh system*, nos. 1–7 (1993–1997); *Butovskii poligon*, vols. 1–4. Similar documents are found frequently in martyrologies of the victims of mass repression.

163. From the report of Dikii of December 26, 1938. GARF, f. 10035, op. 1, d. p-23556.

164. From the report of Tsyganov on December 26, 1938. GARF, f. 10035, op. 1, d. p-23556.

165. GARF, f. 10035, op. 1, d. p-23240.

166. From the report of police sergeant Boriskov, the head of the passport office, on December 26, 1938. This archival file is now closed.

167. The copy of the letter is contained in a now-closed archival file.

168. GARF, f. 10035, op. 1, d. p-7698.

169. GARF, f. 10035, op. 2, d. 30515.

170. Resolution on the handling of the list of forty-nine people connected with the case organized and authorized by Karetnikov. GARF, f. 10035, op. 1, d. p-33920.

171. Explanation of Leonov to the investigatory section of the Moscow provincial NKVD, May 1, 1940. GARF, f. 10035, op. 1, d. p-25482.

172. GARF, f. 10035, op. 1, d. p-53465.

173. GARF, f. 10035, op. 1, d. p-25714.

174. GARF, f. 10035, op. 1, d. p-23240.

175. GARF, f. 10035, op. 1, d. p-61785.

176. GARF, f. 10035, op. 1, d. p-26041.

177. GARF, f. 10035, op. 1, d. p-23556.

178. In Serpukhov district NKVD, a commission from the provincial administration concluded that there had been "a violation of socialist legality" in the previous period. The findings of the committee led to the prosecution of the head of the district NKVD, M. I. Veselov, and the operative V. I. Khvatov. GARF, f. 10035, op. 1, p-67528.

179. See, for example, Zolotov, *Kniga pamiati*, 1:914. Balakina, *Rekviem*, 50–56.

180. The head of Mtsenskii district (Orlov province) NKVD, M. F. Pikalov, received seven years in the camps in November 1939 but received a pardon and had his conviction record wiped clean in December 1941. Balakina, *Rekviem*, 54–55.

181. See Petrov and Skorkin, *Kto rukovodil NKVD*, 491–502.

182. March 28, 1940, interrogation of Iu. S. Drobik, later released during the investigation. GARF, f. 10035, op. 1, d. p-51556.

183. V. M. Kriukov, the director of the USSR's Academy of Architecture, whose investigation was carried out by the fifth department of the Moscow province NKVD, wrote in his petition: "They beat me at night for more than two weeks, not letting me sleep during the day. I was beaten by investigators Bochkov, Omel'chenko, Prishchepa, and others using their fists, feet, belts with buckles, rubber clubs, and rope. They broke two marble paper weights on my shoulders, a chair on my side. They beat my head with a big rolling pin and the leg of a chair. Then Bochkov said, 'We'll beat you until you sign everything . . . We won't beat you to death, but you'll be a cripple crawling on all fours.'" GARF, f. 10035, op. 1, d. p-60179.

184. From the February 9, 1939, interrogation of Karetnikov.

185. For a copy of the petition, see Zolotov, *Kniga pamiati*, 1:896.

186. *Kniga pamiati zhertv politicheskikh repressii Nizhegorodskoi oblasti* (Nizhnii Novgorod: Nizhegorodskii pechatnik, 2001), 2:96–97.

187. From the testimony of an operative in that district, N. D. Petrov. GARF, f. 10035, op. 1, d. p-59771.

188. From the investigation file of V. I. Khvatov. GARF, f. 10035, op. 1, d. p-64568.

189. V. Kudriavtsev and A. Trusov, *Politicheskaia iustitsiia v SSSR* (Moscow: Iuridicheskii tsentr press, 2000), 88.

190. Petrov and Skorkin, *Kto rukovodil NKVD*, 501.

191. From the petition of P. K. Filikhina. Zolotov, *Kniga pamiati*, 1:897.

192. GARF, f. 10035, op. 1, d. p-67528.

193. Testimony from October 4, 1956. GARF, f. 10035, op. 1, d. p-61785. The procurator of Moscow province in October 1957 submitted a resolution to the Moscow provincial party committee to bring Rukodanov to justice for his actions.

Part II: Patterns of Victimization

1. Gosudarstvennyi arkhiv Rossiiskoi Federatsii (GARF), f. 10035, op. 1, d. p-25316, t. 1.

2. GARF, f. 10035, op. 1, d. p-25316.

3. GARF, f. 10035, op. 1, d. p-23240.

4. Fitzpatrick, *Stalin's Peasants: Resistance and Survival in the Russian Village after Collectivization* (Oxford: Oxford University Press, 1996), 14–15.

5. See the case of S. M. Zaitsev. GARF, f. 10035, op. 1, d. p-7934.

6. The true story of Pavlik's denunciation has come under question based on FSB files. See Catriona Kelly, *Comrade Pavlik: The Rise and Fall of a Soviet Boy Hero* (London: Granta, 2005). To protect the identity of the letter's writer, the author has chosen to withhold the name and archival file of the young person.

7. GARF, f. 10035, op. 2, d. 20955.

8. GARF, f. 10035, op. 1, d. p-26195.

9. See the petition of the mother of the arrestee S. G. Zudin, who wrote that she was sure that a neighbor at the dacha orchestrated the arrest because he undertook illegal handicraft manufacturing at home and wanted to rid himself of witnesses. GARF, f. 10035, op. 1, d. p-28856.

10. GARF, f. 10035, op. 1, d. p-63233, l. 36.

11. In the indictment of Avramovich, the uncharacteristic phrase appeared: "Uses the Stalin constitution for the defense of kulaks." GARF, f. 10035, op. 1, d. p-48234.

12. GARF, f. 10035, op. 1, d. p-25316, l. 42.

13. Ibid.

14. GARF, f. 10035, op. 1, d. p-39982.

15. GARF, f. 10035, op. 1, d. p-26549.

16. A. Iu. Vatlin, *Terror raionnogo masshtaba: "Massovye operatsii" NKVD v Kuntsevskom raione Moskovskoi oblasti 1937–1938 gg.* (Moscow: Rosspen, 2004), 216–47.

17. GARF, f. 10035, op. 1, d. p-40549.

18. GARF, f. 10035, op. 2, d. 20713.

19. GARF, f. 10035, op. 1, d. p-48708.

20. GARF, f. 10035, op. 1, d. p-52301.

21. For the purposes of protecting the identity of an informant, the author has chosen to withhold the name and archival file of Snow White.

22. Lynne Viola, *The Unknown Gulag: The Lost World of Stalin's Special Settlements* (Oxford: Oxford University Press, 2007).

23. Operational report from 1934. GARF, f. 10035, op. 1, d. p-70909.

24. See Seth Bernstein, "Class Dismissed? New Elites and Old Enemies among the 'Best' Socialist Youth in the Komsomol, 1934–1941," *Russian Review* 74, no. 1 (2015): 97–116.

25. Although police found Pechnikov with the weapon, he received the lightest sentence of the members of the SR group, three years of exile. GARF, f. 10035, op. 1, d. p-55451.

26. GARF, f. 10035, op. 1, d. p-23962.

27. GARF, f. 10035, op. 1, d. p-56812.

28. GARF, f. 10035, op. 2, d. 20952.

29. GARF. f. 10035, op. 2, d. 20950.

30. GARF, f. 10035, op. 2, d. 50478.

31. GARF, f. 10035, op. 1, d. p-61546.

32. GARF, f. 10035, op. 2, d. 22941.

33. GARF, f. 10035, op. 2, d. 18853; d. 19769; d. 20953.

34. GARF, f. 10035, op. 2, d. 20759; d. 27727.

35. GARF, f. 10035, op. 1, d. p-55451.

36. GARF, f. 10035, op. 1, d. p-60184.

37. GARF, f. 10035, op. 1, d. p-63256.

38. O.A. Del', *Ot illiuzii k tragedii: Nemetskie emigranty v SSSR v 30-e gody* (Moscow: Noies Leben, 1997), 82–91.

39. GARF, f. 10035, op. 1, d. p-61718.

40. GARF, f. 10035, op. 2, d. 14000.

41. GARF, f. 10035, op. 2, d. 28174.

42. The indictment of M. Iu. Ryvkin included a customs declaration for a care package containing food from his son, a British citizen living in London. GARF, f. 10035, op. 2, d. 23043.

43. GARF, f. 10035, op. 2, d. 18543.

44. GARF, f. 10035, op. 1, d. p-72809; op. 2, d. 24149.

45. GARF, f. 10035, op. 1, d. p-46575.

46. GARF, f. 10035, op. 1, d. p-34643.

47. GARF, f. 10035, op. 1, d. p-26301.

48. Irina Shcherbakova, "'Vyskazyval rezkuiu zlobu'," *Nezavisimaia gazeta*, December 4, 1991, 5.

49. GARF, f. 10035, op. 1, d. p-60092; d. p-70435; op. 2, d. 42809; d. 14475; d. 17204.

50. GARF, f. 10035, op. 2, d. 19766.

51. GARF, f. 10035, op. 1, d. p-47738.

52. GARF, f. 10035, op. 2, d. 24746.

53. From the case of P. N. Fateev, exiled during collectivization. GARF, f. 10035, op. 1, d. p-52089.

54. Fitzpatrick, *Stalin's Peasants*, 293–94.

55. GARF, f. 10035, op. 1, d. p-74993.

56. GARF, f. 10035, op. 1, d. p-28856.

57. From the indictment of V. T. Davydov. GARF, f. 10035, op. 1, d. p-31802.

58. From the case of F. F. Abrosimov, an officer of the imperial army. GARF, f. 10035, op. 1, d. p-24913, l. 20.

59. GARF, f. 10035, op. 1, d. p-60092.

60. Statement of S. P. Karetnikov. GARF, f. 10035, op. 1, d. p-28856.

61. GARF, f. 10035, op. 1, d. p-28856, l. 10.

62. GARF, f. 10035, op. 2, d. 18543.

63. On the "Doctor's Plot" and repression against Soviet Jews, see Jonathan Brent and Vladimir Naumov, *Stalin's Last Crime: The Plot against the Jewish Doctors, 1948–1953* (New Haven, CT: Yale University Press, 2003).

64. GARF, f. 10035, op. 1, d. p-18431.

65. GARF, f. 10035, op. 1, d. p-59678.

66. GARF, f. 10035, op. 2, d. 19265.

67. Statements from the testimony of witnesses from 1958 who later refused to acknowledge them. GARF, f. 10035, op. 1, d. p-51292.

68. J. Arch Getty, "State and Society under Stalin: Constitutions and Elections in the 1930s," *Slavic Review* 50, no. 1 (Spring 1991): 18–35.

69. The murder was the work of a lone gunman who broke into Kirov's office, but popular accounts claim that Stalin himself orchestrated the murder to rid himself of a potential rival. Recent archival evidence has dispelled the story of Stalin's involvement. On the Kirov assassination and its future interpretations, see Matthew Lenoe, *The Kirov Murder and Soviet History* (New Haven, CT: Yale University Press, 2010).

70. GARF, f. 10035, op. 1, d. p-60184.

71. *Butovskii poligon, 1937–1938 gody: Kniga Pamiati zhertv politicheskikh repressii* (Moscow: Panorama, 1997–2007), 3:345–46.

72. GARF, f. 10035, op. 1, d. p-23962.

73. On peasant women's resistance, see Lynne Viola, "Bab'i Bunty and Peasant Women's Protest during Collectivization," *Russian Review* 45, no. 1 (1986): 23–42.

74. GARF, f. 10035, op. 1, d. p-34643.

75. GARF, f. 10035, op. 1, d. p-32338.

76. GARF, f. 10035, op. 1, d. p-49320.

77. GARF, f. 10035, op. 1, d. p-49330.

78. GARF, f. 10035, op. 1, d. p-32338.

79. GARF, f. 10035, op. 1, d. p-32338. See also, *Butovskii poligon*, 5:350.

80. GARF, f. 10035, op. 1, d. p-49320. See also, *Butovskii poligon*, 5:349.

81. GARF, f. 10035, op. 1, d. p-49298.

82. Unless otherwise cited, information for this section comes from Muralov's investigation file, GARF, f. 10035, op. 1, d. p-25777.

83. See, for example, the head of Mnevniki village council's investigation. GARF, f. 10035, op. 1, d. p-56832.

84. GARF, f. 10035, op. 1, d. p-44002.

85. GARF, f. 10035, op. 2, d. p-7698.

86. For the investigations of the six Presnovs, see GARF, f. 10035, op. 1, d. p-60950; d. p-60951; d. p-60952; d. p-60958; d. p-60959; d. p-60960.

87. GARF. f. 10035, op. 1, d. p-60958; d. p-60959.

88. GARF, f. 10035, op. 2, d. 23854; d. 23855; d. 23856; d. 23857.

89. GARF, f. 10035, op. 1, d. p-24984; d. p-26041; d. p-29143.

90. GARF, f. 10035, op. 1, d. p-50029.

91. GARF, f. 10035, op. 1, d. p-63240.

92. GARF, f. 10035, op. 1, d. p-20394; d. p-22247.

93. GARF, f. 10035, op. 1, d. p-63233.

94. GARF, f. 10035, op. 1, d. p-8454; d. p-13778; d. p-40663; d. p-40664.

95. Institut für Geschichte der Arbeiterbewegung, *In den Fangen des NKWD: Deutsche Opfer des stalinistischen Terrors in der UdSSR* (Berlin: Dietz Verlag, 1991).

96. See Wilhelm's Comintern file, Rossiiskii gosudarstvennyi arkhiv sotsial'no-politicheskoi istorii (RGASPI), f. 495, op. 205, d. 4660.

97. "Pravdivost' i chestnost'," *Bol'shevik*, June 8, 1937, 1.

98. GARF, f. 10035, op. 1, d. p-65924.

99. Ibid.

100. GARF, f. 10035, op. 2, d. 29552; d. 23689; d. 29549; d. 27651.

101. GARF, f. 10035, op. 1, d. p-34147.

102. GARF, f. 10035, op. 2, d. 28645.

103. RGASPI, f. 495, op. 205, d. 4644; d. 4646.

104. GARF, f. 10035, op. 1, d. p-40549; op. 2, d. 27609; d. 28272.

105. GARF, f. 10035, op. 2, d. 27606.

106. GARF, f. 10035, op. 2, d. 28164.

107. GARF, f. 10035, op. 2, d. 27605; d. 28021.

108. RGASPI, f. 495, op. 205, d. 4651; d. 4652.

109. R. Muller, "'Wir kommen alle dran': Saurberungen unter den deutschen Politemigranten in der Sowjetunion (1934-1938)," in *Terror: Stalinistische Parteisäuberungen 1936-1953*, ed. Hermann Weber and Ulrich Mählert (Paderborn: Schöningh, 1998), 125.

110. Lorsheid was arrested in February 1938 and sentenced to eight years of incarceration. See M. Stark, *"Ich muss sagen, wie es war": Deutsche Frauen des GULag* (Berlin: Metropol, 1999), 256–57.

111. GARF, f. 10035, op. 1, d. p-41532.

112. RGASPI, f. 495, op. 7, d. 24, l. 9.

113. A. Kuusinen, *Gospod' nizvergaet svoikh angelov: Vospominaniia 1919-1965* (Petrozavodsk: Kareliia, 1991), 46.

114. RGASPI, f. 495, op. 205, d. 11788, l. 25.

115. GARF, f. 10035, op. 1, d. 47576.

116. GARF, f. 10035, op. 1, d. p-23556.

117. RGASPI, f. 495, op. 205, d. 3163, l. 1.

118. Rossiiskii gosudarstvennyi voennyi arkhiv, f. 772, op. 1, d. 10, l. 16; d. 19, l. 101.

119. GARF, f. 10035, op. 1, d. p-23478; d. p-22203; op. 2, d. 30515.

120. V. A. Tikhonov et al., *Rasstrel'nye spiski* (Moscow: Memorial, 1993), 1:172.

121. L. S. Eremina and A. B. Roginskii, eds., *Rasstrel'nye spiski, Moskva, 1937-1941: "Kommunarka," Butovo; Kniga pamiati zhertv politicheskikh represii* (Moscow: Memorial, 2000), 416.

122. GARF, f. 10035, op. 2, d. 24455.

123. GARF, f. 10035, op. 1, d. p-23478.

124. GARF, f. 10035, op. 1, d. p-21602; d. p-26061; d. p-23478; d. p-21561; d. p-22180; d. p-23556; op. 2, d. 30515.

125. GARF, f. 10035, op. 1, d. p-22203.

126. GARF, f. 10035, op. 1, d. p-21602.

127. GARF, f. 10035, op. 1, d. p-23556.

128. From the author's interview with Feyerherd's daughter, Vera Feyer-herd, Berlin, 1997.

129. GARF, f. 10035, op. 1, d. p-46575.

130. GARF, f. 10035, op. 1, d. p-29137.

131. This happened frequently. Olga Rosenberg and her husband Vasilii Klimentevskii, the father and son Sommerfeld, and other relatives who were victims had no idea about the accusations against their families. GARF, f. 10035, op. 1, d. p-57225; d. p-24759; d. p-49580; op. 2, d. 27651.

132. GARF, f. 10035, op. 1, d. p-29144.

133. GARF, f. 10035, op. 1, d. p-26041.

134. Ibid.

135. GARF, f. 10035, op. 1, d. p-61786.

136. GARF, f. 10035, op. 1, d. p-48229; d. p-48224; d. p-48225; d. p-48226; d. p-47468; d. p-48227; d. p-49562.

137. GARF, f. 10035, op. 1, d. p-50176.

138. GARF, f. 10035, op. 1, d. p-50167; d. p-49661.

139. GARF, f. 10035, op. 1, d. p-22684; d. p-26549; d. p-25774.

140. GARF, f. 10035, op. 1, d. p-25966.

141. GARF, f. 10035, op. 1, d. p-50163.

142. GARF, f. 10035, op. 1, d. p-52533.

143. Oleg Khlevniuk, *Politbiuro: Mekhanizmy politicheskoi vlasti v 1930-e gody* (Moscow: Rosspen, 1996), 190–91.

144. GARF, f. 10035, op. 1, d. p-34140.

145. *Butovskii poligon*, 1:25–26.

146. GARF, f. 10035, op. 1, d. p-70909.

147. GARF, f. 10035, op. 1, d. p-51107.

148. GARF, f. 10035, op. 1, d. p-52089.

149. GARF, f. 10035, op. 1, d. p-23556.

150. GARF, f. 10035, op. 1, d. p-21839.

151. For example, GARF, f. 10035, op. 1, d. p-55451.

152. GARF, f. 10035, op. 1, d. p-33920; d. p-33922.

153. GARF, f. 10035, op. 1, d. p-33921.

154. *Butovskii poligon*, 5:344.

155. GARF, f. 10035, op. 1, d. p-32338. Similar resolutions are in GARF, f. 10035, op. 1, d. p-49320; d. p-49330.

156. GARF, f. 10035, op. 1, d. p-31357.

157. GARF, f. 10035, op. 1, d. p-47013.

158. GARF, f. 10035, op. 1, d. p-47468; d. p-48224; d. p-48225; d. p-48226; d. p-48227; d. p-48228; d. p-48229.

159. GARF, f. 10035, op. 1, d. p-33618; d. p-29469; d. 48283.

160. GARF, f. 10035, op. 1, d. p-48282.

161. GARF, f. 10035, op. 1, d. p-22114.

162. GARF, f. 10035, op. 1, d. p-34140.

163. GARF, f. 10035, op. 1, d. p-8049.

164. For example, Ia. V. Derov received his freedom on January 2, 1940, after the procurator protested the case. GARF, f. 10035, op. 1, d. p-7808.

165. GARF, f. 10035, op. 1, d. p-20247.

166. GARF, f. 10035, op. 2, d. 20790.

167. GARF, f. 10035, op. 1, d. p-30447.

168. From the author's interview with Vera Feyerherd, Berlin, June 1997.

169. RGASPI, f. 495, op. 205, d. 1258.

170. GARF, f. 10035, op. 1, d. p-65924.

171. RGASPI, f. 495, op. 205, d. 1258.

172. GARF, f. 10035, op. 1, d. p-61546.

173. GARF, f. 10035, op. 1, d. p-25777.

174. GARF, f. 10035, op. 1, d. p-60950; d. p-60951; d. p-60952; d. p-60958; d. p-60959; d. p-60960.

175. A. B. Roginskii, "Posledovie," in Eremina and Roginskii, *Rasstrel'nye spiski*, 488–90.

Index

Abramov-Mirov, Ia., 121
Amin'evo, 47, 113
Anikovich, M. M., 128, 155n109
Artsimen'ev, Maksim and Mikhail, 86
Avdeenko, M. M., 30, 60, 84–85, 130
Avramovich, Kh. A., 83

Babushkina, Evgeniia, 31–32, 128
Badaev, I. P., 54
Baglikov, Iakov, 11–12, 60, 64, 68, 71, 103, 108
Bakovka, 25, 28, 82, 92, 100
Balykov family, 113
Baptists, 90
Barvikha, 28, 87
Batashev, N. E., 97
Belousov, G. I., 118
Belov, A. G., 54
Bel'skii district (Smolensk province), 58, 61, 155n113
Berg, Isai, 11–12, 14–16, 66–67, 77, 157n156
Beria, Lavrentii, xxiv, 67, 134, 135
Blakh, L. P., 46
Blinova, Ekaterina, 138
Boltrukovich, Bronislava and family, 113, 133
Borodina, Aleksandra, 89
Breivinskaia, E. V., 31

Brevdo, B. P. and family, 37, 113
Budennyi, Semen, 101
Bukharin, Nikolai, 106
Burhard, Karl, 117
Bushinov, M. G., 98
Butovo firing range, 6, 49, 77, 139, 142–43

Chenykaev, N. S., 90
Chernov, Mikhail, 28, 49, 106
Chernov, V. S., 50
Cherskii, B. B., 45
children of victims, 112, 116–17, 132–33
Chistov, D. M., 128
Chugunov (Kuntsevo police head), 37, 44
Chuprik, V. M., 82, 113
collectivization, xi, xxi, 81, 87–88, 94–95
Comintern (Communist International), 59, 91–92, 113, 116–17, 119–22; House of Leisure, 119–22
Communist Party of Germany, 114, 117–19, 121
Communist Party of the Soviet Union, 46; relationship to NKVD, 15, 49–58, 106, 155n115
Conquest, Robert, x, xxv

Danich, V. F., 130
Danilovskii house, 117

Deich, I. A., 30
Demidov, A. P., 35
denunciations, 79–85; of family members, 82; of property holders, 83; at workplaces, 79–80, 83–85, 106, 128–29
de-Stalinization, x
Dikii (Kuntsevo NKVD investigator), 33, 45–46, 72, 130, 136
Dimitrov, Georgi, 137
Dimova, P. D., 91–92
Ditbender, Walter, 119
Diuchkov, Ivan and family, 132–33
Domninskii, P. A., 101
Drobik, Iu. S., 74
Dulin, S. G., 132
Dvoretskii, V. I., 30

Efremov, S. K., 33–34, 72, 116
Egorov, V. E., 91
Ermakov, S. I., 62
Ershkov, I. N., 54
Etminus family, 112–13
Ezhov, Nikolai, xxii–xxiv, 21, 56, 67, 71, 105, 117

Favorov, Ivan, 13, 17
Ferapontova, G. G., 34–35, 130, 135–36
Feyerherd family, 121–27, 137
Filatov, N. A., 49, 104
Filikin, P. K., 75–77
"former people," 79, 81, 90–91, 100
Frinovskii, Mikhail, 84
Funk, Peter, 117, 119

Gailesh, A. A., 31, 35, 132
Galeev, K., 98
Geflikh, Gertrude and Karl, 119
Golengrin, M. S., 134
Golke, Arthur, 121, 126–27
Gorbatov (Moscow provincial cropping station director), 51
Gorbul'skii, Solomon, 57
Grietsche, Friedrich, 118
Guenther, Margarita, 117
Gutkin, P. S., 89

Hadrossek, Heinz, 116–17, 137–38
Hadrossek, Luise, 114–17, 137–38

Hadrossek, Wilhelm, 114–16, 118
Harbin, 85, 113
Helei, Georg. See Geflikh, Gertrude and Karl
Huebner, Erika, 117
Hungarian Revolution, 119

Iagoda, Genrikh, xxi–xxiii
Iakubovich, Grigorii, 14, 43, 55, 62–64, 66
Iaroslavl' province, 28
Iliadis, G. Kh., 129
Il'in, Il'ia, 43
Iliukovich, Iosif, 135
International Red Aid, 118
Isakov, Dmitrii, 92
Ivanovskaia, T. P., 99
Izmailova, 25

Jews and antisemitism, 89, 97–98
Jogiches, Leo, 121

Kamenev, Lev, xxii
Karetnikov, Viktor, 8, 18–19, 20, 23, 29, 31, 32, 36, 38, 43, 48, 55–57, 59–60, 62–68, 70–71, 74–75, 87, 90, 101, 104–5, 112, 129, 131, 135, 139, 154n89
Karutskii, Vasilii, 43, 75–76
Kaverznev, Mikhail, 57
Khrushchev, Nikita, 52; and "Secret Speech," x, xxxi, 5, 141
Kim, San-Tagi, 59, 92
Kirov, Sergei, xxii, 99, 162n69
Kliat, R. S., 30, 128
Kokhanskaia, T. S., 55, 134, 156n125
Kokhov, V. T., 54, 57, 156n122
Kolbut, V. V., 126
Konon-Kononov, I. Ia., 34
Kordon, P. K., 90
Kostaki, Elena, 92, 135
Kotsin, Karl, 95–96
Kovalevsky, Arthur. See Steinitz, Wilhelm
Kozlov, Semen, 112
Krestinskii, Nikolai, 122
Kriukov, V. M., 159n183
Krylatskoe, 92–93, 108–12
Krys'ev, Timofei and family, 92–93
Kuborskaia, M. A., 63–65
Kuborskii, V. P., 62–65

Kudriavtsev, A. I., 47, 72
kulaks. *See* collectivization
Kulikov, I. V., 100–101
Kuntsevo, xix, 3, 8–9, 141–44; Communist
    Youth International Factory, 30, 84, 115,
    117, 128–29; Factory 46, 30, 48, 55, 62,
    66, 71–72, 88, 118, 130–32; Factory 95,
    30, 91–92, 128
Kuusinen, Otto, 120
Kuznetsov, Aleksandr, 8, 17–18, 23, 29, 37–
    38, 42, 43–45, 50, 54–55, 59–60, 66–68,
    70–71, 84, 92, 135, 139, 156n122

Lazarev, N. I., 60, 67, 84, 115–16
Leningrad province, 28
Leonov, A. G., 69, 71
Letuchev, V. E., 97
Ligeropulo, Evgeniia, 35
Litvak, Ia. G., 63–66
Lopatin, G. M, 54
Luga district (Leningrad province), 21

Maevskii, I. A., 90
Martkovich, S. A., 130
mass operations, xxiii, 21; arrests in rural
    areas, 24–28; arrests in towns, 30; con-
    tinuation of investigations after, 132–
    38; end of mass arrests, 49; German vic-
    tims, 38, 39, 87, 113–27, 130, 137–38,
    151n22; Greek victims, 129, 135; Latvian
    victims, 35, 86–87, 130–31; motivations
    for, xxvi–xxvii, 77, 88; national opera-
    tions, 40–43, 92, 126, 128–32, 153n80;
    numbers of victims, xii; Polish victims,
    31–32, 128, 129; quotas in, 29, 43–44,
    152n38, 154n89; religion, 88–91, 100;
    remembrance in post-Soviet Russia,
    141–44; sources for study of, xiv–xv,
    xxv, xxx, 6–9, 50, 70, 116, 139–40, 143,
    149n12
Matveevskoe, 25, 28
Meier, Ernst, 39, 118, 153n73
Mekhlis, Lev, 98, 134, 136
Menshevik Party, 46–47, 107
Merkulov, Vsevolod, 135, 137
Miklau, Zhan, 34, 86–87
Mishin, Petr, 57
Mnevniki, 25–27, 47, 107

Monich family, 40
Morozov (Kuntsevo party secretary), 56–57,
    84
Moscow provincial propping station, 21,
    51–53, 79–80, 83, 104, 127
Moscow Provincial NKVD. *See* NKVD
Mtsenskii district (Orel province), 44
Muralov, Sergei, 48, 53–54, 56, 59, 102–8,
    138, 154n101
Mytishchi (Moscow province), 29, 41, 76

Nazi Germany, xxviii
Neiman, R. K., 130
Nemchinovka, 25, 28, 83, 89, 100–102, 120
Nikiforov, M. N., 57
Nikitin, Aleksandr, 36, 101–2, 134
Nikitin (secretary of Moscow NKVD), 65
Nikolaev, N. P., 51–53, 83, 127
Nikulino, 47
Nizhny Novgorod, 76
NKVD (People's Commissariat of Internal
    Affairs): corruption in, 58–65, 157n140;
    counterespionage, 40; hierarchies in,
    20, 37–38, 148n2; ideological influences
    in, xvi, 73; investigatory practices in,
    xix–xxx, 7, 23, 31–36, 43–45, 47–49, 74,
    85–93, 107–13, 128–32, 151n35, 152n52;
    patron-client relationships, xvi, xix, 5,
    12–18, 39, 42, 66, 75, 77–78, 150n9; psy-
    chological breakdown of officers, 44,
    76, 112; purge in 1938–39, 8, 67–77, 108,
    157n156, 158n178, 159n180; recruitment
    practices in, 22, 73; relationship with
    Soviet officials, 103–4; Special Counsel,
    47, 96, 108, 132, 133, 136; use of infor-
    mants, 24, 27–28, 36, 100–102
Novikov, D. V., 130

Ob"edkov, M. I., 57
Ochakovo, 47, 95
Odinkov, V. M., 91
Odintsovo, 47, 107
Osaulenko, I. M, 51–52
Ostroumov, D. I., 88–89
Ozolin, Karl, 130–31

Papakhristodulo, Liubov', 35, 135
Pavlenkovich, N. A., 92

Pechnikov, F. P., 88, 160n25
People's Commissariat of Internal Affairs. *See* NKVD
Pertsits, Mikhail, 37
Petrov, G. P., 90
Petrov (NKVD officer), 42
Petukhov (NKVD officer), 38
Petushkov, V. F., 31, 32, 63, 131
Pieck, Wilhelm, 137
Poda, Ul'iana and family, 82, 113
Polegen'ko, P. I., 90
Popov, A. A., 35
popular opinion and rumors, 93–100; about impending war, 96–97; about terror, 97–99
Postel', A. O., 99
Pozdniakov, K. A., 80
Presnov family, 108–12, 139

Radzivilovskii, Aleksandr, 12–15, 17, 62, 65–66, 84
Ramenskoe, 95
Redens, Stanislav, 15, 84
Red'ko, I. Ia., 134
Remizov, Nikolai and family, 94–95, 113
rehabilitation and appeals of victims, xxxi, 6, 72, 78, 133–40
repression in USSR: denunciations, xxviii; effects on society, xxvii; number of victims, xiii, xix, xxv
Romashkovo, 89, 107
Rostislav (Kuntsevo party secretary), 53, 57
Rukodanov, S. I., 23, 29, 36–37, 46–49, 54, 56, 70, 72, 78, 100–101, 106–7, 113, 136–37, 153n66, 159n193

Sal'nikov, D. P., 101
Schule, Ernst, 109
Selina, Elizaveta, 94, 100
Semenov, M. I., 45
Senenkov, A. F., 69, 71
Serpukhov district (Moscow province), 57, 61, 76
Shchadenko, M. T., 36–37, 82, 100
Shematovich, V. V., 39
Shidlovskii, Etgard, 31
Shnaidruk, Vladimir, 102, 134
show trials, xxii, 20, 40, 48, 106

Shpakova, Aleksandra, 132
Shteklian, Anton, 38
Shtol'der, Elisei, 89
Shtybor, V. M., 96
Shushunov, S. A., 136
Shuvalov, Aleksandr, 112
Sidiropulo, Nadezhda, 32
Sim, A. A., 41
Skladnov family, 112
Skoruk, K. V., 54
Smirnitskii, G. I., 37, 46
Smirnov, B. D., 44, 76, 112, 131
"Snow White" (NKVD informant), 87, 135, 160n21
Socialist Revolutionary (SR) Party, 46–47, 88, 91, 107
Sokolov, Aleksei (priest in Kuntsevo district), 89
Solomatin, G. A., 66
Solov'ev, A. V., 22–23, 31, 32, 46, 72, 74, 129–31
Sol'ts, Aaron, 121
Solzhenitsyn, Alexander, ix–x
Sommerfeld, Adolf, 39
Sommerfeld, Eduard, 38, 117
Sommerfeld, Tatyana, 117
Sorokin, Ivan, 11–12, 18, 29, 37, 42, 62, 66, 75
special settlements, xii
"speculation," 81
Stalin Constitution (Soviet Constitution of 1936), 74, 98–99, 160n11
Stalin, Iosif, xxii–xxiv, 16, 77; as supposed target of terrorism, 80, 97, 101
Stange, Adolf, 120–21
Steinitz, Wilhelm, 117–19
Studenova, Evdokiia, 82
Sukovo, 119, 125
Sukurov, V. M., 57
Sviridov, I. A., 49

Tatarovo, 98
Teplyi Stan, 26
Tereshkovo, 132–33
Tikhonov, V. A., 87
Tomskii, Mikhail, 132
Tropereva, 26
Trotskii, Lev, 98, 106

Tsesarskii, V. E., 62, 64–65
Tsikhotskii family, 113, 128
Tsyganov, A. A., 22, 70, 72, 133

Ugletskii, Vasilii, 136
Ul'ianovsk, 75
Uzunov, 100

Verakso, P. I., 30
veterinarians, 107
Vizula, A. R. P., 35
Vokresensk district (Moscow province), 57
Volkov, M. K., 50, 90
Vyrubova, 25
Vyshinsky, Andrei, xxii, 64, 71, 117

Werth, Fritz, 92

Zaitsev, A. I., 37, 136
Zaitsev, Stepan, 37
Zakovskii, Leonid, 43, 75
Zanegin, I. M., 90
Zavilov, N. I., 53
Zhdanov, Andrei, 75
Zhirnov, S. F., 101–2, 134
Zhivov, A. S., 131
Zhuravlev, V. P., 69, 71
Zinov'ev, Grigorii, xxii, 98
Zirt, Peter. See Funk, Peter
Zuden, S. G., 45
Zverev, A. G., 47, 72

Printed in the United States
By Bookmasters